Reaching the Arabs

A felt need approach

Reaching
the Arabs

A felt need approach

Tim Matheny

William Carey Library

1705 N. SIERRA BONITA AVE. • PASADENA, CALIFORNIA 91104

Library of Congress Cataloging in Publication Data

Matheny, Tim, 1952-
    Reaching the Arabs.

    Bibliography: p.
    1. Missions to Muslims. I. Title.
BV2625.M37   266'.00956   81-2738
ISBN 0-87808-331-6   AACR2

Published by the William Carey Library
P.O. Box 128-C
Pasadena, California 91104
Telephone (213) 798-0819

In accord with some of the most recent thinking of the aca-
demic press, the William Carey Library is pleased to present
this scholarly book which has been prepared from an author-
edited camera ready copy.

PRINTED IN THE UNITED STATES OF AMERICA

Contents

PART TWO: STRATEGY

Diagrams

ix

Tables

Maps

Foreword

In recent years a plethora of books and articles on the Middle East and Islam have been published or republished. These productions have come from and been addressed to people of varying interests: economists, political scientists, travellers, biblical theologians, students of world religion and history, the curious and, at times, the infuriated. But while one may wonder about the advisability of publishing yet another volume on this subject, there are good reasons for paying attention to Mr. Matheny's missiological treatment of the area.

Born of his long-standing interest in and love for the Middle Eastern Muslims and Arabs, Tim Matheny has put together in this volume a good piece of "borderline research," that entity which arises when research results from various disciplines brought together in new combinations. He used his own field work along with judiciously selected materials from the social sciences and biblical studies. While more than a nod is given to past evangelistic work among the Middle Eastern peoples, his primary interests are in analyzing the recent past and present so an informed agenda may be developed for the present and near future.

For a start, Mr. Matheny narrows the scope of his work by focusing on the "transitional Arabs," who, according to both Daniel Lerner's specific studies and general anthropological theory, are likely to be the block of Arabs most receptive to innovations. Whether that is in fact pervasively true

remains to be proven by actual evangelistic efforts, but
one cannot be faulted for recommending an agenda based on
the soundest theoretical approach of which one is aware.

Mr. Matheny has not written as a starry-eyed optimist; he
has an entire chapter on "restrictions" to evangelization.
But a major conclusion he reaches is that "the primary restrictions to evangelism in the Middle East are sociological
not theological (or doctrinal)" (p.160). In his proposed
agenda he certainly does not neglect message, to which he
devotes a chapter and an Appendix. He tries rather to place
it in context so that it comes across to Arabs as "good news."
Overall, he certainly does not major in message as did
Raymond Lull and, in a measure, Samuel Zwemer. Obviously,
evangelizing among Muslims entails the preaching of a "good
news" message, but the most carefully designed and accurate
message can fail to bring about desired and possible results
if it is formulated in ignorance of context and milieu. To
facilitate that outcome Mr. Matheny utilizes the "felt need"
approach, on which he has done some original thinking. He
has sought to tabulate the major "culture themes" (after M.
Opler) to which the Christian response must be made.

Christian response involves much more than an initial
good news message. At the Tambaram Missionary Conference
(1938) Dr. Paul Harrison related in a humorous but moving
speech the story of the five converts that had been made in
Arabia in the previous fifty years (*Tambaram Series*, VII:
54-59). They were mostly isolated individuals. More recently (1966), Professor J.N.D. Anderson claimed that

> We must also sadly confess that throughout
> the greater part of the Muslim world there
> are very few churches into which the lonely
> convert will be welcomed, and where he will
> find the warmth of fellowship and under-
> standing he so greatly needs. (*One Race, One
> Gospel, One Task*, II: 284.)

That was at the 1966 Berlin Conference, but one suspects
that in the fifteen or so years since that conference the
church picture has not changed much in the Middle East. In
view of this it is significant that Mr. Matheny gives attention to "social structure," "channels of communication," and
"goals" because in those sections he grapples theoretically
with questions about small group conversion, networks of
communication, and meaningful relationships in a Christian

community -- the local church. In other words, a part of
his recommended agenda involves front-end decisions which
will help both to win and stabilize converts from Islam to
Jesus Christ.

At pessimistic moments one wonders whether any agenda at
all can be proposed for a rapidly changing Middle East. A
part of the significance of Mr. Matheny's work is that it
deals with the change itself and suggests points along the
gamut of change on which the discerning evangelist should
likely focus his efforts. His agenda is likely to supply
insight for immediate use as well as to stimulate further
research by those on the job in the Middle East.

C. Philip Slate
Harding Graduate School of Religion
Memphis, Tennessee

Preface

My interest in the Arab world stems from the fact that I grew
up there. In 1961 my parents, Carl and Betty Lou Matheny,
went to Beirut, Lebanon, where there was no church of Christ.
I was eight years old at that time. My parents worked
diligently for seven years. Our family returned to the
United States in the summer of 1968, when I was fifteen
years old. During our stay in the Middle East I was deeply
impressed with the need to do evangelistic work in this
neglected part of the world. I shall be eternally grateful
for the godly influence of my parents and for the sense of
purpose they have given to my life.

My sincere appreciation is expressed to Philip Slate,
Mac Lynn, Carl P. Matheny, Evertt W. Huffard, and especially
my wife, Carol, who all took the time to read the first
draft of this thesis and offered many valuable suggestions.
Recognition must also be given to Gary Holmes, Carl Guthrie,
Dave Hogan, Charles Fowler, Gary Williams, and Bob Douglas
who provided assistance in various ways. I am also deeply
grateful to Toy Hicks and Zola Morris who provided help in
typing the manuscript. Appreciation is also due to all the
members of the Applied Missiology class of the Spring of
1977 at Harding Graduate School of Religion who offered
some very thoughtful suggestions.

Tim Matheny

1

Introduction

Western evangelistic efforts have faced extreme difficulty
in the Middle East, primarily because of the strong resistance from traditional Arab society. This resistance is
greatly influenced by Islamic theology and culture. Because
of this resistance, religious workers have healed tens of
thousands of Muslim sick and educated tens of thousands of
their children, but have converted very few.(1) Protestant
missions began their evangelistic efforts by trying to revive
the Eastern churches so that they could have a greater impact
on Islam. When this approach failed because of the uncooper-
ative attitude of the Eastern churches, they began working
with those individuals who, being sympathetic with the evan-
gelicals, formed evangelical churches. The Protestants,
still conscious of their responsibility to Islam, tried the
indirect approach of medical and educational missions. They
did much valuable work in this area but there were still very
few converts as a result.

A historical survey of Protestant evangelistic efforts
among Muslims will indicate that Muslims have been largely
neglected. Although some will categorize the Muslims as very
unreceptive to Christianity, the reason why so few Muslims
have become Christians may very well be explained by the fact
that very few Christians have made serious attempts to reach
them and not necessarily because they are totally resistant
to a culturally meaningful Christian message. Very few of
the religious groups in the Middle East have done any significant work among Muslims, but have instead concentrated
their efforts on members of the Eastern churches who are

easier to convert. The evangelistic efforts of the churches
of Christ in the Middle East have had similar results and
only about eight percent of the total number of converts
have been from among Muslims.

The difficulty of the evangelistic task in the Middle
East is well stated by Cragg: "There are few communities in
the world where the missionary Christian requires more dis-
arming patience and steadiness of purpose than amid Arab
Islam."(2)

Someone has described the task of commending the Gospel
to Muslims in terms like these: it is an attempt to
persuade the proudest man in the world to accept the
thing he hates at the hands of the man he despises.(3)

The blame for the minimal results in the Arab world cannot be put entirely at the foot of the Arab. One important
factor in the failure of religious missions in the Arab world
has been the lack of understanding on the part of the Western
evangelist of the complexities of Arab culture. The task of
introducing new ideas into a culture must of necessity be
based on extensive prior study of the nature of that
society.(4) Such a study should include the world view, the
thought forms, the cultural themes, the social structure,
the authority patterns, and the space-time dimensions of the
culture to be evangelized. Luzbetak has said that "research
into cultural dynamics is perhaps the most urgent and most
basic missionary research called for."(5) This study is an
attempt to use such insights in the construction of an
evangelistic strategy for the Arab world.

DEFINITION OF TERMS

An "innovation" is an idea, behavior, or object that is
perceived as new by an individual or group of individuals
because it is qualitatively different from existing forms.(6)
Evangelism in Arab culture is an effort to communicate innovations since Christianity is a way of life that is qualitatively different from much of Arab life. Innovation does
not imply changing in any way the essentials of the Christian
message. Religious innovations in the Arab world would
include the following: 1) God has communicated with man
through his word, the Bible, 2) the Bible is still a valid
guide for men today who want to obey God's will, 3) one must
accept Christ as Savior and Lord through faith, confession,
repentance, and baptism (immersion) in order to be saved,
4) the concept of equality in Christ across national,

linguistic, sexual, sectarian, or social lines, 5) the priority of biblical authority to tradition, 6) the concept of applying principles of Christian living in contrast to ritualism, and 7) the concept of restoring New Testament Christianity according to command, example, and necessary inference.(7)

"Communication" is the process by which messages are transferred from a source to a receiver.(8) The famous statement: *"Who* says *what,* through what *channels* (media) of communication, to *whom* and with what *results?"* is an over-simplified summary of the communication process.(9)

"Diffusion" is a special type of communication, and is the process by which innovations spread to members of a society.(10) Communication theory encompasses all types of messages, whereas diffusion studies involve messages that are new ideas, which usually emphasize bringing about overt behavior change.(11)

"Modernization" is the process by which individuals change from a traditional way of life to a more complex, technologically advanced, and rapidly changing style of life.(12) Change from the traditional to the more modern necessarily involves the communication and acceptance of new ideas.

A "Transitional Arab" is an Arab who is in the process of modernization. He is a man-in-motion having left the traditional way of life but not yet attaining a completely modern way of life (see p. 5).

ASSUMPTIONS

1. Transitional Arabs are most receptive to evangelism.
2. The results of non-religious social science research concerning the innovation process in Arab culture can be validly applied to efforts to communicate religious innovations.
3. Although theoretical generalizations cannot eliminate the element of surprise, they can help prevent mistakes and reduce the trial and error factor in evangelism.
4. The evangelist is justified in converting nominal "Christian" Arabs to a more accurate and dedicated commitment to God.

LIMITATIONS

Addison says that there are three kinds of problems in
the Christian approach to the Muslim: those which are common
to all mission fields, those which are common to all Muslim
mission fields, and those which are characteristic of
specific Muslim areas.(13) Problems which confront missionaries in all areas of the world are of course important, but
the problems which are the primary concern of this study are
those which are peculiar to the Arab countries of the Middle
East, with special emphasis on the countries of the fertile
crescent.(14) Where it is relevant the author will state his
position on those more general issues, but will leave it to
someone else to argue their validity.

This study will deal only with direct evangelism, and
will not be concerned with indirect work such as medical and
educational work. This study will not be an apologetic
approach to any religious belief common to the area under
study. Rather than discussing doctrinal differences between
New Testament Christianity and Islam or the Eastern Christian sects the emphasis will be on the cultural factors and
how they influence the evangelistic approach.

This study is limited primarily to the diffusion aspect
of the communication process. More specifically, it is an
analysis of the diffusion of religious innovations among
Trasitional Arabs. Although this study is limited to developing an evangelistic strategy among Transitional Arabs,
certain aspects of the Traditional Arab way of life will be
discussed since they are crucial to understanding the
behavior and thought patterns of Transitional Arabs.

This study is not therefore concerned with a strategy for
reaching all the peoples of the Middle East, but only the
pockets of receptivity as identified by Huffard.(15) This
is not an attempt to exclude any individual from the salvation of Christ, but an effort to set forth a theoretical
approach for planting churches in the most receptive segments
of Arab society, which should be much more capable of influencing other segments of Arab society.

Since this study is based on library research it is
limited in that it is of necessity a theoretical thesis.
Any cross-cultural worker knows that journalistic descriptions provide only a very superficial knowledge of the ways
and mentality of a people; and methodology based on such
knowledge will of necessity be as imperfect as the knowledge

itself.(16) The proposals and conclusions made in this
study will need to be tested on the field before their
validity can be totally demonstrated.

The Christian message will be reexamined in light of the
felt needs of Transitional Arabs, but the actual content of
the Biblical message will be dealt with only briefly. It is
beyond the scope of this thesis to provide a complete presentation of the Christian message.

THE TARGET AUDIENCE: THE TRANSITIONAL ARAB

Daniel Lerner identified three typological units of
Middle Eastern society: Traditionals, Transitionals, and
Moderns.(17) The Traditionals live in the villages, have a
fatalistic outlook on life, are resistant to change, and
depend primarily on face-to-face communication rather than
the mass media. The Moderns are educated, consumers of the
media, urbanized, and are characterized by empathy, which
is the capacity to see oneself in the other fellow's
position.(18)

The Transitionals are men in motion, who are in between
a traditional and modern way of life. A majority of the
Transitionals were born in the villages and have since moved
to the urban centers. While Transitionals are not nearly as
well educated as the Moderns, they are highly empathic.
The vast majority of the high school and college students
are Transitional Arabs. Lerner's research documents the
generalization that Transitionals in 1950 tended to be young
unmarried males, relatively well-off, and recruited among
minority groups--in higher proportions than the total population.(19) Among both Muslim and Christian groups the
Transitionals have proven to be the most receptive to the
communication of innovations.(20)

Evertt W. Huffard used Lerner's typology to categorize
the converts to New Testament Christianity in the three Arab
countries of Lebanon, Jordan, and Egypt. His research
demonstrated that the Transitionals were the most receptive
to Christianity as illustrated in table 1.(21) He established that curiosity, media participation, moral consciousness, weakened Islamic strongholds, and decreased impotency
(fatalism) render the Transitionals more receptive to innovations.(22) He also concluded that the potential for
church growth in the Middle East is greater than generally
believed, since receptive pockets do exist.(23)

TABLE 1

TYPOLOGY OF CONVERTS

COUNTRY	TRADITIONAL	TRANSITIONAL	MODERN
Egypt	5%	68%	27%
Jordan	18%	74%	8%
Lebanon	-	85%	15%
Average	8%	75%	17%

SOURCE: Evertt W. Huffard, "An Agenda for the Evangelization
of Egypt, Jordan, and Lebanon with Specific Reference to the
Effect of Modernization on Receptivity," (M.A. thesis,
Harding Graduate School of Religion, 1973), p. 69.

The thesis of this study is that Transitional Arabs should
be made the target audience of the evangelistic outreach of
the churches of Christ. It is the purpose of this study to
develop an evangelistic approach which will most effectively
reach the Transitional Arabs. Not only will this proposed
strategy be based on an analysis of the innovation process in
Arab culture, principles of culture change, and communication
theory; but it will involve a reexamination of the Christian
message. Research indicates that if this evangelistic
strategy is followed the chances for successful evangelism
in the Middle East will be much greater, more souls will be
won to the Christian way of life, and Christianity will be
more relevant to the Arab people.

ORGANIZATION OF THESIS

Part one is primarily descriptive in nature, dealing with
those cultural factors which are crucial in constructing an
evangelistic strategy to reach the Transitional Arab. Part
two is prescriptive in nature in that it sets forth the
essential criteria for an evangelistic strategy in the Arab
world. Eugene Nida has demonstrated that there is much to
be learned from applying social science models to religious
behavior.(24) In looking for a comprehensive framework
with which to analyze religious innovations in Arab culture,
several possibilities were considered. Hesselgrave sets

forth seven dimensions of cross-cultural communication; Hall
categorizes ten Primary Message Systems (PMS); Niehoff
defines seventeen categories of innovator and recipient
characteristics; and Doob identifies twelve variables of
communication in Africa.(25)

Hall's Primary Message Systems emphasize the non-verbal
aspects of communication, and though suggestive, they are
not the most helpful for the purpose of this thesis.
Hesselgrave's list is also thought provoking but not as comprehensive as Doob's variables. Of these studies Doob's
treatment is the most thorough. Therefore, Doob's variables
are used in this study as a basic framework for analyzing
religious innovations among Transitional Arabs. Doob's purpose is to indicate in some detail all the variables that
have at least on one occasion affected communication in
Africa. Doob's list of variables can help to uncover the
hidden assumptions that must be made before practicing or
analyzing communication anywhere.(26)

As demonstrated in diagram 1 there is a dynamic interrelationship between Doob's twelve variables in the communication
process.

The goal of the communicator (II) depends in a large
part on himself and his position in the society (I) as
well as upon what he has learned about the audience in
the past (XII). The site at which the audience is
located (V) influences the kinds of basic media to be
employed (III) and may or may not require extending
media (IV). The contents of a communication (VII) are
affected by all sorts of taboos or restrictions (VI)
and by the mood of the audience (VIII). Whether or
not changes occur in people (XI) can be traced to the
way in which they perceive (IX) and react (X) to
communication.(27)

It is very unlikely that all of the above variables would
be critical in any single situation. In fact only a glance
will be necessary in many cases to determine that one or
more of them is not critical. But the author agrees with
Doob that it is at one's peril to discard one or more of the
dozen variables or their subcategories. "Ideally an investigation of each variable and subcategory is demanded."(28)

DIAGRAM 1

DOOB'S VARIABLES

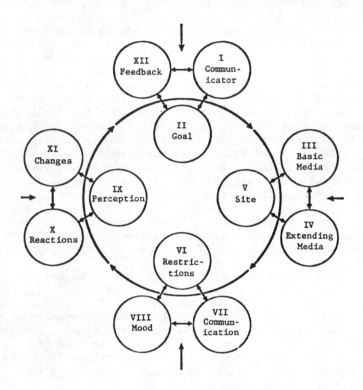

SOURCE: Leonard W. Doob, *Communication in Africa* (New
Haven: Yale University Press, 1961), p. 11.

As is apparent in the table of contents Doob's variables
are used with a varying degree of emphasis.(29) In most
social situations more than one variable turns out to be
critical. In a multivariant situation the relevant variables
must be empirically determined. The author identifies those
variables which at one time or another will be crucial in
the process of communicating religious innovations among
Transitional Arabs.

However, it must be emphasized as strongly as possible
that no matter how well informed one might be on the innovation process, every communication is unique and is likely to
have some new or surprising element in it. Yet in order to
construct an effective evangelistic strategy one must draw
certain generalizations. Therefore, the conclusions of this
study serve only to reduce that unexpected factor and not to
eliminate it completely.(30)

The study that is probably more directly related to this
thesis than any other is Fisher's STM thesis at San Francisco Theological Seminary.(31) After a study of the
"kerygma" and some fundamental principles of Christian
communication he sets forth in his conclusion certain areas
where research is still needed in this field. These include
those elements which enable the evangelist to make a closer
identification with the Muslim, the use of meaningful
symbols, the extent to which the mass media can replace
personal communication, and the type of Christian community
which will be most relevant and meaningful to the Muslim.(32)

The demand for a study of this nature has been long over-
due as Kraemer emphasized:

> A radical rethinking and reshaping is imperiously
> demanded, if we discern the signs of the time and are
> willing to learn to walk in the new way of obedience
> to the Lord Jesus Christ. It is this that is implied
> in "missionary adequacy." The deeply humbling fact
> remains that the Muslim world in its whole history has
> never had a chance to *see* the Christian Church as she
> is according to her true nature and calling, but has
> always been presented with lamentable caricatures.
> The chance as far as the Christian Church is concerned,
> is now there. The great question is: will the oppor-
> tunity be taken? If so, then a new dimension of think-
> ing and of spiritual and intellectual preparation
> emerges and calls for new inventive answers and a new
> kind of commitment.(33)

Part one begins in chapter two with an analysis of the
cultural themes which regulate the behavior of the Transitional Arab. These cultural themes become very important
in constructing a relevant Christian message and other
details in the evangelistic strategy.

Part One

Analysis

2

Cultural Themes

The study of cultural anthropology has created a strong
interest in the totality of each culture. It is commonly
believed that hardly any trait of culture can be understood
when taken out of its general setting. Culture is more than
its functionally organized parts; it has a "soul" that gives
direction to the functions. Anthropologists have offered
various theories to explain this principle of life, dominating idea, or configuration.

Ruth Benedict suggested that a whole culture might be
dominated by a single, all pervading principle or pattern.(1)
Her insights were helpful in emphasizing the fact that different segments of a culture provide only a very superficial
knowledge of the ways and mentality of a people, unless
viewed in terms of the whole. However, more recent researches
indicate that there are few, if any, cultures in which a
single pattern dominates all others.(2) Opler suggests that
each culture has not just one dominating pattern but a set
of related underlying "themes." A theme may be defined as a
multi-individual value which controls behavior or stimulates
activity, which is tacitly approved or openly promoted in a
society.(3) These themes may be formalized or unformalized,
primary or symbolic, material or non-material.(4) Opler
points out that there are four ways to evaluate the importance of these themes: 1) the number of expressions, 2) the
degree of concern when the theme is violated, 3) the number
of facets of the total system of ideas and practices in
which it appears, and 4) the limiting factors which control
the number, variety and force of a them's expressions.(5)

Here a comprehensive treatment of the cultural themes of
Transitional Arabs is not possible. But an attempt will be
made to isolate those themes that would be of crucial importance to the communicator of religious innovations. Anyone
who plans to work among the Arabs should definitely read
some of the more comprehensive treatments of the values and
themes of Arab culture.(6)

Nothing is more basic to making Christianity relevant
than insight into the **value** system of the local culture.
Luzbetak emphasizes the importance of a discussion of cultural themes:

> Modern **anthropological** theory tells us that a
> society seems to have its own basic set of as-
> sumptions, values, and goals. These are usually
> closely related and it would be possible to for-
> mulate a list of basic psychological "themes"
> permeating native thought, sentiment and action...
> Since missionary work consists essentially in
> communicating, convincing, and persuading, any
> light cast on methods of analyzing basic assump-
> tions, values and goals of a people would be a
> tremendous asset to the missionary.(7)

Christian values are supracultural as distinct from
cultural, and were originally communicated to people of
Hebrew and Greek culture, who had their own set of culturally
determined values, in light of which the new values had to
be interpreted and taught. This is turn has been mediated
to the American evangelist in terms of his own value system.
(8) The evangelist has next to communicate these values to
members of an Arab culture who have their own culturally
established set of values. It is not surprising that there
are so many cases of missionary work which have not succeeded
in adequately relating the essential supracultural values of
Christianity to the background of the Arab.

HONOR

The most important cultural themes of Arab society are
honor and hospitality, the one governing the Arab's protection of and behavior toward his kinsman, the other governing his protection and behavior toward his guest.(9)
Honor is not only the value of a person in his own eyes, but
also in the eyes of his society.(10) The Arabic word for
honor, *sharaf*, comes from a root which implies "highness."
All good achievements, whether realized by personal effort

or by laborious efforts of other members of the kin-group to
which a man belongs, build up his *sharaf* or at least contrib-
ute to it. Thus a man's honor is largely determined by his
own personal behavior and by the behavior of his kinsmen.(11)
There is a strong correlation between honor and group sur-
vival. Honorable behavior is that which is conducive to
group cohesion. The Arab family enjoys a solidarity that
has resisted the changes of time. The individual is expected
to suppress his personal needs and interests if they interfere with those of the family.(12)

Honor in the Arab world is a universal concept that finds
expression in many different spheres of life. Honor involves
maintaining the proper relationship between the sexes. A
man of honor sees that his daughters and sisters do not act
sensually toward men. Sexual crimes are considered crimes
against honor.(13) Any injury done to a man's honor must be
revenged, or else he becomes permanently dishonored. To illustrate the deep fear of the loss of honor, consider the
story told by a Marsh Arab and published by Fulinain.

> In an argument a man claims that the sister of his
> antagonist is "dishonoring" the tribe in her rela-
> tionship with a man. The man goes home, says to
> his sister, "the price of adultery is death," and
> stabs the girl to death, despite his presumed great
> love for her. The story is told to illustrate how
> young men should act, and clearly reflects a cul-
> tural value.(14)

Such stories are common in many parts of the Middle East.
The stains on one's honor are regarded as so important that
Arabs will kill those dear to them rather than be disgraced.
These stories necessarily have a profound influence on the
Arab's code of conduct.

It is honorable to engage in certain types of work. Arab
society despises manual labor. Many middle class Americans
quite willingly engage in tinkering around the house, but
this "do it yourself" attitude contrasts sharply with the
Arab unwillingness to engage in any type of manual labor.(15)
Darity tells how most Arabs that have any western influence
will not accept a job unless they can wear a coat and tie to
do the job, even if such jobs as construction work pay considerably more.(16) Seventy percent of all Arabs live in
villages and are engaged in agriculture.(17) Nevertheless,
the aversion to such work is very much a part of the village
atmosphere. This is dramatically illustrated by the answers

given by the majority of adolescent boys in a Muslim Lebanese
village to the question: "If there were things about your
life that you could change, what would you change?" Twenty
out of thirty-five boys answered: "Not to have to work with
my hands," or words to the same effect.(18) Among the des-
pised varieties of work, agricultural labor is the one most
emphatically rejected.(19)

After the Israeli air attack in 1967, in order to "save
face," Nasser suggested to King Hussein that a communique be
issued to the effect that American and British aircraft
were collaborating with Israel and attacking Egypt from
their aircraft carriers.(20) Similarly, in his attempt to
"save face," a hungry Arab will often refuse an invitation
to a meal, pretending that he has already eaten, for fear
that the host may suspect that he was too poor to have
enough food.(21) All the different kinds of honor in Arab
life interlock to surround the Arab ego like a coat of armor.
(22)

Another area where the cultural theme of honor finds
expression is in the Arab's high respect for the elderly.
Respect for the aged is a moral duty, and everyone defers
to members of the older generation as a matter of course.(23)
Respect for the elderly is expressed in polite behavior and
in tolerance for attitudes and actions, which among younger
persons would be treated with scorn. A Christian missionary
asked an Arab audience which son in the New Testament parable
(Matt. 21:28) is the better: the one who, when asked by his
father to do something, replies that he will and does not,
or the son who replies that he will not and then does what
his father asks. Nearly all the Arabs answered that the son
who lied was the better because, even though he did not
carry out his father's wish, he showed proper respect in his
reply.(24)

The concept of honor is a cultural theme not only for
Traditional Arabs but also for Transitionals and Moderns.
A look at the daily newspaper or a visit to the local cinema
in any Middle Eastern city will demonstrate that the crime
of honor is very frequent--"it occurs, it is understood, it
is applauded, and it is celebrated--it is not satirized."(25)
Films such as "Seduced and Abandoned" or "Divorce Italian
Style" are foreign to the Middle Eastern way of life. There
is hardly a subject one can investigate--law, morality,
family life, social control, social change, politics--without
at some point impinging on the domain of honor.(26)

HOSPITALITY

The theme of hospitality is a bedouin value that goes
back to biblical times. Because of the rules of hospitality,
the fugitive becomes an honored guest whom the host must
protect even at the risk of his own life.(27) Hospitality,
like other bedouin values, serves the goal of strengthening
the group. The extending of hospitality is inherently
related to the systems of honor. One can show his unself-
ishness and his wealth, and increase his prestige. It can
be dangerous to refuse Arab hospitality because this offends
their honor by indicating that one thinks they might not be
good hosts or might do one harm.(28) By practicing hospitality lavishly one increases one's reputation. If a visitor
is not received hospitably, the failure reflects on the
entire tribe or village and blemishes its reputation.(29)

Most discussions of Arab hospitality describe its bedouin
origin. In the desert, hospitality was practiced as a means
of overcoming the individual's helplessness in a harsh
environment. However, Berger points out that in the villages
and cities, hospitality has a different function. It reduces
the tendency of the ever-present hostility to burst into
violence at every moment. Exaggerated hospitality and politeness are reactions to exaggerated hostility, at least in
part.(30) Berger describes how and why there is a great
deal of what may be called "free-floating" hostility. Politeness is a means of maintaining enough distance to prevent
aggressive tendencies from becoming actual. Conflict is so
much on the verge of breaking out that interpersonal relations to a great extent attempt to avoid the slightest tendency toward the expression of difference. There are few
informal mechanisms for the serious discussion of opposing
beliefs without a display of intense anger. Therefore,
except among a few highly educated groups, people do not
discuss their differences. People seem to feel that the
slightest tendency toward verbal disagreement may lead to
something unmanageable, and therefore, must be suppressed
or channeled through a mediator.(31) In relation to this
Hamady notes that religion is not touched upon for fear that
the participants might be condemned as atheists.(32) Obviously, such circumstances pose a problem for the evangelist
who is interested in converting people to a new way of life.
Since hospitality is best demonstrated in the home, should
serious discussions of religion take place elsewhere? Would
a geographical location outside the home be more conducive
to the goals of the evangelist? Ways in which these problems
can be overcome are discussed more thoroughly in chapter five.

Because of the fear of hostility described above social
intercourse follows a precise pattern. Formal, stereotyped
greetings and inquiries are almost inexhaustible, and each
has its own stereotyped response. Arabs may engage in this
sort of dialogue a long time without becoming intimate. It
provides a useful means for each to size up the other and
avoid arousing easily ruffled tempers and pride.(33) How
one is greeted, where to sit, and how one is seen off all
has a tremendous significance. The host assigns the place
to sit, but even then the visitor, unless he is undoubtedly
of higher social rank, does well to sit a little lower than
indicated.(34) Once all are seated another period of elaborate welcoming phrases follows. Periodically thereafter,
the host expresses in diverse and repeated formulas his welcome to his guest. Hamady points out that there are limitations on subjects that are socially acceptable for conversation. In such a gathering people do not feel obliged to
speak and entertain with light conversation once their main
topics are exhausted. They know how to keep quiet. That
silence is interrupted only by intermittent phrases of welcome and good wishes. The host seldom terminates a conversation or dismisses a guest no matter how busy he may be.
At the end of the visit elaborate phrases of thanks, compliments, and good wishes are exchanged again between the host
and departing guests.(35)

No matter how short the visit, the guest is never allowed
to leave before he is offered some food or drink. The usage
connected with food and drink have an almost ritual significance far exceeding a Westerner's idea of mere good manners
and politeness. This is especially true of the intricate
ceremony of serving coffee, which is described in detail by
Dorthy Van Ess.(36) From the humblest tent in the desert to
the sheikh's pavilion one can be sure of a cup of coffee or
a sumptuous meal. Sometimes a casual caller is almost
forced to stay till meal time. To provide only enough food
for him is considered mean; there should always be a surplus.
(37) It is not uncommon to be served seven or eight courses,
each about twice as large as an average American soup bowl.

Regardless of their economic situation, Arabs make every
effort to treat their guests in the most lavish manner possible. Even the poor man does his best to live up to this
expectation, and will literally kill the last animal he
possesses in order to provide a banquet for a guest who may
be a complete stranger. Village folklore is full of stories
about persons who borrowed money to be hospitable to their
guests or who were rich and became poor because they enter-

tained so generously.(38)   The best illustration is the true
story of Hatem At-Taei. Hatem owned the fastest, most beautiful, and powerful horse of Arabia. One day about dinner
time a stranger stopped by Hatem's tent. In the normal manner Hatem insisted that the visitor stay for dinner. After
the meal Hatem asked the visitor about the purpose of his
visit. He answered that the king had heard about Hatem's
horse and he had been sent to ask for it. Hatem cried in
great sorrow, and explained that having nothing else to offer
his guest that he had ordered his son to kill the **horse** and
that **they had** just eaten it.(39)   Although it is not difficult for an Arab to understand this, it is very difficult
for a Westerner to comprehend the motivation behind such
behavior. But Hatem would much rather slaughter his much-
beloved horse than be thought of as a deficient host.

Unless the foreigner understands the nature of the relationship he is involved in as seen by the Arabs, he can permanently damage his influence as is pointed out by Vinogradov:

> Social exchange can function to establish a rela-
> tionship of friendship and equality as well as one
> of superordination/subordination. A relation of
> equality is maintained through strict adherence to
> the rules of balanced reciprocity where obligations
> incurred are repaid in full. Negative or unbalanced
> reciprocity leads to the establishment and maintenance
> of status differentials between the participants.
> The refusal to participate in an exchange relation-
> ship may be tantamount to a declaration of hostility.
> (40)

THE FAMILY

Most of the authors who deal with Arab society, have a
section on the family.(41)   Additionally, several articles
in the journal literature are excellent introductions to
the Arab family.(42)   Of all the component features of
Middle Eastern social structure the family is undoubtedly
the most fundamental and most important.(43)   In Arab
society the welfare of the individual is far less important
than that of the group; and the family, not the individual,
is the social unit.(44)   It is difficult for Westerners to
comprehend the dominant role played by the family in Arab
society. The individual's position in society, his chances
of success, his expectations of education, and attainments
of wealth are largely determined by the family into which
he is born.(45)   The individual has two principal sources

of social identity--his family and his religious community.
Family loyalty is a dominant cultural theme. It is expected
that an individual's first allegiance will always be to his
kin group and the family ties will take precedence over
others in any circumstance.

Empirical evidence of this is provided by studies done
among college students in Beirut.(46) In a rapidly changing
culture affiliations to groups that are not a part of the
traditional culture sometimes conflict with the traditional
loyalties required of the individual. Therefore, Melikian
and Diab sought to determine the hierarchy of group affiliations. They concluded that the core group in the culture --
the family -- still seems to have maintained its position.
The family is still the main source of security, and to win
the approval of one's family and to maintain its confidence
is still of primary importance.(47) In Tomeh's study sixty-
two percent of the students surveyed indicated that both
parents play a primary role in their educational and occupational aspirations.(48) In a survey conducted by the
author among fifty-five Arabs in 1975, the family was rated
as the most important factor in their religious decisions
(table 2).(49)

TABLE 2

WHO IS THE MOST INFLUENTIAL IN THE MAJORITY
OF THE RELIGIOUS DECISIONS YOU MAKE?

Item	Total Response		Response of Christians	
	N	Percent of N	N	Percent of N
Family	17	58.82	5	41.67
Priest	9	26.47	4	33.33
Teacher	2	5.88	2	16.66
Friends	3	8.82	1	8.33

SOURCE: Tim Matheny, "Teaching the Gospel in an Arab
Culture, Field Notes," unpublished paper, Summer 1976,
p. 10.

THE FUNCTION OF RELIGION

Raphael Patai draws an interesting comparison of the role
of religion among the Arabs and among Westerners.(49) He
compares the normative function, the psychological effect,
the supernatural component, and the religiocentric aspect of
religion in Middle Eastern culture and western culture. In
the West the function of religion has shrunk considerably
and covers only one area of life, but in the Arab world it
is the fundamental motivating force on which most cultural
traits and behavior rest; it is the hub from which all else
radiates; and religious convictions influence practically
every act during each moment in life. For example, Jennings
tells of a train in Iran that stopped near sundown and
delayed the journey until the faithful Muslims completed
their prayers.(50)

Islam has always been a civilization and an orientation
to the world. It is not merely a religion in the limited
modern sense. In the Muslim view, there are few or no aspects of individual and social life that may not be considered as immediate expressions of Islam or the working
out of its implications. According to the Muslim world view
the religious commitment is seen as the central point from
which all else flows. It is nearly impossible to draw the
line between those facets of Islamic experience that are
religious and those that are not. Indeed, many Muslim
thinkers would insist that it is illegitimate to try to do
so.(51)

In the Arab world, religion is an asset, the psychological
value of which cannot be overestimated, in that it lends an
unfailing spiritual sustenance to the majority of the population. Rebecca West, in comparing her Christian guide with
his Muslim neighbors, observed:

> The lad was worse off for being a Christian; he
> had not that air of being sustained in his poverty
> by secret spiritual funds that is so noticeable in
> the poverty-stricken Muslim.(52)

In the West, religion has largely lost its function as an
inner sustaining force.

Concerning the supernatural component, both Islam and
western Christianity are monotheistic, but in the Arab
world there remain many animistic beliefs on the popular
level beneath this thin veneer of official doctrine. In the

religiocentric aspect there is a marked similarity between
Christianity and Islam in that they are both characterized
by exclusivity. To sum up, the main differences between
Islam and western Christianity lie in their normative and
psychological functions. This means that the crucial difference is more functional than doctrinal.(53)

John Gulick provides a useful analysis of certain features
of religious behavior in the Arab world which seem to recur
in different sects.(54) They reflect either vestiges of
practices which antedate all present sects, or certain
cultural uniformities. These recurrent elements are as
follows:

1. De-emphasis of hierarchies of authoritarian religious
officials. Their social lives are not particularly separate
from those of the rest of the population.
2. The most important rites of passage are birth and
death. Marriages are primarily secular in tone.
3. A pervasive sense of both positive and negative
supernatural power which can be identified with God and
Satan only by rationalization. The positive aspect is most
clearly revealed in visitations to saint's shrines. The
negative aspect is represented most clearly by belief in the
Evil Eye.
4. Personalization of these concepts of supernatural
power in the form of saints and various mischievous and
malevolent goblins. The Muslim jinn is the **classic** example.
Often these superstitions are violations of formal religious
doctrine. The anthropologist is inclined to suspect that
most Arabs who are internally committed to religious beliefs
are more intensely committed emotionally to the beliefs and
rituals referred to as "superstitions," than to any formalized theological doctrine.

FATALISM

Fatalism is "the degree to which an individual perceives
a lack of ability to control his future."(55) It causes
people to believe that the events of their lives are pre-
ordained and determined by fate or supernatural forces.
Their attitude toward self-control of future events involve
passivity, pessimism, acceptance, endurance, pliancy, and
evasion.

Fatalism is supposedly typical of Middle Easterners and
is often linked with Islam. Though often mentioned, it has
not, until recently, been studied with enough precision to

warrant discussion as a cultural theme.(56) Paydarfar's
survey in Iran indicated that fatalism appeared to be far
less common in urban centers than in the villages. He could
account for it only by suggesting that urbanites are more
exposed to modernization and that modernization is best
indicated by innovativeness.(57)

   The crucial question is: How does fatalism affect an
individual's propensity to change, to accept innovations?
There are two views on the relationship of fatalism and
modernization. First, it has been said that fatalism is
a barrier to modernization and the acceptance of innovations.
Many missionaries in the Middle East have taken this position.
Lerner also takes this position and asserts that such factors
such as literacy, empathy, urbanization, and mass media exposure tend to decrease fatalism, thus making people more
receptive to innovations.(58) The second view is that
fatalism is not an impediment to modernization, but merely
a post hoc rationalization by people to account for obstacles
they feel they cannot overcome. Magnarella takes this position and suggests that once they are presented with con-
vincing evidence that they can change their destinies, they
often act with surprising spontaneity.(59) Roger's research
suggests that the second view is more valid, although evidence on this point is far from definite.(60) More research
is needed before a decision can be made as to which of the
two viewpoints of fatalism is more correct. The question is
not whether fatalism decreases when people become literate,
empathic, urban and exposed to the mass media; the question
is whether fatalism causes people to be less receptive to
innovations.

   Recently, the concept of fatalism has been challenged as
an accurate description of an Arab's behavior.(61) Westerners **have** often emphasized the Arab's fatalistic approach
to life by the following story:

   When all the birds were gathered together to make
   their final arrangements before starting on a pilgrimage to Mecca, they passed a resolution saying:
   "If God wills, we will start tomorrow." But the
   hens cried out "If God wills or not, we will start
   tomorrow." When the time came to start they were
   punished for their irreverent words by finding
   themselves unable to fly.(62)

   Rather than being proof of fatalism, this story really
illustrates a punishment for opposing God's will. In

reality Arabs are afraid of opposing God's will, and a careful examination of their beliefs indicates much that is not
fatalistic.(63)

The Arab world still sees the universe running its pre-
destined course, determined by the will of God, who not only
guides the world at large, but also predestines the fate of
each and every man. Hence, Islam means "submission to the
will of God."(64) There is a lack of a sharp distinction
between the natural and the supernatural. In dealing with
Arabs it is imperative that Westerners have some grasp of
this traditional world view, in which there are strong subconscious motivations radically different from those of
Westerners.(65)

Hamady points out that the Arab's attitude of resignation
is due to many factors: 1) religious indoctrination, 2) subsistence economy, 3) long centuries of foreign domination,
and 4) the pressure of family and public opinion.(66)
Although the Muslim belief in predestination is firmly en-
trenched in the Koran, there are many passages that contradict the spirit of determinism. The impact of fatalistic
philosophy on the Arabs is therefore due not so much to religious doctrine as to the vicious influence of political subjugation, economic poverty, and social tyranny.(67) If fatalistic resignation is due more to political subjugation,
then should not political freedom, nationalism and and modernization lead to a rejection of fatalism?

Fatalism is not a major cultural theme of the Transitional
Arab because there is a basic conflict between fatalism and
modernization. However, although fatalism is not a cultural
theme regulating the behavior of the Transitional Arab, it is
a part of Traditional Arab society out of which the Transitional has recently come.

ANIMISTIC SUPERSTITIONS

In contrast to the view that one should not take action
lest he go against God's will, one finds in daily life all
sorts of efforts to change an existing situation and to act
in many ways which appear to be logically irreconcilable
with the religious belief in predestination. Nida diagrams
the essential features of the communicative relationships in
popular Islamic faith in diagram 2. Under Allah there are
a whole series of spirit beings, from archangels to the
jinns. These spirits are very real in popular Islam and are
regarded by some as more important goals of communication

than God himself. Magic is one of the techniques whereby
fate may either be foretold or escaped. Since fate is impersonal the impersonal techniques of animism seem fitting in-
struments to control it.(68)

DIAGRAM 2

COMMUNICATIVE RELATIONSHIPS IN ISLAM

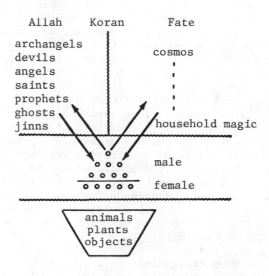

SOURCE: Eugene A. Nida, *Religion Across Cultures* (New York:
Harper and Row, 1968), p. 39.

Several works deal extensively with this aspect of Arab
religious behavior.(69) Beneath the thin veneer of official
doctrine are old popular beliefs, held by the masses who
know little of the theological tenets of their religion.
In the West little of this popular religiosity has survived.
(70) In the Arab world there is a great deal of emphasis on
belief in innumerable demons, spirits, jinn, the evil eye,
and ritual worship of saints who wield supernatural powers.
(71) Magic beliefs and practices are found among villagers
in all Arab countries. Simple practices are known to every-
body, but if more effective action is required, the services
of magical specialists are available for a fee.(72) Arab
superstitions may be divided into four categories: the evil
eye, spirits, shrines, and vows and phrases.

The Evil Eye

The evil eye is the most widespread of these animistic
beliefs and it is not confined to the Middle East. The concept of the evil eye implies that things or persons one
holds dear are continually vulnerable to damage or destruction
caused by other people's envy projected through their eyes.
(73) The possessor of an evil eye usually has no control
over his unconscious wishes and their workings.(74) Belief
in the evil eye is different from witchcraft in that everyone can be an agent of the evil eye. It is a projection of
the destructively envious feelings that large numbers of
people harbor.(75) It is believed to cause sickness, death
and bad luck.(76)

The belief system itself includes no cures for the evil
eye, only a large variety of defensive protective rituals
and devices. Children, animals, and taxi cabs have blue
beads or other amulets attached as symbolic protection
against the evil eye.(77) Compliments are supposed to bring
evil because they make the inhabitants of the spirit world
jealous, and they get even by causing illness. Therefore,
it is customary not to compliment very young children, since
they are especially vulnerable. Male children are often
dressed as girls till the age of five to keep the evil eyes
from focusing on them.(78)

Envy is very understandable as a commonly felt emotion
in a land where subsistence is precarious. Gulick explains
the evil eye not as an irrational superstition, but as a
realistic reaction to styles of life in which people are
both agents of peril to others and also imperiled themselves
by others.(79) In other words, it is an answer to a felt
need.

Spirits

Many Arabs believe in invisible creatures and occult
forces including: angels, devils, and the jinn. The jinn
are shadowy beings without any distinct personality whose
principal abode is the underworld, but are essentially dangerous when they visit the earth.(80) The jinn are mentioned
in the Koran, but while some Muslims ignore the idea, the
belief of others goes far beyond what is said in the Koran.
(81) Jinn are believed to live in many empty and deserted
places including door sills. Arabs invoke the name of God
when passing such places to protect themselves from such
spirits.(82) One must be very careful not to offend the

jinn for fear of dire consequences such as bodily injury or disease.(83)

Saint's Shrines

Saint's shrines are very common in the Middle East, being used by Muslims and Christians alike.(84) The souls of these saints are still believed to be present and are believed to hover over the body or get out to stay at a distance. The souls visit their bodies on those days when the living choose to visit the graveyard.(85) Arabs come to the shrines to seek favors, swear oaths, take vows, prove innocence of any crime, cure disease, take care of other medical problems, and to bring gifts to gain the saint's blessing *(baraka)*.(86)

Although many of the shrines are used by both Muslims and Christians, some of the more important elaborate Shia shrines in Iran are limited to Muslims, such as the one described by Elizabeth **Fernea**.(87) Gulick describes his visit to the tomb-shrine of Abdul-Qadir al-Giland in Baghdad:

> It was not a crowded day, and so I was able to observe one pilgrim with some care. He stood close to the grillwork facing the tomb and grasped the grillwork with both hands so tightly that his knuckles were white, and his mouth opened and closed in silent prayer or entreaty. Every few moments he would release his grasp, step backwards a couple of paces, run the palms of his hands all over his body, and then step forward grasping the grillwork again. To this man, it would seem, that baraka of the saint was a palpable though invisible substance, applicable to his body like an ointment. This was no "superstition-ridden" peasant or laborer. He was dressed in a western-style business suit, with shirt and necktie, and he had set his briefcase on the floor beside him.(88)

Gulick's observation points to the significant fact that it is not just Traditional Arabs who are involved in such practices, but Transitionals and sometimes Moderns believe in the value of this type of behavior.

The saint complex is present virtually everywhere in the Middle East except for Saudi Arabia, where the Wahhabi sect has suppressed it. It enables the ordinary Muslim to get emotional reinforcement through exposure to *baraka* and emotional release by means of spiritual and physical exercises.

The rationale behind this type of activity is that it constitutes immediate communion with God. Many observers say
that classical (the great tradition of) Islam is deficient
in its provision of this kind of emotional and spiritual
satisfaction. Evidently, the emotional needs met by these
rituals are still felt needs, and the saint complex is not
dying in the Middle East.(89)

Vows and Other Phrases

Many phrases, formulas, and vows such as "God protect
him" and "let it be far from you" and God's name on him" are
used to ward off disease and other evil influences.(90)
Uttering the name of God or saying the phrase "in the name
of God" (*bismillah*) is believed to be a protection against
evil of all kinds.(91)

The question arises: Do Transitional Arabs really hold
such superstitions? Has not modernization and westernization
caused much of this superstition to disappear? Yes, modern
medicine does seem to have contributed to the abandonment of
visits to the shrines, and Gulick observed in 1952 that no
one was wearing or using amulets or religious medals in the
Lebanese village that he studied.(92) However, Gulick argues
that the mentality which lies behind the superstitious behavior persists inspite of modern innovations.(93) Additionally, Darity tells of a western-trained Lebanese techni-
cian who sincerely rejects many traditional aspects of Middle
Eastern culture and equally sincerely protects his children
against the evil eye.(94)

Therefore, the needs fulfilled by these various superstitious practices continue to be felt needs among many
Arabs. These pagan remnants in the Arab's system of beliefs
occupy a more important place in the life of the Arab masses
than do the official doctrines of Islam.(95) The very fact
that these superstitions have survived is evidence of the
age-old human readiness to engage in activity that promises
to fulfill certain basic needs. It appears that the doctrine
of predestination is believed on one level of consciousness,
while everyday behavior is determined on a different level.
(96)

What does this say for the evangelist who encounters the
Arab only at the intellectual or doctrinal level? Even if
converted, his everyday behavior will not change. The needs
supposedly satisfied by the animistic behavior must be determined, and then Christianity should be presented in terms of

those needs. Thus the study of the animistic behavior and
beliefs of Arabs becomes significant in determining their
felt needs.

The construction of a message to meet the felt needs is
dealt with in chapter seven. McCurry says that these animistic practices must be dealt with since they are the express
felt needs and point to the inevitability of "power encounters"
if its practitioners are to come to Christ.(97)

In the Arab's response to Christianity he may accept certain aspects without adopting a logical system. The American
evangelist, whose cultural background has prepared him to
notice logical inconsistencies often assumes that the Arab
reader of scripture will draw "logical" conclusions of the
same type that were presented in the books on doctrine and
theology which he studied. But unless such items as the
animistic practices are specifically dealt with, the Arab
may continue to rely on them in spite of the fact that he
has become a Christian.(98)

CONCEPT OF TIME

The Arab's concept of time is another cultural theme that
sets Arab culture apart as being distinctive. The value
attached to time by the Arab can be an endless source of
culture jolts for the evangelist.

> What does it mean to hurry? When is a person on
> time? When is he prompt? What should the mis-
> sionary's reaction be when someone fails to keep
> an appointment? How long may the missionary keep
> one waiting? How serious must the reason be before
> the missionary may be disturbed?...The answer to
> all these questions will be found to be closely
> associated with the culturally defined value
> attached to time.(99)

The values attached to exactness and punctuality, as the
evangelist understands these terms may differ considerably
from the value the Arabs attach to such exactness and punctuality. As anyone who has lived among Arabs can testify,
they are much less concerned with time than Westerners.
Advance planning and scheduling is a basic part of the
Westerner's everyday life. Under the influence of westernization, some of this has penetrated in recent decades to
the Arab world as well. Work schedules, timetables, and
the like have become important ordering factors of life in

the Arab cities. But even there, and much more so in the
villages, the traditional lack of concern with time still
predominates in many areas of life.(100)

Edward T. Hall isolates five dimensions of time: appointment time, discussion time, acquaintance time, visiting time,
and time schedules.(101) An examination of these five dimensions of time will illustrate the many ways in which the
Arab's concept of time is expressed in the various facets of
the total cultural system of the Arab. The Westerner will
find much of Arab behavior confusing if he tries to interpret
it in terms of a western concept of time.

Appointment Time

The value attached to exactness and punctuality by the
evangelist may differ considerably from the value the Arab
attaches to such exactness. Rarely does the Arab finish an
assigned job by the time he has promised. He procrastinates,
and does not feel pressed by the element of time. Nor does
he operate on schedule, and if he does, he is either too
early or too late. He will come several hours early to
catch a train, but may arrive several hours late for an
appointment. Punctuality, precision, and haste are beyond
his perception.(102) A forty-five minute wait may not be
any more unusual in the Arab world than a five minute wait
would be in the United States. No insult is intended, the
time pie is just cut differently.(103)

A Westerner would say, "May I come to see you at five in
the afternoon?" but an Arab would say "I shall come to see
you tomorrow afternoon, God willing." The "afternoon"
referred to may be any time from noon to late in the evening,
or any other afternoon within the next few days. The phrase
"God willing" stamps any advance commitment with a note of
uncertainty, which is a carry-over from the cultural theme
of fatalism discussed previously. In light of this it becomes clearly impossible, and to some extent improper to fix
the time of a future act with greater exactness.(104)

A few years ago in Kabul, Afghanistan a man appeared
looking for his brother but could not find him. The next
year he was back doing the same thing. One of the members
of the American embassy who had heard about his inquiries
asked whether he had found his brother. The man answered
that he and his brother had agreed to meet in Kabul, but
neither of them had said what year.(105)

In the United States there are eight time sets regarding punctuality and the length of appointments: on time, five, ten, fifteen, twenty, thirty, forty-five minutes, and one hour early or late. But the Arab makes fewer distinctions than most Westerners do. His scale has only three discernable points, not eight. These are: no time at all; now (or present) which is of varying duration; and forever (too long). In the Arab world it is almost impossible to get someone to experience the difference between waiting a long time and a very long time.(106) An evangelist who reacts to Arab behavior by saying, "How can you depend on these people when they arrive an hour late for an appointment and then just mutter something?" has obviously not understood the Arab's concept of time and is apt to do a great deal of damage to his effectiveness.

Discussion Time

Suppose one has been waiting forty-five minutes, does he then try to get down to business and stop "wasting time"? For most Westerners discussion is a means to an end, which means that one makes his point quickly and efficiently. But the Arab does not tend to separate rigidly business and non-business. Therefore, discussion time also becomes something of a social event. The Arab disregard of time often finds its expression in the inability to begin and end sessions at appointed hours.(107)

Acquaintance Time

Acquaintance time means how long one must know a man before he does business with him. In the United States a salesman may walk away from the first meeting with an order in his pocket. But in the Arab world, several meetings of social visiting may be required before one can "get down to business." Therefore, the use of timing to introduce an innovation requires that the evangelist know a fair amount about the local scene.(108) An evangelist who tries to begin talking about the serious matters of the Gospel too soon could rapidly ruin his effectiveness. In the Middle East refusal of one party to come to the point and discuss the topic of a meeting often means he cannot agree to your terms but does not want to turn you down, or simply that he cannot discuss the matters under consideration because the time is not yet ripe. He will not, moreover, feel it is improper to meet without ever touching on the topic of the meeting.(109)

Visiting Time

Visiting time involves the question of who sets the time
for a visit. In the United States a telephone call very
early in the morning during breakfast or after 11:00 P.M.
usually signals a matter of utmost importance and extreme
urgency.(110) The parts of the day have different meanings
for different people, and it is improper to assign a western
meaning to Arab behavior which is drastically different in
many cases. An American girl would feel insulted if she was
asked for a date at the last minute by someone she does not
know very well. How different from the Middle East where it
is pointless to make an appointment too far in advance, because the informal structure of their time system places
everything beyond a week into a single category of "future,"
in which plans tend to slip off their minds.(111)

A Westerner may be casually invited for a drink in a
Middle Eastern home in Cairo or Beirut, and many times the
hour is not given. The underlying implication is that the
guest is always welcome and free to come at any time, though,
of course, within the unwritten rules of the code of visiting
etiquette in the Middle East. The Westerner might ask directly
or indirectly, and an hour around eight or nine in the evening
might be settled on. That is definitely after dinner time
for an American, and so he eats dinner and later goes to the
home of his Middle Eastern friend. There he is likely to
find a huge meal waiting for him and the Middle Eastern friend
is offended when the American does not eat because he has had
dinner.(112)

The role of time in a visit itself is also important. The
hostess gauges the serving of various items depending on the
nature of the visit and importance of the guest. The final
cup of coffee is the cue that one would be free to leave.(113)

Time Schedules

When Westerners interact with people in the Arab world,
both quickly become aware that their outlook in regard to
time is different. For Westerners, "time is money." A person works for a stated number of dollars per hour, and an
employer literally buys the time of his worker. Equating
work with time implies using the least amount of time to produce the largest amount of work. Such a precise concept of
time is foreign to many Arabs.

The cities in the Arab world have all adopted the western
concept of time to some degree, but frequently the traditional
pattern is still maintained in modified form in the urban
context. Individuals simply do not keep hours or appointments precisely and are surprised when they learn that a
Westerner is irritated by a missed appointment.(114)

One can imagine the fundamental conflicts that arise when
a Westerner attempts to communicate with people who are just
as strongly oriented away from time schedules as he is toward them. Not only is the western idea of time schedules
no part of Arab life but the mere mention of a deadline to
an Arab is interpreted as a threat. In his culture, a
western emphasis on a deadline has the same emotional effect
on him as backing a Westerner into a corner and threatening
him with a club.(115) One effect of this conflict of unconscious habit pattern is that hundreds of American-owned sets
are lying on the shelves of Arab radio repair shops, untouched.
The Americans made the serious cross-cultural error of asking
to have the repair completed by a certain time.

How does one cope with this? How does the Arab get
another Arab to do anything? Every culture has its own way
of bringing pressure to get results. The usual Arab way is
one which Westerners avoid as "bad manners." It is needling.
An Arab businessman whose car broke down explained it this
way:

> First, I go to the garage and tell the mechanic what
> is wrong with my car. I wouldn't want to give him
> the idea that I didn't know. After that, I leave
> the car and walk around the block. When I come back
> to the garage, I ask him if he has started to work
> yet. On my way home from lunch I stop in and ask
> him how things are going. When I go back to the
> office I stop by again. In the evening, I return
> and peer over his shoulder for a while. If I
> didn't keep this up, he'd be off working on some-
> one else's car.(116)

The overriding pattern with Westerners is that once the
time is scheduled it must be used as designated. All of
this seems very strange to an Arab. He starts at one point
and goes until he is finished or until something intervenes.
Westerners cannot shift the partitions of schedules without
violating a norm; Arabs can.(117) Westerners treat time
much like a material; one can earn it, spend it, save it,
and waste it. People who cannot schedule time are looked

down upon as impractical.(118)   Since the Arab does not consider time as an item of value, time is neither accumulated
nor budgeted.(119)

   In view of this unconcern with time it is not surprising
to find that the concept of punctuality does not exist in
traditional Arab culture, and that the introduction of rig-
orous time schedules, demanded by modernization, has encountered great difficulties. Nor will it come as a surprise
that lateness for appointments or not showing up at all has
remained to this day a fairly common phenomenon in Arab life.
(120)

   Few efforts will serve to confuse the Arab more than those
which attempt to have him grasp the western concept of time.
The American evangelist can plead that "Behold now is the
acceptable time; behold, now is the day of salvation" and
mean a point of time in terms of a day or an hour.(121)   But
to many Arabs this "now" must not refer to the present moment but to an indefinite duration in which group consideration may occur.(122)

                          BARGAINING

   The Arab conducts his business, social duty, and pleasure
at the same time. He is subjective and likes to deal with
people on a personal level. This is seen in the personal
method of buying and selling in bargaining.(123)   Coon tells
how the buyer and seller may argue over the price of a pair
of slippers for as much as half an hour.   Friends and by-
passers may even join in the sport.(124)   The foreigner may
ask, "Why do they go to all this trouble? Why not just tag
the merchandise with a fixed price?" Because the seller
likes to bargain with his customers. It is his job and he
enjoys it. From his point of view it is not a waste of time.
Someday he will get a gullible customer and make a killing.
But that is less important than the pleasure this kind of
interaction gives him.

   Another reason bargaining is not a waste of time is
because it is a form of developing social relationships. In
traditional society, the buyer and seller as a rule are well
known to each other, each of them knows the male members of
the other's family, and for this reason the seller will offer to reduce the price "for the sake of your father" or "for
your sake." The common feature of this game of bargaining
is that it not only leads to successful conclusion of a bargain, but also cements the personal relationship between the

two men.(125)   Even in large cities such as Tripoli, Lebanon
most businesses are known by the personal identity of their
owners, not by an impersonal trade name.(126)

When a shop keeper is asked the price of his goods, he
usually asks more than he expects to receive; the customer
declares the price exorbitant, and offers about half or two-
thirds of the sum first named. The shop keeper lowers his
demand and the customer bids somewhat higher and they usually
meet about halfway. Bargaining even over insignificant items
many times involves a great deal of vehemence of voice and
gesture and a person ignorant of Arabic would imagine that
they were quarreling and very angry.(127)

To understand the function of bargaining in Arab culture
it is necessary to apply the anthropological concept of
form and meaning to this practice. A Westerner can easily
detect and see the form of bargaining in the Middle East,
but it is much more difficult to detect the meaning that it
has to the Arab. In the Middle East bargaining is an underlying theme which is significantly different from the activity
which goes under that name in American culture. Yet what is
seen on the surface (form) looks familiar and is assumed to
be the same. It is easy for Westerners to make a mistake in
assessing the meaning of bargaining in the Middle East, and
the role it plays in everyday life. Americans tend to look
down on people who haggle, but to the Arab bargaining is
not only a means of passing a day but is actually a technique
of interpersonal relations.(128)

The American pattern of bargaining is predicted on the
assumption that each party has a high and a low point that
is hidden. The function of the bargaining is to discover
what the opponent's points are without revealing one's own.
(129) The American in the Middle East will ask, "What percentage of the asking price do I give as my first offer?"
This procedure is not only wrong but it can end in trouble.
What the American does not know is that the Arab has many
different asking prices, each with a different meaning. The
principle to be remembered is that instead of each party
having a high and a low there is really only *one* principle
point, which lies somewhere in the middle. Much like the
latest stock market quotation in the United States, this
point is determined not by the two parties, but by the market or the situation, constituting a set of circumstances
which are known to both parties.(130) Khuri tells what some
of these circumstances are. Shop keepers in Beirut are
extraordinarily perceptive of people's accents, dress,

cleanliness, names, and the way these correlate with specific
backgrounds. Names often suggest sect and clan membership;
accents and dialects suggest regional and sometimes village
membership; dress and cleanliness suggest class membership.
(131) The point is determined by such factors as these as
well as others. Ignorance of the position of the pivot opens
one up to the worst type of exploitation, as well as loss of
face (honor), of which the author himself has been guilty.
Above and below the central points there are a series of
points which indicate what the two parties feel as they enter
the field.(132)

TABLE 3

A BARGAINING SCALE

Piasters		Meaning
Seller's asking prices	12	complete ignorance on the part of the seller
	10	an insult, arguments, and fights ensue, seller doesn't want to sell
	8	will sell, but let's continue bargaining
	7	will sell under the market
pivot	6	market price
Buyer's offering prices	5	buyer really wants the squash, will pay over the market
	4	will buy
	2	arguments and fighting, buyer doesn't want to buy
	1	ignorance of the value of the item on the part of the buyer

SOURCE: Edward T. Hall, *The Silent Language* (Garden City,
New York: Doubleday, Anchor Books, 1959), p. 128

An Arab from Damascus describes the process in a case
where the pivotal point for the price of squash is six
piasters. Any one of the four prices above the pivotal point
(see table 3) might be the first price asked by the seller.

Any one of the lower four represents the first offer made by
the prospective buyer. Notice the hidden meaning that is
given beside each point in table 3. This meaning is not
exact but represents a clue as to the attitudes of the two
parties as they enter the bargaining process.

Considering the difference of meaning which carried by a
variation of one piaster, the question, "What percentage of
the asking price do I give?" seems meaningless. Other variations on this pattern have as many as five or six points
above and below the pivot, each with its own meaning. Understanding the Arab concept of bargaining could mean the difference between success and failure in many personal relationships the evangelist might have. Research in areas of
culture such as this is very difficult. Even the best of
informants can never describe the meaning of all the cultural
themes which regulate Arab behavior, even though he has been
born and raised· in that culture.

CONCEPT OF NATURE

The Traditional Arab is surrounded by the world of nature.
Earth, rock, water, and growing things are to him the handi-
work of God. God created the natural world and sustains it.
Toward all nature's forms the Arab has a sense of piety,
since they are signs of deity and since they relate closely
to his own welfare.(133) The Transitional Arab is not as
closely attached to nature, but these traditional attitudes
constitute the background of his mentality. Family and kinship sentiments are deeply tied up with the land. The amount
of land owned is a sign of the family's social and basic economic status in the village. Fuller describes how the different festivals and ceremonies of the village are closely
connected to the land and the natural seasons.(134)

In Lebanon, approximately one-fourth of the village is
absent during the winter season. Young unmarried men drift
off to find work in Beirut or in the citrus groves along
the coast. Persons away from home for the winter season
attempt to find work in the same general neighborhood of one
another. As a result the sense of tie with the mountain
community is not entirely disrupted.(135)

One does not have to know a Lebanese very long before one
is invited to his village for a visit. The evangelist can
use the Arab's concept of nature to his advantage in communicating the Christian message. Much of the Bible is more
relevant to the Arab because of his concept of nature (see
chapter seven).

CONCLUSION

This discussion of the cultural themes of Arabs has involved many references to the traditional way of life. It
is the impression of many that the impact of the West in
the Arab world thought modernization will transform it into
a copy of the West.   However, Gulick declares that there is
"little doubt that there remain in the Middle East cultural
themes that are distinctive and special."(136)   Therefore,
although the way of life in the Middle East is radically
changing, most of the cultural themes discussed in this
chapter will continue to find expression among Transitionals
in one form or another, and will continue to be relevant to
evangelistic strategy in that part of the world.

Another aspect of Arab culture which is crucial in constructing an evangelistic strategy is its social structure.
The social structure influences the ways in which innovations
diffuse through a society. It can act as a restriction or
as a channel of effective communication depending on how it
is approached. The following chapter will include an examination of the five categories of identity of Arab society,
its vertical class structure, and its opinion leaders.

3

Social Structure

Social structure may be so defined as to include several categories of customs which involve extensive interpersonal relations and the groups that form as a result.(1) Social structure includes groups formed on the basis of kinship, religion, language, sex, and geographic location. The social structure of a society affects the diffusion pattern of an innovation in several ways. It may act to impede or facilitate the rate of diffusion and adoption of new ideas through what are called "system effects."(2) The social structure can provide serious resistance to change unless efforts are made to adapt to it. Where significant ethnic groups exist, the change agent can simplify the change process if he takes into account the vested interest of these groups.

After a careful analysis of the social structure of a people, the evangelist should be able to recognize the direction and relative force (or persuasive influence) of the various currents of communication.(3) It is wrong to assume that once the social and intellectual elite accept an innovation the rest of the society will inevitably follow. The currents of communication in many cultures are not vertical but horizontal. Society strongly influences every aspect of what a man says, thinks, and does. Therefore, when the evangelist comprehends the social structure of a particular segment of the total population, he will know better how churches are likely to increase and ramify through it.(4)

It is one thing to analyze the structure of a society in order to discover the fundamental lines of communication; it

is quite another to develop a message relevant to the different social groups. This chapter is primarily concerned with
the former; that is, it is descriptive in nature. Chapter
seven discusses the construction of a relevant message. Nida
points out that despite the fact that Americans usually sense
the importance of different social structures, they rarely
recognize the degree to which these factors influence a people's
religious thinking and tend to condition their response to
new ideas, especially to the presentation of the gospel message.(5)

   The numerous groups of Arab social structure fall into two
planes, the horizontal and the vertical. The horizontal
plane divisions are based on five basic categories of identity:
the same ancestor (kinship), the same religion, the same language, the same sex, and the same territory (geographical
location).(6) These various categories of identity very often overlap thus producing a very cohesive unit. A man who
resides in a certain neighborhood is likely to find himself
with others who are also kinsmen, coreligionists, members of
the same ethnic group, and engaged in the same occupation.
Categories on the vertical plane are based on various combinations of income, political power, education, style of
life, and family reputation. The vertical plane is what may
be called the social stratification or the class structure.
There is almost no mobility on the horizontal plane, but
vertical mobility is extensive.(7)

HORIZONTAL STRUCTURE

   Of the categories of identity, religion and kinship are
the most pervasive and enduring loyalties in the Middle East.
(8)   The psychologists Melikian and Diab found that students
at the American University of Beirut affiliated themselves
with family first, ethnic group second, religion third,
citizenship fourth, and political party fifth.(9) A more
recent study of students of the above university showed that
they are less alienated from family than from religion, university, and government, and none showed a high feeling of
alienation from the family.(10)

Kinship: The Extended Family

   The patrilineal kin group is a major unit of identity in
Arab culture. Kinship is the pattern of responsibilities
toward and rights expected from relatives.(11)   The smallest
kinship group is the nuclear family which consists of husband,
wife, and their dependent, unmarried children. In the Middle

East the nuclear family is normally assumed to be strongly affiliated with the husband's brothers, their parents, and the brother's children (this larger group constituting what is called the patrilineal extended family.(12)

The section on the family in chapter two stressed the dominating influence of the Arab family on the individual. This section will go further than that in seeking to bring out those aspects of family structure that influence the diffusion of innovations.

McGavran affirms that a homogeneous unit of society may be said to have "people consciousness."(13) The degree of people consciousness is an aspect of social structure that has a tremendous influence on when, how, and to what extent innovations will flow through that segment of society.

Many discussions of Arab culture sometimes convey this stereotyped impression of the Arab family:

> The basic family unit is the patrilocal, patriarchal,
> extended family, often linked to a larger lineage.
> For the Muslim majority, polygyny is permitted and
> patrilateral parallel-cousin marriage is preferred,
> hence both may be presumed to be frequent. Where
> monogamous nuclear families as independent units oc-
> cur, they are due to urban influences.(14)

Gulick asserts that the above image is only partially true, and many of the assumptions are of questionable validity. Although cousin marriage is a formal ideal among Muslims, the evidence indicates that only a small minority of such marriages actually occur.(15) Less than five to ten percent have more than one wife simultaneously.(16) The literature is very careless in its references to "urban influences" and so far few significant differences in kinship patterns between villages and cities have been discovered.(17) The available data show that the nuclear family and not the extended family is the typical residential unit of the area.(18)

Farsoun examined the functions of the extended family among Transitional Arabs in Beirut in the economic, political religious, and stratification structures.(19) First, in relation to the economic structures in the Middle East, the employment of relatives whenever possible or feasible is generally admitted as good practice. The extended family functions as an informal group for the collection, storing and transmission of information on available jobs. Pierce indicates

that many times when new jobs are created close friends
would approach him to hire their relatives. Usually they
were unqualified for the position, and the average American
reaction is that these people are dishonest or immoral. But
it is of significance to note that it would be dishonorable
for an Arab to do otherwise. He is honor bound by all that
he holds sacred to promote the welfare of his extended family
group.(20)   To accept western values forces an Arab to be
dishonorable in the eyes of his family and friends, and yet
to follow his own cultural values is to appear dishonorable
in the eyes of Americans. The evangelist may be misled by
the apparent westernized and modern looks of many Arabs.
However, these cultural themes run deep, having been learned
at an early age, so that although they appear to be westernized, they operate on the basis of a set of subconscious
values. They are not being dishonest but simply human.

The implications of this are that the individual partici-
pates with the larger groups of society--economically, politically, socially, and religiously--through his family membership rather than as an individual. An individual does not
usually make important decisions without conferring with his
family, to which he usually subordinates his wishes.(21)

Herbert and Judith Williams conducted a very significant
study on "The Extended Family as a Vehicle of Culture Change."
(22)   They examined the role of the extended family in culture change in a small Lebanese village community. They are
primarily concerned with the extended family as a functional
unit and not as a residential unit.(23)   They discovered
that the innovations in the village were largely brought
about by those families who have acted as particularly well-
integrated and cohesive units.(24)   Although the extended
family was widely scattered in residence it remained functionally intact and integrated. Its very level of integration
seems to be a prime factor in making change possible.(25)   In
other words, the cohesiveness of the Arab extended family,
which has been the primary barrier to individual religious
conversions in the Middle East, can become the primary vehicle
of culture change and innovations. The Williams add that
change has enhanced the extended family cohesion and rein-
forced and preserved the lineage structure.(26)   The Williams'
study becomes even more significant when one is reminded that
no significant differences have been found in the function of
the extended family in villages and cities.(27)

In Farsoun's study of kinship patterns among the Transitionals in Beirut, four aspects of interaction among kinsmen

were discovered.(28) The first consists of the religious
celebrations, personal festivals, rites of passage, and
serious illness that bring the entire extended family together
several times a year. The second kind of interaction is the
weekly gathering of grandparents, children, spouses, and
grandchildren. The third consists of daily visits among
adult siblings, and between parents and married children.
These visits are the basis for the major source of entertainment and satisfaction the individual has. The fourth
kind is dependent on the telephone and the automobile, which
are used as auxiliary mechanisms when convenience or distance
make immediate face-to-face contact impossible.(29)

   Table 4 shows the results of Farsoun's survey which asked
how often extended family kinsmen had face-to-face interaction
with each other. If the "daily" and "weekly" categories are
combined into an "at least weekly" category, all respondents
interact with almost all members of their respective extended
families in Beirut every week.

TABLE 4

FREQUENCY OF INTERACTION WITH EXTENDED FAMILY LIVING
WITHIN BEIRUT

Frequency of Interaction	Extended Family			
	Parents	Own Married Children	Married Siblings	Married Nieces and Nephews
Daily	73%	94%	46%	0%
Weekly	27%	6%	51%	93%
Less than weekly	0%	0%	3%	7%
Total	100%	100%	100%	100%
Number of kin	89	18	187	29
Number of Respondents	98	98	98	98

SOURCE: Samih K. and Karen Farsoun, "Class and Patterns of
Association among Kinsmen in Contemporary Lebanon," *Anthro-
logical Quarterly* 47 (January 1974): 105.

Religion

Religious identity serves as a very important means of
social differentiation in the Arab world. Consciousness of
social distance is clearly marked among the Arabs.(30) Muslims are an overwhelming majority in every Middle Eastern
country except Israel and Lebanon. A great deal has been
written on the religious social structure in the Middle East,
of which only the highlights can be touched upon here.(31)

John Gulick makes a distinction between religion and sect:

> A *religion* is a system of beliefs and symbolic acts
> concerned with the superhuman and with human beings'
> beliefs about their relationships with the super-
> human. A *sect*...is a group of people that has a
> religious identity but also has its own internal
> social structure and its own external political
> relationships, with other sects and groups.(32)

Sectarian behavior is therefore social behavior and is
quite distinct from symbolic religious behavior concerning
the superhuman. This distinction between religious and sectarian is not the same as the classification in which a "religion" is divided into "denominations," and these are sub-
divided into "sects."(33) Sectarian behavior represents a
spectrum of behavior in which the non-religious concerns of
group dynamics are combined with religious concerns. Gulick
traces out the historical process of the formation of the
various religious sects in the Middle East of which the geneology of the various Christian sects are illustrated in
diagram 3. These sects (both Christian and Muslim) are known
as cultural communities and remain divided long after the
reasons for division have disappeared. Gulick proposes that
sectarian concerns may be far more important than religious
ones in the on-going Middle Eastern experience.(34)

Although Lebanon is not typical of the Middle East in a
number of respects, its political structure is consciously
and deliberately organized along sectarian lines, and exem-
plifies many of the issues of Middle Eastern religion and
sectarianism. The last official census was taken in 1932,
and its sectarian enumerations were used as the basis for
the proportionate representation of the sects among the
elected members of parliament.(35) The 1932 census established
an offical ratio of five Muslims for every six Christians in
the country, and no census has been taken since, lest the
delicate balance be upset. But the organization of the

DIAGRAM 3
GENEOLOGY OF THE CHRISTIAN CHURCH

N.B.
THE SIZE OF THE VARIOUS BRANCHES OF THE CHURCH
IN THIS DIAGRAM DOES NOT REPRESENT THEIR
NUMERICAL STRENGTH.

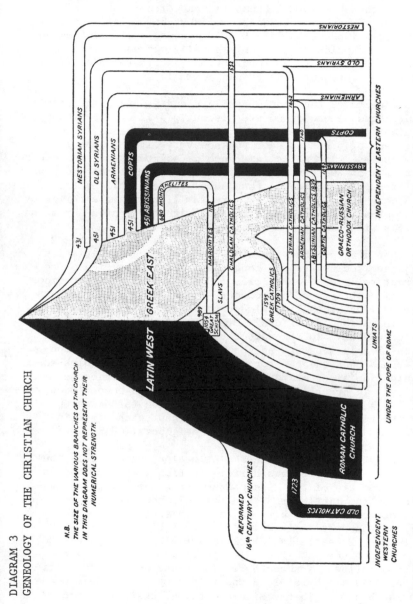

SOURCE: Gabriel Baer, *Population and Society in the Arab East* (New York: Frederick A. Praeger, 1964), p. 85.

Lebanese social structure around religious communities goes
back to Ottoman times. A Lebanese can neither vote nor in
effect hold Lebanese citizenship without belonging to a recognized religious sect.(36) Every Lebanese adult carries an
identity card which designates his religious community and,
regardless of his personal convictions, he is regarded by
others as a representative of his community.

These sects of the Middle East are endogamous on principle
and marriages between them are discouraged if not forbidden
altogether.(37) One result of this social distance is that
the members of one sect seem to know very little about life
in the others. The social distance is so great that a Lebanese
Christian knows more about the religious convictions and practices of a French Catholic than about those of his next door
Muslim neighbor. A Muslim is more familiar with the religious
beliefs of an Indonesian Muslim than with those of a Christian
who lives with him in the same building.(38)

Barakat affirms that one of the dominant characteristics
of Lebanese society is the geographical concentration of the
different religious communities.(39) He examines the various
electoral districts of the country and shows how the members
of the various sects live almost to the total exclusion of
others in various districts. Even where the different religious groups live in the same city, town, or village, they
tend to live in separate neighborhoods. This situation obviously has consequences for interpersonal relationships and
communication among members of the different religious communities. In order for these relationships to become deeply
extensive and intimate and for communication to become open
and authentic, Lebanese will have to accept each other in
marriage and not just as friends or neighbors.(40)

Not only does Gulick make a distinction between religion
and sect, but he makes another distinction in the religious
social structure of the Middle East: that of the great tradition and the little tradition.(41) In the previous chapter
a distinction was made between the intellectual (doctrinal)
level and the emotional (animistic superstitious) level (see
pp. 28-29). Essentially Gulick is applying these labels to
the same distinction. Each diverges from the other, yet
each also influences the other. The great and little tradition concepts are helpful in understanding the religious and
sectarian behavior in the Middle East. Classical Arabic is
the language of the Koran which is the scriptural base for
all Muslims. It is thus the foundation of the religious
great tradition of Islam. Their recognized custodians and

interpreters--the ulama--are the sectarian personnel of that
great tradition.(42) But as demonstrated (pp. 24-29), there
is much more to the religious and sectarian reality of Islam
than this. It is in this connection that the concept of the
little tradition is utilized. The four cells of diagram 4
are intended to indicate different emphases of great and
little tradition, religion, and sect, rather than sharp
boundaries. There are those who reject the little tradition
phenomena contemptuously as superstitious and do not recognize
them at all as being aspects of religion. But a realistic
view of religion in the Middle East must account for both.

DIAGRAM 4

GREAT TRADITION AND LITTLE TRADITION

	GREAT TRADITION	LITTLE TRADITION
RELIGION	The "Five Pillars"	Reverence for saints Dhikr Zar and Evil Eye prophylaxis
	jinn life-crisis rituals	
SECT	Ulama and specialized functionaries	Marabouts Brotherhoods

SOURCE: John Gulick, *The Middle East: An Anthropolotical Perspective* (Pacific Palisades, California: Goodyear Publishing
Co., 1976), p. 172.

   Based on the two distinctions made by Gulick, religion
and sect, and great tradition and little tradition, he
discusses the religious social structure under four categories. In order to understand Gulick's distinctions, it
will be helpful to note what he discussed under each category.

   1. *The religious great tradition* includes the five pillars of Islam, the Koran and Hadith, the Jinn, and three
rites of passage: getting married, giving birth, and dying.

2. *The religious little tradition* includes the animistic
superstitious behavior such as the saint comples, the dhikr,
and exorcism.
3. *The sectarian little tradition* includes such groups
as the major Sufi orders of brotherhoods which many times
are organized around the charisma of a saint.
4. *The sectarian great tradition* constitutes only a part
of the whole social structure of Islam, just as the religious
great tradition constitutes only a part of the religious
whole of Islam, and it includes the officials of the various
sects of the Middle East.(43)

Gulick claims that this is a more realistic, more humane,
and more complicated account of religion in the Middle East.
Permeating the mass media of the West are some seriously
distroted assumptions about Islam which have affected the
Christian approach to Islam. Some of the common ones are:

> Islam is a cold, formalistic religion; it has
> no priest or ministers to provide the comforts
> of sacramental rituals; its prayers are merely
> rote-memorized formulas that are impervious to
> personal involvement and are recited in a rigidly
> prescribed calisthenic fashion. What emotional
> support can such a religion give? What sort of
> emotions is it likely to generate in its followers?
> ...Isn't such a religion fundamentally defective,
> and aren't its followers ripe for conversion to
> more emotionally satisfying religions like Chris-
> tianity?...Isn't Islam obviously a block to liberal
> modernization?(44)

Gulick rejects the assumptions implied by the questions
above. The saint complex of the little tradition abundantly
facilitates emotional discharge providing many supportive
communal activities for the faithful. In addition, the
mosque is a marvelous adaption to the needs of the modern
Arab, and such has been argued by Christian missionaries
for more than a century. Islam appears to be a viable and
adaptable system of belief that has spread to many different
cultures, and there are signs that it is adapting to new
conditions and remaining a need-fulfilling religion in the
process.(45) This in no way justifies the conclusion that
Islam is just as valid a way to approach God as Christianity,
or that Christianity is not superior to Islam in any way.
But it is essential to recognize the needs that Islam fills
in the lives of the Arab people if the evangelist is to effectively introduce the religious innovation of the Christian

message in such a way that the Arab people will accept it as a viable alternative.

Language

When an Arab affirms that "God gave the Frenchman a head, the Chinese hands, and the Arab a mouth," he is indicating the deep significance of language for the people in question. (46) When the inhabitants of two or more countries speak the same language, the common tongue constitutes a bond among them, but linguistic identity is of greater importance in the Arab world than mnay other places.(47) Middle Eastern people are highly sensitive to the diversity of their languages and dialects, to the cultural identities, and to the antagonisms that are likely to come to the surface when speakers of divergent languages and dialects come into contact with one another.(48) Wherever Arabic is in common usage, the people who speak it share a number of common ideas--religious, social, and intellectual. The Arabic language is one of the strongest bonds, is the primary criteria of ethnicity, and is a potent force for unity throughout the Middle East.(49)

The possession of the language is a highly charged emotional symbol, both of ethnolinguistic identity and of aesthetic involvement. The great verbality of Arab culture is one generalization that has been made which need not be hedged with provisions.(50)

Languages of the Middle East. Arabic is the most widely spoken language in the Middle East. However, there are other significant language groups in the Middle East which ought to be noted here.(51) The various languages spoken in the Middle East represent the different ethnic groups that exist. Most ethnic groups share the same Middle Eastern culture, but no group has been so isolated as to develop its own distinctive culture.(52) The ethnic groups in the Middle East would include the following: Arabs, Armenians, Turks, Kurds, Assyrians, Jews, Persians, and Syriacs. Armenians constitute six percent of Lebanon's population and they tend to inhabit separate neighborhoods in the cities, particularly Beirut. Many still speak only Armenian, and few speak Arabic well.(53) The Kurds live in various parts of Iraq, Iran, Turkey, Syria, and Lebanon. The Assyrians are the Nestorian Christians who speak a language related to Arabic and most have become assimilated into Arab culture. The ethnic group tends to have some influence on the types of employment found among the different groups. The Armenians tend to be urban and are principally craftsment, small traders, and office workers. Most Kurds and Assyrians are unskilled laborers.(54)

French and English are the most widely known western languages. Fluency in English or French generally marks the
educated man.(55) Despite the widespread use of Arabic, its
various dialects are so diverse that the colloquial spoken
in Morocco is so different from that spoken in Iraq that they
are mutually unintelligible. Therefore, the Middle East has
no lingua franca. French and English are spoken as secondary
languages by many Middle Easterners, but their primary purpose is to communicate with non-Middle Eastern people or
about western or international business and professional matters.(56)

Sex

All cultures provide means of accomodating the basic differences between the sexes. One way of doing this is by the
segregation of women. If a cross-cultural scale of intensity
in this matter were to be constructed, Arab culture would
undoubtedly rate high on it.(57) Sexual segregation is basic to Arab social life, and sex is one of the most important
determinants of social status. Men dominate women in most
aspects of life. Men and women constitute separate sub-
societies, each with its own values, attitudes, and perceptions of the other.(58) Since the concern of this study is
Transitional Arabs, the urban dimension of the segregation
of women is of primary concern here. In cities women are
more likely to encounter strangers than they are in the villages, and for this reason they are more fully veiled in
public than are women in the villages. Veiled women are
still very frequent in many sections of Middle Eastern cities.
(59) However, western dress has been adopted by many Arab
women.

One of the most marked changes in the Middle East is concerning the status of women. The young women in the cities,
towns, and more modern villages, have begun to demand greater
freedom and equality. In modern-educated families relations
between the sexes tend to be more westernized.(60) In general,
the possibilities for movement and the degree of freedom are
greatest for the women of educated and middle and upper income groups in an urban area, especially Beirut.(61)

From the anthropological point of view, it is probably
better for the evangelist to look upon the status of women
in the Arab world as being an aspect of a very complex cultural configuration rather than as a phenomenon which must
be changed.(62)

McCurry declares, in reference to Pakistan, that it is
concerning the status of women that the greatest violence
has been done by the western missionary women. Modesty in
the Middle East demands that a woman's limbs be covered. To
expose either arms or legs is to say in effect, "I invite
your amorous attentions."(63) By patterning the church
after the western model, Christianity has been highly offen-
sive to the Muslim community where strict segregation is
practiced. Of course, segregation is practiced more by
Traditionals than by Transitionals, but this category of
identity is an important one for the evangelist to remember.

Territory

The categories of identity that have been discussed have
clearly recognized territorial expressions. There is a tendency for individuals of the same family, sect, language, and
dialect to live in the same geographical area, not only in
the villages and small towns, but also in the large cities.
These territorial, ethnic, and sectarian groups are not only
different subcultures but also, in many cases, political
units.(64) The study of the territorial expression of these
categories of identity is a relatively recent phenomenon.
In 1963 Gulick claimed that there was virtually no information on kinship organization in the cities.(65) But recently
some significant research has been done on kinship organization in the cities.(66) Below attention is given to the
rapid growth of the cities, the residential patterns in the
cities, and the structure of the Middle Eastern town.

Rapid growth of the cities. More and more villagers are
looking for employment in the towns and cities contributing
to the rapid rate of urbanization in the Middle East. Cairo
is the largest city in the Middle East and all of Africa,
containing six million.(67) Gulick estimates that twenty-
five percent of the population of the Middle East are city
dwellers.(68) However, the percentage is much higher for
the countries with which this study is primarily concerned.
The estimated urban population in Lebanon is from fifty to
seventy-five percent, Jordan is fifty percent, Israel is
fifty-three to eighty percent, Syria is thirty-seven percent,
and Egypt is forty percent.(69)

The high estimates of urban population in these countries
becomes vitally important to this study because most Transitional Arabs are those that have moved from the village to
the city; they are the migrants. Therefore, it is the cities
of the Middle East that have the highest concentration of
Transitionals.(70)

Residential Patterns. The clustering of the various sects
into their own quarters of districts is one of the conspicuous
features of Middle Eastern cities, including Beirut, Damascus,
Cairo, Jerusalem, Baghdad, and many others.(71) Beirut, for
example, has a number of quarters in which inhabitants are
predominantly Christian and Muslim. The two maps on the following pages of Beirut and Amman show the clearly marked
quarters of the city.(72) Recent immigrants who are coming
into the cities from the villages in large numbers generally
follow this same pattern.(73) Farsoun's study of kinship
patterns in Beirut notes that Lebanese sectarianism is phys-
ically expressed in religious-ethnic residential quarters,
so that kinsmen find themselves not only in the same quarter
but even in the same neighborhood.(74) Table 5 shows this
tendency. Kinsmen belonging to different classes tend to
live in the same quarter but not necessarily in the same
neighborhood. The majority of the closest members of the
extended family live virtually within shouting distance of
each other.

TABLE 5

PROXIMITY OF RESIDENCE OF EXTENDED FAMILY UNITS LIVING IN
BEIRUT

Location of Residence	Extended Family Kinsmen			
	Parents	Married Children	Married Siblings	Married Nephews and Nieces
Same Building	26%	17%	11%	0%
Same Neighborhood	43%	61%	55%	52%
Elsewhere in Beirut	31%	22%	34%	48%
Total	100%	100%	100%	100%
Number	89	18	187	29
Number of Respondents	98	98	98	98

SOURCE: Samih K. and Karen Farsoun, "Class and Patterns of
Association Among Kinsmen in Contemporary Lebanon, *Anthropological Quarterly* 47 (January 1974): 103.

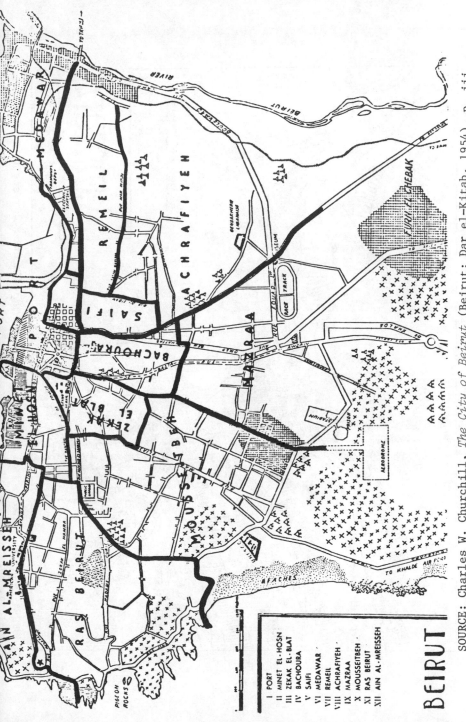

BEIRUT

I	PORT
II	MINET EL-HOSN
III	ZEKAK EL-BLAT
IV	BACHOURA
V	SAIFI
VI	MEDAWAR
VII	REMEIL
VIII	ACHRAFIYEH
IX	MAZRAA
X	MOUSSEITBEH
XI	RAS BEIRUT
XII	AIN AL-MREISSEH

SOURCE: Charles W. Churchill, *The City of Beirut* (Beirut: Dar el-Kitab, 1954), p. iii.

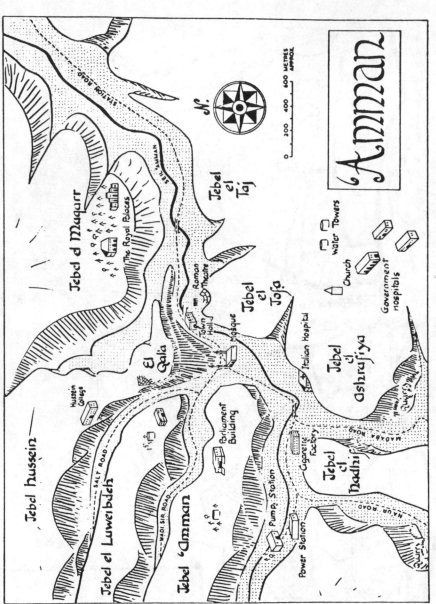

SOURCE: Jane M. Hacker, *Modern Amman: A Social Study* (Durham: University of Durham, 1960), p. 46.

One exception to the tendency for religious sects to cluster together in their own quarter of the city is that of the Greek Orthodox. Khuri, in a comparative study of migration patterns in a Greek Orthodox village and a Shia village noted that the Shia migrants tended to cluster together into one geographical area in Beirut, but that the Greek Orthodox migrants tended to disperse.(75) The Shias tended to localize because of their homogeneity in occupation and education, but the Greek Orthodox held occupations of diverse income, status, and family connections. Khuri's discovery becomes quite significant in light of the previous evangelistic work done by the churches of Christ (see p. 131).

The Structure of the Middle Eastern Town. A typical Middle Eastern city consists of five main parts.

1. *The madina* is the old pre-automobile city, with its narrow streets, old houses, traditional markets, and historic sites. Now generally inhabited by the poorer people, the old city is usually divided, with each ethnic or religious group inhabiting its own quarter.
2. *The modern business district* with streets designed for automotive traffic, hotels, cinemas, and tall office buildings.
3. *The modern residential section* includes villas, apartment houses, wide streets and retail commercial establishments which are inhabited by the middle and upper classes.
4. *The new slums*, on the fringes of the city, are often shanty towns with shacks, narrow muddy paths, and little electricity or water or sewage service. The poorest new immigrants to the city live in these sections.(76)
5. *The industrial and suburban area* is located along the main highways leading out of the city. These are different from the far-flung suburbs inhabited by commuters in western countries, because they are relatively independent of the city and their wage-earners work in them.(77)

Khuri did a study of two adjacent suburbs of Beirut that grew out of the village of Chiyah, largely by the migration of Maronites and Shia villagers to them. He draws a distinction between the suburb in contrast to the village and city. In the village and city the community relationship is relatively stable, but suburban society is in the process of transformation. "It is a society that is coming into being." The implication is that it is in such areas that the greatest concentration of Transitional Arabs are likely to be found. If this pattern is common in other Middle Eastern cities, these suburbs may be the location of a large number of Transitional Arabs who are most receptive to the Gospel.

The categories of identity examined above (kinship, religion, language, sex, and territory) constitute the horizontal social structure of Arab society. These categories of identity have a great deal of influence on the ways in which people make decisions and the groups with which they choose to identify themselves. An awareness of this aspect of social structure is crucial for the effective communication of religious innovations (see chapter six).

VERTICAL STRUCTURE

The vertical structure differs from the horizontal structure in many important aspects: 1) there are no definite boundaries between the groups, 2) one is generally born into the horizontal group, but social mobility is freer within the vertical structure, and 3) social interaction tends to be among those with whom an individual has ties other than social class, such as family or religion.(78) The factors which determine social class are wealth, education, type of occupation, political activity and power, and family reputation. The various social classes are not totally unrelated to the five categories of identity discussed above, because they have a determinative effect on one's social class.

There are many and various ways to classify the social classes of the Middle East. Table 6 represents a modification of James Bill's categories of social class in the Middle East which can serve rather well as a model.(79)

TABLE 6

VERTICAL SOCIAL STRUCTURE OF THE MIDDLE EAST

UPPER CLASS	MIDDLE CLASS	LOWER CLASS
Land owners	Bureaucratic	Traditional
Tribal nobility	*Merchants	*Industrial workers
Economic elite	Cleric	Unskilled workers
Political leaders	*Professional	
Military elite	Educators	
High ulama	*Students	
Foreign capitalists		
Rentier elite		

* Indicates the social classes which have the highest concentration of Transitionals.

An analysis of the vertical class structure in the Middle
East is crucial to this study because it aids in locating
the Transitional Arabs. Huffard suggests that the Transitionals may be thought of as the middle class of Arab society.
(80) In the various case studies that Lerner made of the
countries in the Middle East, he classified the respondents
on a different basis in the different countries.(81) The
Turkish respondents were classified by the range of their
opinions, the Lebanese by their radio-listening habits, the
Egyptians by their jobs, the Syrians by their political views,
and the Jordanians by their place of residence. Lerner's
classification of the Egyptians by their jobs is of most relevance to this discussion of vertical structure. The 262
respondents are presented in four large occupational categories: professional, white collar, workers, and farmers.(82)
The white collar group clusters at the upper limit of the
Transitional type and the workers aggregate closer to the
lower limit of the Transitional type.(83) Learning where in
the vertical class structure one is most likely to find the
Transitional Arabs not only is helpful in locating the Transitionals themselves, but also in locating the opinion leaders
who can have the most persuasive influence on the Transitionals
who are most receptive.

OPINION LEADERS

Individuals play a variety of roles in the social system
and one crucial role is that of opinion leader. Opinion
leadership is "the degree to which an individual is able to
informally influence other individual's attitudes or overt
behavior in a desired way with relative frequency."(84) The
leadership pattern is undoubtedly the most significant element of any local culture to work through in presenting new
ideas (innovations).(85) There is probably no way to ruin
the chances for an innovation more quickly than to ignore
the traditional leaders or to choose the wrong ones.(86)
Opinion leaders are usually members of the culture in which
they exert their influence.

The role of the opinion leader in the communication process was introduced by Lazerfeld, who pointed to the prominent role they played in conveying information from the mass
media to the less active sections of the population.(87) He
introduced what is called the two-step flow of information,
the first step being from the sources to opinion leaders,
and the second step from the opinion leaders to their followers. Although this model provided a usable conceptual
framework, it cannot serve as a model basically because it

does not tell one enough.(88)   Therefore, Rogers proposed a
multi-step flow model which does not have any particular
number of steps.(89)

    In the traditional Middle East the opinion leaders have
been the older men, the heads of families, and the priests,
but there is evidence that with the impact of modernization
that the opinion leaders in the Middle East are changing.(90)
The mobile young Transitionals are in the process of taking
over the opinion leadership from the village elders.   They
go off to the cities, take jobs under modern discipline, and
learn from newspapers and movies.   On many matters they are
better informed and so others (including their elders) turn
to the young men for opinions and advice.   The structures of
influence thus changes in the community and in the family.(91)

    The following are generalizations concerning opinion
leaders which are based on cross-cultural research of Rogers
and Shoemaker.(92)

Generalizations on Opinion Leaders

    1. *The change agent's success is positively related to
the extent that he works through opinion leaders.*(93)   The
success of the political career of Gamal Abdul Nasser as a
change agent seems to have been related to his use of opinion
leaders.   Early in his career he attributed his disappoint-
ments to a dependence on the mass media alone.   Then he decided to seek the views of the leaders of opinion, such as
the intellectuals, the elite, the large landholders, and the
politicians.   But they seemed to be more concerned with their
own personal desires.   Then Nasser turned to what proved to
be the two strongest forces of influence in the society: the
army and the ulama (Muslim preachers).(94)   The position of
the ulama and the Friday sermon had high credibility in the
Muslim society, and the legitimacy of the sermon made the
traditional people more willing to listen to it and comply
with the modern messages communicated through it.(95)

    2. *Interpersonal diffusion is mostly homophilous.*(96)
Homophily is the degree to which pairs of individuals who
interact are similar in certain attributes, such as beliefs,
values, education, social status, and the like.(97)   One of
the most obvious and fundamental principles of communication
is that the transfer of ideas most frequently occurs between
a source and a receiver who are alike and similar.   Homophilic
diffusion patterns cause new ideas to spread horizontally,
rather than vertically, within a society.   This generalization

makes a great deal of sense in light of the five categories
of identity in the Middle East discussed above (pp. 40-56).
It is a fact that Middle Easterners tend to interact primarily
with those who are their kin, or who are members of their
religious sect of ethnic group. In support of this, Khuri
affirms that professional associations in Lebanon pursue
their interests as long as they do not conflict with the
family, sect, or regional loyalties of the members.(98)

   3. *When the norms of a community are more modern, opinion
leadership is more monomorphic.*(99)   Monomorphism is the tendency for an individual to act as an opinion leader in only
one area rather than on many issues.(100)   In more traditional communities the leaders are more likely to serve as
opinion leaders for all issues. In Lerner's interview with
the chief of a Turkish village, when asked on what topics he
was influential, replied: "About all that you or I could
imagine, even about their wives and how to handle them, and
how to cure their sick cow."(101)   In Harik's study of opinion leaders in an Egyptian community, he discovered that the
information that the opinion leaders passed on tended to be
specialized. The various government officials and organizations tended to pass on information in which they had a special interest.(102)

Characteristics of Opinion Leaders

   1. *Opinion leaders have greater exposure to the mass
media than do their followers.*(103)   Related to this characteristic is the fact that opinion leaders are more cosmopo-
lite and have greater change agent contact than their followers. In the community studied by Harik, thirty-seven percent of the adult male population depended on mediators for
political information. Usually those who owned no radio sets
would go to the market place where they could listen to the
radio or have the newspaper read to them.(104)   However,
Harik discovered that the shop keeper and the newspaper
reader, as news mediators, had no personal influence on
those who got their news in the market place.(105)   If this
is true in this community, can it also be said to be true in
other Middle Eastern communities where the market, coffeehouse, or cafe is a strategic site for the "geography of information seeking"?

   2. *Opinion leaders are more accessible.*(106)   This is
because they have greater social participation than their
followers. Borthwick's study of the role of the ulama (Muslim preachers) supports this characteristic because they are

very accessible to the people. (107) Abu-Lughod's study also
confirmed that those who interacted the most with the people
were the ones who were the opinion leaders, not the government officials who were outsiders to the community. (108)
Dawn identifies the bureaucrats and the businessmen as being
much more likely candidates for being effective opinion
leaders than are the intellectuals. (109) The businessmen
and bureaucrats are much more likely to be in greater social
contact with the people than are the intellectuals. However,
there are exceptions to the rule. In Khuri's study of migration patterns of two Lebanese villagers, he found that the
opinion leaders of the Shia village tended to live outside
the village, such as in Beirut, but that in the Greek Orthodox village, the opinion leaders must cultivate prestige by
returning to live in the village. (110)

   3. *Opinion leaders have higher social status than their
followers.* (111) In Khuri's study of the class structure in
Lebanon, he isolated four classes of which the notables were
said to be the opinion leaders and the affluent (just below
the notables) were said to be the most receptive to modernization. (112) Among the higher class are the entrepreneurs
which, according to Sayigh, are the opinion leaders in the
business world in Lebanon. (113)

   This characteristic does not contradict an earlier generalization (p. 58) that interpersonal diffusion takes place
between people who have similar attributes. The difference
in social class is very slight as illustrated in diagram 5.
Thus, innovations tend to spread within the homogeneous or
ehtnic unit and not between these units and not in a vertical
fashion.

   4. *Opinion leaders are more innovative.* (114) Harik's
study confirmed that the opinion leaders were modern, young,
and educated individuals. (115) Lerner points out that in
Lebanon it is becuase the youth have become mobile, literate,
and exposed to the media that they are taking over the opinion
leadership of Lebanon. (116) Sayigh also found that the entrepreneurs of Lebanon were more innovative. He also discovered
that four-fifths of the entrepreneurs studied were of the
Christian faith and that Muslims constituted only about one-
sixth of the entrepreneurial group, thus indicating that the
Christian segment of the population is more innovative. (117)

   5. *Opinion leaders conform to the norms of their followers.*
(118) Leaders lead not so much because they possess certain
characteristics, but rather because they are easily accessible

DIAGRAM 5

OPINION LEADERS AND SOCIAL STATUS

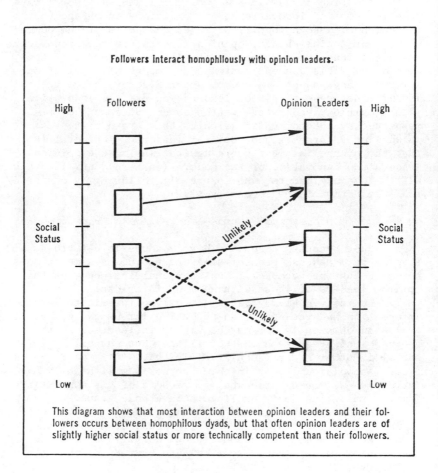

This diagram shows that most interaction between opinion leaders and their followers occurs between homophilous dyads, but that often opinion leaders are of slightly higher social status or more technically competent than their followers.

SOURCE: Everett M. Rogers and F. Floyd Shoemaker, *Communication of Innovations*, 2nd ed. (New York: Free Press, 1971), p. 211.

to their followers, more competent, and in general conform
to the norms of the society.(119) How can opinion leaders
be most conforming to the norms of the society and also lead
in the adoption of new ideas? Opinion leaders do not always
lead in adopting innovations, but sometimes encourage the
rejection of innovations.(120) When the norms of the community favor social change, opinion leaders are more innovative
and hence function in close conformity to the norms of the
community. This concept contains an important implication
for the change agent. A common error made by change agents
is that they select opinion leaders who are too innovative.
(121) Opinion leaders are what they are because they are
respected by the community of which they are a part. This
is why innovators are poor opinion leaders. The moral is
that the evangelist must guard against making the opinion
leaders too innovative or too modern (western), or else they
will become ex-leaders, who lost their following by deviating
from the norms of the community.(122)

Guidelines for Locating Opinion Leaders Among Transitionals

1. Just because someone is highly accessible (such as a
shop keeper) and has greater exposure to the mass media does
not mean that he necessarily has personal influence on the
opinion leaders of those with whom he interacts.
2. An individual may be an effective disseminator of
information and yet not be an effective influencer of opinion.
3. An opinion leader may be highly influential in the
geographical area (such as the village) but not highly influential in other areas (such as the city).
4. An opinion leader in the Arab world will usually have
influence only over those who are members of his own extended
family, religious sect, or linguistic ethnic group.
5. An opinion leader may live among the group with whom
he is most influential or he may live away from the group.
6. As the community becomes progressively more modern
the opinion leaders are more likely to be younger than their
followers.(123)

CONCLUSION

A descriptive analysis of the horizontal and vertical
aspects of Arab social structure reveals that although mobility on the horizontal plane is very limited, it is extensive
on the vertical plane. The five categories of identity (kinship, religion, language, sex, and territory) become important to the evangelist when he is trying to make Christianity
relevant to the Transitional Arab. The vertical structure

(or social class) becomes significant when the religious
worker is trying to locate the receptive pockets of Transitionals. The horizontal and vertical structures are not
mutually exclusive categories, but have a great deal of influence on each other.

Nida gives the following suggestions for adapting Christian
communication to social structure: 1) effective communication follows the patterns of social structure, 2) the initial
approach should be to those who can effectively pass on communication within their family groupings, 3) time must be
allowed for the internal diffusion of innovations, 4) the
challenge for any change of belief or action must be addressed
to the persons or groups socially capable of making such decisions, and 5) a relevant evangelistic approach will incor-
porate valid indigenous social structures.(124)

The implications of these principles in Arab society is
that the initial approach may be made to a younger person,
but the challenge for a decision to change may be made to
the head of the nuclear family or extended family. Allowing
sufficient time for the making of decisions is indispensable
in the group oriented Arab society. The evangelist's tendency to encourage some especially responsive persons to
step out and make an individual decision, may often cause the
people as a whole to reject the message. Until a people are
able to make what seems to them a valid decision, any pulling
out of members of the group immediately raises the fear of
loss of solidarity.(125)

The last analytical chapter in part one examines the
restrictions to evangelism in the Middle East. It is very
important to understand the barriers one must overcome if
innovations are to be introduced and diffused effectively in
Arab culture.

4

Restrictions to Evangelism

Research on evangelism in the Middle East is inadequate
because there is, to the author's knowledge, no systematic
treatment of the barriers and restrictions to evangelism.
Kraemer and Warren proposed that the restrictions can be
divided into two categories: social and theological.(1)
Kraemer emphasizes the necessity of understanding both of
these categories:

> Whosoever nods impatiently, thinking, let us go
> on to more concrete and practical subjects, never
> has understood the root of the Moslem missionary
> problem and probably never will.(2)

Even as late as 1966 a grave lack of understanding concerning
the restrictions to evangelism in the Arab world was apparent
at the conference of evangelical missionaries to Islam. There
it was said that the primary barrier was the theological
teaching of Islam.(3) The theological teachings of Islam are
an important factor to deal with, but Christians have studied
Islamic theology extensively for over a century and such understanding has still produced very meager results in the
Middle East. McGavran and McCurry seem correct in claiming
that the primary restrictions to accepting Christianity in
the Middle East are sociological not theological.(4) The
harvest is ripening in many parts of the Muslim world, and
through Bible correspondence courses thousands of Muslims
have been convinced of the validity of the Bible and the
divinity of Jesus Christ, and some are even seeking baptism.
But since they are not willing to be incorporated into ex-

isting churches, McCurry stressed the importance of devising
a culturally relevant model for accepting Muslim converts
into Christian fellowship.(5)

Upon an examination of the various handbooks for communicating the Gospel to Muslims, one finds a tremendous emphasis
on the theological issues, but very little on the sociological
factors involved in accepting Christianity.(6) Therefore,
since there is more than adequate material on the theological
issues between Christianity and Islam, this study will be
primarily concerned with the sociological restrictions.

THEOLOGICAL RESTRICTIONS OF ISLAM

Keay has stated three reasons why Muslims have been so
hard to win for Christ, the first being "that Islam is the
only religion which presents a definite theological barrier
in the teachings of the Koran to the teachings of Christianity."(7)

The evangelist does well to remember that the various
sects of Islam interpret the Koran differently, and so the
major theological barriers may differ from one group to the
next. These theological issues are important, but the author contends that most Muslims are unprepared spiritually,
ethically, or intellectually for the fundamental Christian
way of life.(8) In addition, the method of controversy and
argument over theological differences has been tried and
found to fail. For this reason it is usually a mistake to
discuss theological issues before some preliminary teaching
has been done.(9) It is indeed important to note the theological barriers,(10) the most prominent of which are now
mentioned.

The Trinity

Unless one understands the Muslim's idea of God he cannot
understand the Islamic creed, judge his philosophy, or intellectually communicate the Christian idea of God to him.(11)
The strong unifying force of Islam is not in its ritual or
its ethics, but in its fanatical grasp of one great truth:
monotheism. As illustrated in diagram 6, all the laws,
teachings, and morals of Islam hang on the Muslim creed. It
is commonly believed that Muhammad was ignorant of the true
doctrine of the trinity as held by Christians, and that his
idea of the trinity consisted of the Father, the virgin Mary,
and Christ.(12)

DIAGRAM 6

ANALYSIS OF ISLAM AS A SYSTEM DEVELOPED FROM ITS CREED

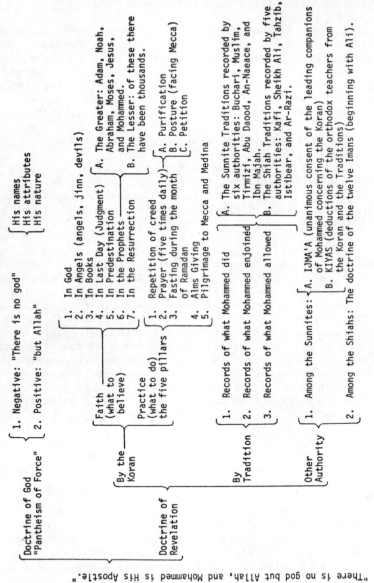

Doctrine of God "Pantheism of Force"
- 1. Negative: "There is no god"
- 2. Positive: "but Allah" — His names, His attributes, His nature

Doctrine of Revelation

By the Koran

Faith (what to believe)
- 1. In God
- 2. In Angels (angels, jinn, devils)
- 3. In Books
- 4. In Last Day (Judgment)
- 5. In Predestination
- 6. In the Prophets — A. The Greater: Adam, Noah, Abraham, Moses, Jesus, and Mohammed. B. The Lesser: of these there have been thousands.
- 7. In the Resurrection

Practice (what to do) the five pillars
- 1. Repetition of creed
- 2. Prayer (five times daily) — A. Purification B. Posture (facing Mecca) C. Petition
- 3. Fasting during the month of Ramadan
- 4. Alms Giving
- 5. Pilgrimage to Mecca and Medina

By Tradition
- 1. Records of what Mohammed did
- 2. Records of what Mohammed enjoined
- 3. Records of what Mohammed allowed

A. The Sunnite Traditions recorded by six authorities: Buchari, Muslim, Tirmizi, Abu Daood, An-Naeace, and Ibn Majah.
B. The Shiah Traditions recorded by five authorities: Kafi, Sheikh Ali, Tahzib, Istibear, and Ar-Razi.

Other Authority
- 1. Among the Sunnites:
  - A. IJMA'A (unanimous consent of the leading companions of Mohammed concerning the Koran)
  - B. KIYAS (deductions of the orthodox teachers from the Koran and the Traditions)
- 2. Among the Shiahs: The doctrine of the twelve Imans (beginning with Ali).

"There is no god but Allah, and Mohammed is His Apostle."

SOURCE: Samuel M. Zwemer, The Moslem Doctrine of God (New York: Young People's Missionary Movement, 1905), p. 14.

For many centuries Christians have defended themselves against the Muslim attack on the trinity. They have used similes, metaphors, and symbols in order to prove the doctrine, but in spite of all this they have failed.

> No amount of discussion and argument over these points will ever convince anybody, because the truth of these doctrines does not lie on the intellectual level where it can be reached by the power of reasoning.(13)

Calverley claims that the best and most effective way to present the trintiy to Muslims is by explaining the meaning of Spirit.(14) To Muslims the term "spirit" applies only to created beings such as angels, demons, and all kinds of jinn. Men also have spirits in their bodies which are intangible but material. The human spirit exists in man like sap in trees.

Nida affirms that since infinite truth cannot be absolutely revealed in finite language, one must come to grips with the problem of biblical symbolism.(15) He suggests that the trintiy should be interpreted in terms of functions and not form. But whatever one's interpretation it is important to realize that the Bible does not explicitly indicate the real nature of God, in terms of substance or form, and therefore one should not presume to know more than God has chosen to reveal. Since the Bible does not give a description or explanation of the trinity, the mystery of the real essence of God will remain a mystery. Some real attempt must be made to convey this truth in a meaningful way if Muslims are to make a valid decision about the Gospel.(16) One of the key issues in Islam's rejection of the trinity is the rejection of the divinity of Christ.

The Divinity of Christ

The Muslim's view of Christ is directly related to their view of God.

> In bringing Christ to Muslims we face a difficulty which is to be met nowhere else. That is that Muslims assume that they know Christ and that their knowledge of him is more accurate than ours...By no other religion is Christ's position challenged in such a definite manner as it is in Islam.(17)

The source of Muhammad's ideas about Christ will probably
remain a mystery, but the Koran does indicate that he was
aware of the controversy over the nature of Christ.(18)
Jesus is honored in the Koran and is regarded as another one
of the prophets. According to the Koran, Muhammad believed
that Jesus was strengthened by the Holy Spirit, but did not
believe that the Holy Spirit was a separate person in the
Godhead. Jesus is known throughout the Koran as the Messiah,
but there is no evidence that Muhammad knew the significance
of this term. The Koran also regards Jesus as the Word of
God which God cast upon Mary, the Word of Truth, a Spirit
from God, an apostle, and a prophet of God.(19)   So much
concerning the nature of Jesus in conceded in the Koran that
it is difficult to understand why Muslims do not accept his
divinity.

The Crucifixion

The orthodox Muslim denies that Christ was crucified, but
claims that when the Jews came to crucify him, God could not
allow his chosen prophet to die, and so caught him up alive
to heaven. Someone else was then crucified in Christ's
place. Why do Muslims believe in a divinely arranged escape?
It is not because they have been confronted with strong evidence that Jesus, in fact, circumvented death. Rather, this
belief originated because of the presupposition that if a
prophet of God is killed it constitutes divine failure.(20)

There are three references to the death of Christ in the
Koran, but orthodox Muslim tradition ignores the two clear
passages which plainly refer to the death and resurrection
of Christ, and bases its argument on an obscure passage.(21)

The Koranic failure to grasp the meaning of the cross is
crucial in determining the nature of Islam. The disastrous
effects of sin are recognized by Islam but it provides no
adequate means for removing man's guilt and restoring man to
a right relationship to God.(22)   Once again the Christian
advocate begins from a position of rebuttal and must somehow
turn resistance into understanding.(23)   It makes no difference whether the Christian advocate is discussing the
trinity, the divinity of Christ, or the crucifixion; the
encounter is difficult because the Muslim categorically
denies the validity of scripture.

Scripture and Revelation

Muhammed at first believed that he was sent to preach the
same message that was contained in the scriptures of Jews

and Christians, and he instructed his followers to consult
the earlier scriptures in support of his own teaching.(24)
But in Medina the Jews mocked some of his references to Old
Testament persons and incidents. Since Mohammed could not
tolerate this he accused the Jews and Christians of corrupting
and misinterpreting their scriptures. Today Muslims account
for discrepancies between the Koran and scripture in terms
of deliberate falsification. The tragedy is that Mohammed
was never familiar with the New Testament, and had he been,
the course of history might have been very different.(25)

Another crucial factor is the Muslim's view of inspiration and revelation in contrast to the biblical concept.
The Muslim believes that all prophets are bearers of the
words of God as a verbal transmission from heaven and not
as a result of a divine enabling of their mental and spiritual powers.(26) Therefore, the Koran did not go through
the mental understanding of the reporters. It is more as-
suredly God's word if man is in entire abeyance. The Muslims see the Old and New Testaments as having human authors,
whereas the Koran has no author but God. Therefore, when
there is a discrepancy between the Koran and the Bible, the
Koran is to be preferred since it contains the direct words
of God.(27)

It is noteworthy that at the Bhamdun Conference of Christians and Muslims in 1954, the New Testament was quoted by
Muslims more often than the Koran was by Christians. There
was no overt suggestion that the New Testament had been cor-
rupted.(28)

Sin

The Muslim concept of sin is different from the Christian
concept of sin, and to this extent it becomes a barrier when
attempting to communicate the Biblical concept of forgiveness and atonement. According to scripture sin is a state
of rebellion against the righteousness and holiness of God,
but the Muslim thinks of sin only in terms of disobedient
acts and their respective punishments.(29) Blasdell declares
that conscience troubles the Muslim so little that many have
wondered if it exists among the rank and file of Muslims.
Actions, attitudes, and motives that would cause much uneasi-
ness to the Christian leave the Muslim but little affected.
A slight sense of sin produces a slight regard for the
Savior from sin.(30) On the other hand, Huffard observes
that the Muslims he has seen have sensitive consciences, and
are probably more guilt ridden than they need to be.(31)

To the Muslim the power and the will of Deity cannot be
so resisted as to frustrate his desire. In contrast, the
Christian views sin in relation to the holiness and righteousness of God, rather in relation to the dominating will of
God. This concept will need attention in responsible evangelization.(32)

Linguistic Barriers

Watt points out that if Christianity is really to take
root among the Arabs it must produce a theology thought out
in the Arabic language, which is genuinely Christian and at
the same time in accordance with the Arab mentality.(33)   A
major obstacle to achieving this is that the Arabic of Islam
and the religious Arabic of Christianity have become two
languages. And this dichotomy is more confusing because to
a great extent both use the same vocabulary, with meanings
that have grown further and further apart.(34)   It is imperative that the evangelist working with Muslims must become
conversant with the religious vocabulary of Islam.

Key religious terms. The whole subject of the use of
Christian terms and phraseology in mission work with Muslims
is one that needs examination.(35)   The Muslim uses many of
the same religious words as the Christian; but when the
Christian uses these words they carry many connotations which
the Christian never intended. Some of these words are:
forgiveness, mercy, thankfulness, patient endurance, inspiration, Son of God, spirit, atonement, reconciliation, grace,
redemption, and sin.(36)   The evangelist cannot escape the
difficulty of presenting "spiritual things" through the
medium of a "secular vocabulary." The problem is to present
the Christian message and to remain aware of the ways in
which we can be misunderstood.(37)

Bible version language. From an examination of the journal literature one discovers that the Arabic version of the
Bible is a problem in the Middle East.(38)   The vast difference between the religious Arabic of Christianity and Islam
has led some to suggest that there ought to be two versions
of the Bible, one for Arab Christians and another for Muslim
converts.(39)   At the Bhamdun conference at least two Muslims
were candid in their criticism of the Arabic version of the
Bible, and one of them preferred to read the New Testament
in English. He pleaded for an Arabic version that the Muslims could enjoy.(40)

The name of God. Watt argues that since "Allah" in Islam and "God" in Christianity refer to the same being, that it is wrong to use the "Allah" in English, because that implies that "Allah" is something different from "God."(41) When the evangelist admits that the Muslim has knowledge of God and worships him then he has laid the foundation stone of a bridge between the two religions. Once Muslims and Christians agree that they are both speaking about God, they can go on to discuss such questions as, "What is he like?" and "How does he reveal himself?"

Once the Christian has thoroughly examined all of the theological difficulties in dealing with Muslims he has only just begun to understand all of the restrictions that are involved in evangelism in the Middle East.

RESTRICTIONS OF EASTERN CHRISTIANITY

Many will point out that one factor that complicates evangelistic efforts in the Middle East is the existence of the various sects of Eastern Christianity. The Eastern churches have taken a policy of *laissez-faire* toward Islam. Their attitude toward Islam has greatly hindered evangelistic efforts in the Middle East.(42) So long as the majority of the Christians known personally to Muslims give by their life a distorted picture of the Gospel of Christ, it is unlikely that Muslims will be attracted to the Christian message.(43)

> When a Muhammad or an Ahmad in Egypt thinks of
> Christians he thinks in terms of his neighbors
> Girgis and Faheem, who are nominal members of the
> Coptic Church. It is by their lives, by their words,
> their actions, and their ideals, rather than by
> occasional contact with a missionary,...that he
> forms his conception of what Christianity teaches
> and what Christians do. Were our friends Girgis
> and Faheem true disciples of Christ, they could
> accomplish far more for the spread of the Christian
> message by the influence of their ordinary daily
> life than the missionary could ever hope to achieve
> by years of preaching.(44)

The churches of Christ do have an advantage over Protestant religious groups, because they are seeking to restore pure New Testament Christianity, and therefore do not claim to be just another denomination. Restoring New Testament Christianity appeals to many Arabs who have seen the corruption in the churches around them.

ATTITUDES OF THE EVANGELIST

Many missionaries, full of good intentions and usually
from a western cultural background, have brought the Gospel
to the Middle East without really knowing or understanding--
sometimes not really trying to understand--the cultural
milieu, historical background, social structure, and religious mentality.(45)   Several aspects of the attitudes of
the evangelist are relevant to evangelism in the Middle East.

Misunderstandings of Islam

Unfortunately there are still some spokesmen for Christianity who continue to look upon Islam as the work of the
devil.(46)   Because of misinformation, lack of information,
or traditional prejudices, communication is almost non-
existent in situations where Islam is dominant.   Whatever
criticism the Christian may level against Islam as a religious faith, it has obviously provided religious satisfaction
and spiritual strength to many people through many centuries.
What is the source of this strength?   How do Muslim devotions satisfy man's needs to worship God?   To what aspects
of his faith does the modern Arab turn when confronted with
the problems of life?   Until such questions as these are
investigated more deeply and sympathetically, evangelistic
efforts in the Middle East will continue to be hindered by
unnecessary restrictions.(47)

Mohamed Al-Nowaihi discusses those aspects of Islam which
have been most liable to misunderstanding by Christians. He
includes the following aspects: oneness of God, crucifixion
and the atonement, the greatness and powerfulness of God, God
is not inaccessible, God is a God of love and mercy, the
ethical aspect of Islam, and the social aspect of Islam (all
encompassing).(48)

Premillennialism

An evangelist does not stand on good ground at all with
the Arab when he claims that Israel's activity in reclaiming
the land of Palestine is all a part of God's plan.   The cre-
ation of the State of Israel and the subsequent wars have
made millions of Palestinian Arabs homeless, and it is very
difficult for an Arab to believe in a God who has this as a
part of his divine plan.   The open advocacy of premillennialism is highly detrimental to evangelistic efforts in the
Middle East.

Ethnocentrism

People are enculturated when quite young to believe that
their culture is the right one and the best. Ethnocentrism
is "the term used by anthropologists to represent that point
of view which we all have to varying degrees, that our own
culture, our own way of doing things, is best."(49) Ethnocentrism cannot be changed in most people by a little study
of other ways of life, but the evangelist who intends to
cross cultural boundaries must learn to recognize when he is
applying ethnocentric standards. If the evangelist is not
aware of the function of the cultural themes of Arab society
such as their concept of time and their attitude toward work,
he may always be complaining about their inability to keep
appointments and their laziness. It behooves the evangelist
to leave his attitudes of superiority behind him when he goes
forth to serve Christ in the Arab world.(50)

SOCIOLOGICAL RESTRICTIONS

In the two previous chapters considerable space was given
to the analysis of group solidarity, fatalism, and the concept of honor in Arab culture. Rather than giving additional
analysis here, this section will indicate how these sociological factors can restrict evangelistic efforts. Suggestions for overcoming these restrictions will be offered. It
has already been stated that the primary restrictions to
evangelism are sociological and not theological. No other
religion in the world has so successfully and thoroughly
integrated itself into the very fabric of the society of its
adherents as has Islam. In spite of tremendous significance
of the sociological restrictions only one of the three most
recent handbooks on evangelizing Muslims deals at length
with the sociological barriers an Arab must overcome before
becoming a Christian.(51) The other two by Marsh and Miller
are aware of the restrictions and make passing references to
them but do not deal with them extensively.(52)

Group Solidarity

Westerners cannot really fathom the depth of the concept
of group solidarity that is found in the Arab world. Indi-
vidualism as known in the western world scarcely exists in
the Middle East. Identity is discovered through membership
in groups as was emphasized in the previous chapter. (pp. 40-
56). For a Muslim to accept Christ as Savior means that he
is apostate and has been cut off from the body. Hence to
deny the faith of one's fathers is to bring upon oneself

social ostracism, a much more intolerable condition in a kinship oriented society.(53) To cut oneself off from the
Islamic community in order to become a Christian seems to a
Muslim like committing suicide.(54) Social ostracism is not
a barrier just for Muslims but also for members of the sects
of Eastern Christianity. Although it can be argued that
group solidarity in the Middle East has a religious foundation in Islam (that being the law of apostasy),(55) the
theme of group solidarity is found among all Middle Easterners including those claiming to be Christians. Therefore,
the restriction is more sociological than it is theological.
Many missionary leaders have regarded the homogeneity of
Arab culture as one of the greatest factors in the failure
of the Christian church to grow in Muslim lands.(56)

One reason why group solidarity has been a major restriction to Christian conversion is that the missionary has
sharply emphasized the right of the individual to make his
own religious choices. This is not a basic Arab conception,
for Arab culture is not an individualistic but a communal
society. So long as the Christian missionary effort appears
to be a frontal attack against this group solidarity it will
effectively oppose the progress of the Gospel.(57) This is
one area where changes must come if there is to be any significant response to Christ in the Arab world.

There are ways to reduce the restrictiveness of group
solidarity to the cause of Christ. Two solutions have been
proposed to overcome this restriction. First, the evangelist
should always be looking for the possibility of a group of
people turning to Christ together. This may be in the form
of a whole family, an extended family, or a group of people
who work together.(58) Second, the possibility of establishing homogenous (ethnic unit) convert churches deserves
more serious attention.(59) Incorporating converts into
ethnic unit churches would minimize the societal and cultural dislocation that often occurs.

Goldsmith argues that group solidarity need not be viewed
only as a restriction to Christian conversion, but that this
concept can cut both ways if one is creative enough to take
advantage of it. He argues that the community in Arab culture is a felt need at which the Christian message can be
aimed if the evangelist is wise.(60)

Fatalism

Since a more thorough analysis of fatalism is given above
(pp. 22-24), this section will give primary attention to ways

of overcoming fatalism as a restriction to evangelism. The
previous discussion of fatalism suggested that it may not be
due so much to religious doctrine as to the vicious influence
of political subjugation, economic poverty, and social tyranny. Although the modern Arab tends to be much less fatalistic, this cultural theme does not disappear completely
with westernization.

There are possible ways of overcoming this restriction.
First, when dealing with Muslims, those passages in the Koran
which emphasize man's free will should be pointed out.
Second, Pierce recommends that when presenting innovations
to Arabs also present evidence that they have worked elsewhere.(61) If an Arab knows that an idea has been tried
elsewhere and has worked, then it must be acceptable to God,
and he will work hard for it. Third, Huffard suggests that
rather than pointing to "what the Bible says" one would do
well to put more emphasis on "what God's will is" and set
out to reveal what his will is as seen in the Bible.(62)
People may not care what the Bible says initially, but would
listen to know God's will.

Concept of Honor

The Arab's concept of honor serves as a barrier to change.
The Arab measures the vital essence of culture quite differently from the Westerner. A high standard of living and
technological progress are vital to success in the West.
The Arab claims superior cultural attainment by emphasizing
social forms, attitudes, and religious beliefs. He reacts
strongly to any suggestion of western cultural supremacy.

The concept of "loss of face" is very strong among the
Arabs. Any admission of inferiority would cause a sense of
shame to the Arab community. Therefore, pride becomes a
strong deterrent to change.(63) Once an Arab convert was
trying to convince the author's father that he was the best
man to be hired as a translator. In the course of his appeal he claimed that he knew every word in the English language! An Arab's pride and concept of honor is something
that must be handled very delicately by the effective missionary.

Foreignness of Christianity

Christianity is both a native and a stranger in the Middle East. Christianity began in the Middle East yet today
it is regarded as a religion of the West.(64) In most cases

Christianity is preached in the historical, theological, and
institutional forms that have been developed in the West.
Christian missionaries have preached the same presentation
of truth which converted them. For the most part they have
not made serious attempts to adapt the message to make it
relevant to the hearers.(65) Anderson wrestles with the
problem of the Christian versus the "cultic" approach to
Islam.(66) He examines the problem of why so few have been
converted into the church, and suggests that the Christian
is responsible for a great deal of the failure. As long as
Christianity continues to be regarded as a western man's
religion its success in the Middle East will continue to be
limited. Christians must find new ways of making the Gospel
relevant to the Arab people. In 1938 Morrison suggested that
the churches of the Middle East need to examine afresh their
traditional forms of worship in order to determine whether
these are repelling the Arabs whom they wish to win to Christ.
(67) At Lausanne it was suggested that certain Muslim worship forms could be retained by converted Muslims; prayer
five times a day, fasting, scripture memorization, and the
removal of one's shoes and bowing for prayer.(68) These
forms of worship could be a non-compromising identification
with the Muslim convert's religious background. Of course
such forms of worship would not be relevant in a congregation
containing converts from the sects of Eastern Christianity,
but in ethnic unit churches containing only converts from
Islam such might be very effective.

Failure of Churches to Welcome Converts

This sociological restriction applies primarily to Muslims. Suspicion and distrust of Muslims is so deeply in-
grained in Middle Eastern Christians that it is difficult
for church groups to open the doors of their hearts and
homes and churches to people of Muslim background.(69)
Therefore, not only is the convert expelled from the Islamic
community, but he does not find another community in which
he feels at home. Until now there have not been enough converts from Islam in one place to constitute a strong group
or church of those who have come out of Islam.(70)

PSYCHOLOGICAL RESTRICTIONS

Phil Parshall suggests that there are psychological barriers to change.(71) Foster has used the term "differential
cross-cultural perception" to indicate the manner in which
people perceive words and actions differently in bicultural
situations.(72) Many workers in the Middle East will readily

admit that Arabs find it difficult to think as logically as
Americans do. Western evangelists have often made the mistake of trying to influence the Arab with the same arguments
they would have used at home. In many cases an illustration
is vastly more persuasive than a syllogism, and is more
likely to convince the Arab and win his allegiance.(73)   Slate
suggests that various modes of perception are used in different cultures to receive ideas, and that the religious worker
does well to examine these modes of perception as keys to
the selection of channels for the Chrsitian message.(74)   It
is recommended that story-telling, poetry, and drama are well
accepted channels of communication.(75)

   MacDonald brings out another difficulty presented by the
Arab's mode of perception.

> The Oriental has the most astonishing keenness in
> viewing, grasping, analyzing a single point, and
> when he has finished with that point, can take up
> a series of others in the same way. But these
> points remain for him separate; he does not co-
> ordinate them. They may be contradictory; that
> does not trouble him. When he constructs systems--
> as he often does--it is by taking a single point,
> and spinning everything out of it; not by taking
> many points and building them up together. Thus
> he may criticize one point and be quite indifferent
> to the consequent necessity, for us, at least, of
> criticizing other points.(76)

   Levonian has done extensive study in the psychological
relationship between Islam and Christianity.(77)   He met
with many Muslim leaders and discovered that Muslims did not
respond to the Christian faith because they could not understand it rightly and they could not understand it rightly
because they had initial psychological difficulties.(78)
Levonian says that the root trouble is in the Muslim's conception of the spirit and the spiritual. To the Muslim,
spirit belongs to the sphere of the physical, and since God
is non-physical he has no "spirit" (see p. 118). The basic
psychological restrictions (modes of perception) are closely
related to the linguistic restrictions discussed above. If
Christian truths could be restated in modes of thought which
the Arab could relate to, many of the misunderstood doctrines
would not be obstacles, and the Arab would be much more
receptive to the Gospel.(79)

POLITICAL RESTRICTIONS

   The work of evangelization is directly affected by events
in the political world. A half-century ago most Muslim
countries were under the control of western nations and in
many of these countries Christian missionaries were allowed
to carry on their work with great freedom. During the past
twenty-five years most of the Muslim countries have gained
their independence. The freedom formerly granted to religious workers has been continued in some countries, but in
others it has been greatly curtailed. It has been difficult
for missionaries to obtain visas to enter several countries
in the Middle East. The countries of Lebanon, Jordan, and
Israel are presently the most open for missionaries to live
in. Egypt, Syria, and Iraq may be entered on tourist visas
without any problem.

Government Restrictions

   Government restrictions are still a hindrance to evangelism in several parts of the Middle East. These restrictions concern such matters as proselyting, holding public
meetings, use of the mass media, use of Bible correspondence
courses, and in some cases changes of faith from Islam to
Christianity.(80) As a result of aid given by the United
States to Israel in the 1967 war, all American missionaries
were expelled from certain Arab countries. This has resulted
in increased opposition throughout the Arab world to all efforts to convert Muslims to the Christian faith.(81) Presently, ten years after the war in 1967, hostility towards
Americans is greatly reduced, and does not pose a serious
problem for American evangelists in most countries of the
Middle East.

Freedom of Religion

   Wilson has aptly said that "freedom of religion is an
idea foreign to Islam."(82) The Islamic law of apostasy
makes it very difficult for a Muslim to become a Christian
since it can incur the death penalty. Even in countries
where this may not be the law, individual converts to
Christianity may be in danger of their lives and liable to
suffer the loss of their possessions, their jobs, their
homes, and their families.(83) In most Arab countries
freedom of religion means that each minority non-Mulsim
group is permitted to minister to the spiritual needs of its
members within the precincts of its own churches, but it
does not include permission to do evangelistic work designed
to win outsiders to Christ.(84)

Foreign Policy of the "Christian" Nations

Muslims have gained the impression that the West, which
they tend to equate with Christianity, gives uncritical support to the State of Israel, and fails to understand the
plight of the Palestinian refugees.(85) Wrongs and injustices
of any kind should be resisted and the legitimate interests
of displaced Palestinians cannot be denied. In 1953 two
Muslims wrote a book in which their purpose was to show that
foreign religious people are responsible for political and
communal division in the Middle East.(86)

The Millet System

Non-Muslim communities are considered separate legal en-
tities within the mechanism of government. This system is
called the millet system, the millet being the religious
community organized as a legal entity within the state. Each
recognized church body has its community court that adminis-
ters the community laws regarding personal status--marriage,
divorce, and inheritance. Under such a system, any change
in faith also means a change in the legal status of the convert. It is not merely a matter of accepting one set of
religious beliefs for another, but of appearing before a
different court to be judged by different laws. And when a
religious group has not been recognized by the government
the convert must continue either to be legally a member of
his old community or have no legal rights in those matters
with which the religious courts are concerned.(87) If Gulick's
distinction between religion and sect (p. 44) is valid, would
it not be acceptable for a convert to remain a part of his
old community culturally, socially, and politically and still
become a Christian? If the sect can be defined as basically
social and cultural as opposed to religious then could not
an Arab change his religious beliefs without necessarily
having to change his sectarian affiliation?

CONCLUSION

The foregoing discussion of restrictions to evangelism in
the Middle East makes it easier to understand why the church
has made such slow progress in winning the Arab people to
Christ. However, most of the literature previously written
on evangelism in the Middle East has placed the emphasis
where it ought not to be. The major restrictions to evangelism are not theological but sociological. If the evangelist would approach the problem with this perspective the
chances for success would seem to be greater. Another impor-

tant factor to consider is that several of the sociological
restrictions need not be as great a hindrance to the spread
of the Gospel as they have been made out to be. Much of the
group solidarity can be overcome by aiming at multi-individual
group conversions. The barrier of fatalism can be avoided
by aiming at the Transitional Arab for whom fatalism is not
as much of a problem. The foreignness of Christianity can
be overcome by making the church, the forms of worship, and
the message much more relevant to the Arab culture, which
will be discussed in chapters six and seven.

Thus the presentation of the present situation in the
Middle East in this and previous chapters is discussed from
a different perspective from previous analyses. Part two of
this thesis deals with evangelistic strategy in the Arab
world. It deals more specifically with how the evangelist
ought to go about his task of introducing religious innovations into Arab culture in light of the material discussed
in the previous chapters.

It will be proposed that the theological restrictions
can be best overcome by constructing a Christian message
based on the felt needs of Transitional Arabs. This subject
is discussed in chapter seven. It is proposed that many of
the sociological restrictions can be turned into avenues of
communicating the Christian message. Rather than allowing
the group solidarity of Arab culture become a barrier to the
communication of the Christian message, the religious worker
can use the group structure as the basic unit to which the
message is communicated. A new methodology is proposed (in
contrast to what has been used by the churches of Christ)
for introducing religious innovations which better fits the
cultural themes and social structure of Arab society. This
subject is discussed in chapters five and six.

Part Two

Strategy

5

Channels of Communication

The evangelistic methods previously used in the Middle
East are similar to the process that an oil company goes
through when it drills test holes in search of oil; some
produce and others do not. As a result of this random guess
work type of approach in evangelism some methods have been
found to be quite useful and others have not been very successful.

This study of Arab culture and the innovation process
sheds significant light on effective ways of communicating
the Gospel to the Transitional Arab. This chapter will discuss the various channels that are open to the religious
communicator. It will be seen that several of the previous
missionaries used channels of communication that proved to
be effective. Suggestions will be made on how these channels
and others, which have not yet been tried, can be used most
effectively to reach the Transitional Arab.

"If no adequate patterns of communication are established,
the other innovation techniques cannot take place."(1) Communication is the "process by which messages are transmitted
from a source to a receiver," and a communication channel is
"the means by which the message gets from the source to the
receiver."(2) The information theory model in diagram 7 is
concerned with the problem of message transmission: what
happens to the information in a message from the time it is
transmitted by a source until it is received at a destination.
In essence this model describes a process in which a transmitter acts upon information from a source to put it into

a channel in the form of a signal. This signal together with
additional stimuli (noise) is picked up by the receiver at
the destination.

DIAGRAM 7

AN INFORMATION THEORY MODEL

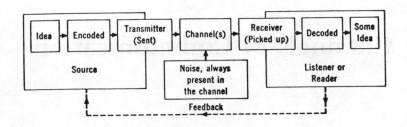

SOURCE: Kenneth E. Andersen, "Variant Views
of the Communicative Act," in *Speech Communication*, eds. Howard H. Martin and Kenneth
E. Andersen (Boston: Allyn and Bacon, 1968),
p. 16.

This model draws attention to the important function of
the channel of communication. Noise (additional but unwanted
stimuli) is indicated as always being present in the channel
to be picked up by the receiver along with the desired signal. The information theory model focuses quite specifically
upon the problem of accuracy of signal transmission.(3) The
communicator can increase the accuracy of his communication
if he pays attention to feedback.

Channels of communication may be classified into two categories: basic media and extending media.(4) A distinction
is made in terms of the communicator's location in relation
to the audience: 1) he may be present (that is heard, seen,
touched, and smelt), 2) he may be distant when one or more
of his attributes are not transmitted (for example: telephone or radio), and 3) he may be absent and cannot be perceived directly, but one or more of his attributes can be.(5)
The media used by the communicator who is present shall be
called basic media. Media which do not demand the actual
presence of the communicator are called extending media,

because they extend the range of the original message in
time or space. Mass media is extending media, but not all
extending media are mass media.

Rogers gives three criteria for selecting the proper channel: 1) the purpose of the communication, 2) the audience
to whom the message is being sent, and 3) the receiver's
stage in the innovation process.(6) An important distinction
is that the channels used depends a great deal on whether
the society is traditional, transitional, or modern. In
traditional societies information travels along lines of
social hierarchy (basic media); in transitional societies
there is a dual system of extending media and basic media
which is not integrated; and in modern societies the dual
system is integrated by means of opinion leaders.(7) Lerner
states that a shift in the channels of communication of ideas
and attitudes is the key to culture change and innovation.(8)
Therefore, the amount of attitude change that can be reason-
ably expected through the various channels deserves thorough
investigation.

THE INNOVATION-DECISION PROCESS

Rogers and Shoemaker have constructed a model of the
innovation-decision process (diagram 8) which will help the
reader to conceptualize the process a person goes through in
making his decision either for or against the acceptance of
an innovation. Diffusion researchers have long recognized
that an individual's decision about an innovation is not an
instantaneous act. Rather, it is a process that occurs over
a period of time and consists of a series of actions.(9)
The model of the innovation-decision process depicted in
diagram 8 consists of four functions:

1. *Knowledge*. The person is exposed to the existence of
New Testament Christianity and gains some understanding of
how it functions.
2. *Persuasion*. The person forms a favorable or unfavor-
able attitude toward the innovation.
3. *Decision*. The person engages in activities which
lead to a choice to adopt or reject the innovation.
4. *Confirmation*. The individual seeks reinforcement
for the innovation-decision he has made, but he may reverse
his previous decision if exposed to conflicting messages
about the innovation.

Different aspects of this process are discussed in the
following chapters. At this point the study is concerned

DIAGRAM 8
THE INNOVATION-DECISION PROCESS

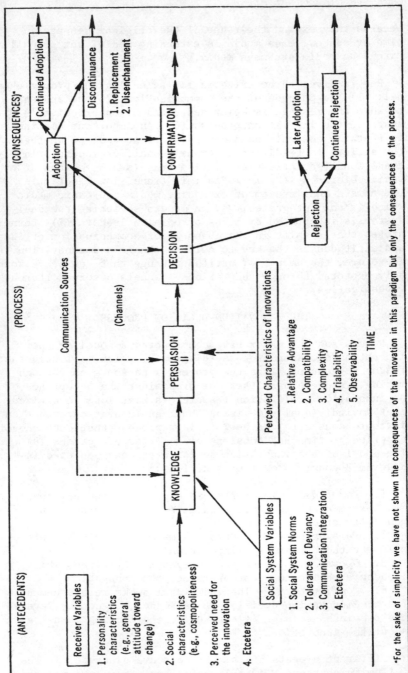

(ANTECEDENTS)

Receiver Variables

1. Personality characteristics (e.g., general attitude toward change)

2. Social characteristics (e.g., cosmopoliteness)

3. Perceived need for the innovation

4. Etcetera

Social System Variables

1. Social System Norms
2. Tolerance of Deviancy
3. Communication Integration
4. Etcetera

(PROCESS)

Communication Sources

(Channels)

KNOWLEDGE I

PERSUASION II

DECISION III

CONFIRMATION IV

Perceived Characteristics of Innovations

1. Relative Advantage
2. Compatibility
3. Complexity
4. Trialability
5. Observability

(CONSEQUENCES)*

Adoption

Continued Adoption

Discontinuance

1. Replacement
2. Disenchantment

Rejection

Later Adoption

Continued Rejection

TIME

*For the sake of simplicity we have not shown the consequences of the innovation in this paradigm but only the consequences of the process.

SOURCE: Everett M. Rogers and F. Floyd Shoemaker, *Communication of Innovations* (New York: Free Press, 1971), p. 102.

with selecting the proper channel in relation to the receiver's stage in the innovation-decision process. At the Lausanne Congress James Engel emphasized the importance of
realizing where the audience is in the process. In diagram
9 Engle conceptualizes the process a religious worker must
go through in making disciples in all nations by bringing
people from no real awareness of Christ to some level of
spiritual maturity. Engle's four stages are essentially
parallel to Roger's four stages in the innovation-decision
process: proclamation (knowledge), persuasion (persuasion),
regeneration (decision), and cultivation (confirmation).

> Christian communication must be directed to people
> in terms appropriate to their current spiritual
> status, recognizing the extend to which a need for
> change is felt or not felt, and employing symbolism
> which is valid for their cultural background. For
> example, if the majority of those who compromise an
> audience have only a distorted awareness of Christ
> (as is the case for most Muslims), it is likely
> that a presentation of the plan of salvation will,
> at that point, have little or no impact, especially
> if they do not feel a need for change. A more
> realistic strategy would be to focus on presenting
> a clear biblical picture of Jesus. This, in turn,
> would represent successful evangelism if it suc-
> ceeds in moving a person closer to Christ and dis-
> posing him to understand the plan of salvation when
> presented later.(10)

It is unjustifiable to assume that all types of Christian
communication should result in conversion. The purpose of
the proclamation stage in diagram 9 is to bring about awareness or knowledge. The purpose of the persuasion stage is
to bring about a decision. Many western evangelists have
made the mistake of initially communicating a persuasive
message based on western-style models of evangelism when
there existed in the audience a lack of sufficient awareness
of the Gospel message along with no felt need for change.
Most methods of evangelism in North America assume a basic
awareness of biblical teaching and the identity of Christ
because the audience is primarily Protestant or Catholic.
But it is a mistake to take correspondence courses and film
strips and other evangelistic material that has been prepared for a North American Protestant audience to the Arab
world and expect that they will communicate the Gospel message in such a way as to bring about a valid decision. Such
techniques will not be successful in the Arab world because

DIAGRAM 9

SPIRITUAL DECISION PROCESS

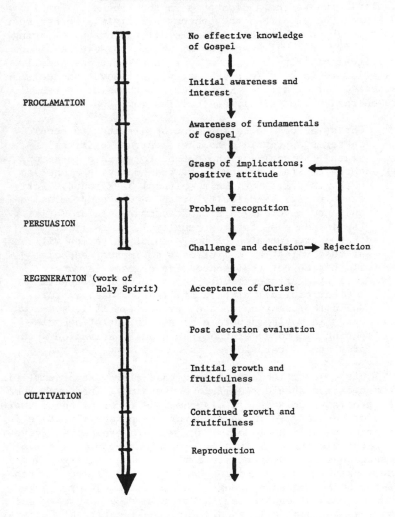

SOURCE: James F. Engel, "The Audience for Christian Communication," in *Let the Earth Hear His Voice*, ed. J. D. Douglas (Minneapolis: World Wide Publications, 1975), p. 535.

they are based on assumptions that are not valid when communicating to an Arab audience.

EXTENDING MEDIA

Extending media are used when the communicator is either
at a distance, disappears altogether, or may never be known.
His message, however, is extended over some distance and
over periods of time.(11) Extending media may be categorized
into two types: instantaneous and preserving. Instantaneous
channels only increase the distance over which a message
travels such as megaphones, telegraph, drums, horns, and
smoke. Preserving channels increase the period of time
during which a communication can reach an audience such as
handwriting, movies, recordings, photos, models, and printed
material.

In the Middle East there are certain government restrictions on various channels of extending media which make
them unavailable for evangelistic purposes. Except for
Lebanon and Kuwait, the governments either control or own
the communication media. What is disseminated must first
be approved by the regime in power.(12) The latest survey
of press freedom around the world ranked the Middle East as
the most oppressive region of the world regarding press
freedom.(13) Since most western missionaries have not been
allowed to use the channels of radio and television in the
Arab countries they have depended heavily on the medium of
the printed page.(14)

Extending media have a much smaller potential for attitude change than do basic media. It is a generally held
view in communication theory that extending media do not
change attitudes but, rather, tend to reinforce pre-existing
ones.(15) Rogers points out that the extending media can:
1) reach a large audience rapidly, 2) create knowledge and
spread information, and 3) lead to changes in weakly held
attitudes but not in strongly held attitudes.(16) Therefore,
in general the extending media will function effectively at
the knowledge stage in the innovation-decision process but
not at the persuasion stage. Lerner affirms that mass media,
in modernizing societies, are most influential in shaping
the lives of people newly located in the sectors of maximum
transition. The new urban workers are such a group in Egypt
today.(17)

Before discussing specific types of extending media, it
is important to notice some general characteristics of ex-

tending media in the Middle East.

1. Mass media and literacy tend to be concentrated in
the urban areas.
2. Person-to-person contact is still the main channel
for the dissemination of information.
3. The press is characterized by a multiplicity of newspapers which to a large extent is a reflection of the diversity of religious, political, and linguistic minorities.
4. The press is characterized by a high birth and mor-
tality rate.
5. The credibility of many newspapers and broadcast programs is low and the people's view of the accuracy of the
press and radio is notoriously pessimistic.(18)

Printed Material

Because of government restrictions the medium of the
printed page is the most widely used of the extending media.
Since extending media are most effective in creating awareness and knowledge and not in attitude change (p. 89), the
religious worker should use printed material for the first
exposure of Arabs to Christianity. Printed material should
not aim primarily in bringing about a decision on the part
of the reader.

The first stage in the innovation-decision process (knowledge) is crucial in the Arab world because the vast majority
of Arabs have a distorted view of Christianity.(19) This is
why the great value of the printed page as an evangelistic
tood can hardly be overemphasized, especially for the Muslim.
(20) Unless the Muslim is able to overcome the long-time
deep seated prejudice and misunderstandings of Christianity,
conversion will be very unlikely.(21) For the Muslim, the
medium of the printed page has an additional advantage in
that it can be used as a device to avoid controversy which
has greatly hindered evangelistic efforts in the Middle
East. All experienced workers in the Arab world agree that
oral controversy and debate must be avoided at all costs,
because such a technique has never proved to be an effective
means of persuading Arabs.(22)

Central to this study is the question: Is the medium of
the printed page a valid channel for reaching the Transitional Arab? Lerner discovered that as a person becomes
modern he moves to the city, becomes literate, and partici-
pates in the media.(23) The majority of Transitional Arabs
were literate in 1958 and would therefore have access to

the medium of the printed page. Therefore, the printed page
is a valid channel for reaching the Transitional Arab.(24)
Table 7 shows the current literacy rates in the countries of
primary concern in this study.

TABLE 7

LITERACY RATES

Lebanon	Jordan	Syria	Egypt	Israel
86%	33%	40%	40%	88%

SOURCE: *Rand McNally Illustrated Atlas of
the Middle East* (Chicago: Rand McNally,
1975), p. 48

Because of the linguistic barriers (p. 70) it is inadequate to translate Christian literature from the West even
of the best quality. It has to be rewritten to make it
suitable especially for the understanding of the Muslim.
This does not mean that truth should be watered down or
even hidden. But it does mean that the message should be
presented in such a way that it does not offend the person
from the very outset. Only a man who is well acquainted
with Islamic thought and deeply versed in its literature
will be able to produce such material.(25)

Correspondence Courses. Bible correspondence courses
have been used very successfully by the churches of Christ
in all three Arab countries where extensive work has been
done.(26) To date Bible correspondence courses have proved
to be the most effective means of locating areas of receptivity and they are also significant because all initial
contacts where congregations are today were made by the
Bible correspondence courses.(27) To use correspondence
courses to locate areas of receptivity is a valid procedure
in light of the innovation-decision process. However, it is
recommended that future religious workers not translate correspondence courses that were originally designed for North
Americans such as was done with Monroe Hawley's Study of the
Bible.(28) Material in such courses is not aimed at the
needs of Transitional Arabs. The religious worker who is
interested in a Bible Correspondence course for the Transitional Arab should first examine those used in the Middle

East by Evangelical Protestant groups which have been written
especially for Muslims.(29) One could use the material that
has already been geared to the Muslim mind as a guideline
in producing material which would present the cause for New
Testament Christianity to the Transitional Arab. Schneider
has offered some helpful suggestions for correspondence
course work.(30) Initial contacts can be made for the
courses through newspaper advertisement and through giving
present students flyers to pass on to interested friends.
Because of family influence it is advisable to add a note
to the introductory letter, which is sent with the first
lesson, saying that children should have the permission of
their parents to take the courses. In following up on Muslim contacts it is advisable to make the initial contact
with them through a personal interview rather than through
a group meeting. It is best to avoid true and false questions and multiple choice questions because these cause perception problems for many Arab students. Gift books should
given upon the completion of a course rather than a certifi-
cate that might bring trouble if displayed. Enclosures
should be developed to help answer frequently asked questions
such as, "How does a Christian pray?" or "Why do Christians
say that Jesus is the Son of God?" A correspondence course
ministry should be kept separate from other works such as
reading rooms, offices, and places of assembly so that in
case the government closes one operation it will not interfere with the others.(31)

   Tracts. Up to the end of 1972 eleven tracts had been
printed in Arabic by the churches of Christ. Some were
translated from English material while others were written
to meet the specific needs of the area.(32) In producing
tracts in the future to reach the Transitional Arabs, it is
recommended that an investigation be made of tracts that
have been written especially for Muslims by various religious groups.(33) In addition, the messages in many of
these tracts should be aimed at the felt needs of the Transitional Arab, a subject which is discussed in chapter
seven.

   Newspapers. There are in the Arab world three hundred
dailies and two hundred weeklies. However, except for the
Egyptian papers, *Al-Ahram, Akhbar al-Yom,* and *Al-Akhabar,*
which circulate more than 250,000 copies daily, few other
newspapers sell over 20,000 per issue.(34) Considering the
fact that evangelists cannot use the radio in the Arab
countries, the newspaper becomes a primary channel of the
mass media for religious workers to use. The large number

of papers in the Middle East makes it necessary to determine
which one will be most widely read by the target audience,
the Transitional Arab. In spite of the fact that newspapers
have low credibility in the Arab world in comparison to
radio their wide circulation indicates that they are an important channel of communication. In Lerner's index of
media preference, fifty-one percent of the Moderns got their
most recent news from radio, forty-five percent of the Transitionals got their most recent news from the newspaper, and
fifty-eight percent of the Traditionals got their most recent news from word of mouth.(35)

The most important paper in the Middle East is *Al-Ahram*,
and it is surprising that Douglas was allowed to advertise
correspondence courses in the paper in 1962.(36) Since
Al-Ahram is the most influential paper in the Arab world, the
most widely circulated, and widely read by Transitionals, it
would be the preferred choice for advertising correspondence
courses or other communications, especially if there was a
worker in Egypt to follow up on the contacts in that country. Not only does *Al-Ahram* have a wide circulation in
Egypt but also in many other Arab countries.(37)

Another factor to consider in newspaper work is the freedom of the press. The press has more freedom in Lebanon
than anywhere else in the Arab world.(38) It is this freedom that made it possible for G. W. Childs to write a weekly
column in Arabic in one of the leading local Lebanese papers.
(39)

Newspapers are an effective channel of communication for
messages which are aimed at increasing the knowledge and
awareness level of the audience and for locating areas of
receptivity. The religious worker is reminded that newspaper work is of little value unless a feedback mechanism
is provided to enable one to evaluate the response.

Wilson suggests four categories of literature for use in
the Arab world: 1) for the first approach, 2) for follow-up
work, 3) to bring conviction to the reader, and 4) to build
up in the faith.(40) Notice how closely these four categories are parallel to the four functions of the innovation-
decision process in diagram 8 (p. 86). Tracts used for the
first approach should be aimed at creating an initial awareness of Christianity, and should therefore not call for a
decision or present the plan of salvation. Many of the
tracts used for follow-up work would be designed to answer
frequently asked questions and to clear up misunderstandings

and misconceptions about Christianity. Although tracts are
useful at this stage in the innovation-decision process,
they are not sufficient--personal contact is necessary.
Only those tracts in the third category would be designed to
bring about a decision. The fourth category of tracts is
very important if new converts are expected to grow to maturity in the Christian faith.

Audio-Visual Media

The audio-visual media are being used by the leaders of
the Middle East for both propaganda and educational purposes.
(41) Therefore, they would be a viable alternative for the
religious worker to use in communicating religious innovations. Audio-visual media have several advantages over
printed material being used alone: 1) instruction time can
be reduced as much as thirty to forty percent, 2) there is
a fifty percent improvement in permanence, and 3) audio-
visuals can modify attitudes or opinions.(42) However,
audio-visual material cannot be brought in from the West
without consideration to how they will affect the Arab mind.

Radio and television. Government restrictions on these
media in the Arab countries still prohibit their use for
evangelistic purposes. However, Evangelical Protestant
groups have done broadcasting into t he Arab world from
Ethiopia, Sudan, and Cyprus.(43) Therefore, assuming access
to the media, would they be a valid channel of communication
for reaching Transitional Arabs? Lerner indicates that
radio has a much higher credibility rating among both Transitionals and Moderns.(44) In addition, there are nearly
twelve million radio receivers and over two million television sets in the Middle East.(45) According to a report
on communications in the Middle East the majority of the
radio sets are in the urban areas.(46)

In some countries like Kuwait, Sudan, and Jordan, radio
broadcasting has advanced more rapidly than the press and
it is the primary source of news.(47) In view of the tremendous impact of radio and television in the Middle East
it appears that it would be worth investigating the possibilities of using radio as a means of locating areas of
receptivity.

Film. Evertt L. Huffard tried using a slide series from
the United States in home Bible studies, but it proved to
be inadequate for two reasons: 1) the pictures were such a
novelty that they were distracting, and 2) the message was

aimed at middle class Protestant Americans.(48) Obviously
such slide presentations are not effective in reaching Arabs.
But the channel of film (slides, filmstrips, or motion pictures) should not be discarded as an effective channel of
communication in the Middle East. Film-going is now among
the most popular forms of entertainment in the Middle East
even in the more traditional countries.(49) Crawford discovered that even in more traditional sections of Morocco
film was the most effective channel of communication.(50)
The foreign movies are appreciated only by the Modern Arabs,
but the majority of the population prefer locally produced
films since they cannot understand a foreign language or
even read the Arabic subtitles.(51) This indicates that for
film to be an effective channel of communication in the Arab
world it will have to be especially geared for the Arab mind
and show scenes that are familiar to the Arab people. Joyce
affirms that drama (whether on stage, film, or radio) is a
channel of communication that is almost unsurpassed in
reaching the Muslim heart and mind, as long as the scripts
are geared to their religious background and culture.(52)

Recordings. There is a great opportunity for reaching
Arabs through recorded messages. Various organizations
have recorded short messages on records and cassettes in
many of the languages spoken in the Muslim world.(53) Card-
board record players are also available which are given out
free with the records.(54)

Credibility of the Channel

Communications theory places an emphasis on the credibility or believability of the message.(55) The higher the
credibility of the transmitter and the channel, the more
weight or faith will be placed in the message. One variable
that affects credibility is proximity. The words of a neighbor are trusted before the words of a stranger are trusted,
even though the message may be new (an innovation). This is
why short-wave radio is rarely as believable as medium wave
or local radio.(56) Of the above channels of communication
discussed which would seem to have higher credibility?
Lerner indicates that among both Transitionals and Moderns,
radio is regarded as more credible than newspaper.(57) However, the newspaper will still need to be used in the Middle
East as a primary channel of locating areas of receptivity
because of the government restrictions on radio.

The more localized the channel appears to be the more
credibility it is likely to have. Local films are more

likely to communicate effectively than foreign films.

   The extending media discussed above are able to reach a
large audience rapidly and to create knowledge and spread
information. However, to diffuse innovations meaningfully
and successfully, people must not only be exposed but they
must be brought to accept the innovation. Since exposure
does not guarantee acceptance, the purpose of the communication is vital in selecting the channel. Basic media have
much greater potential for influencing opinion change.

BASIC MEDIA

   Basic media implies that the communicator is present when
the communication takes place.(58) In the innovation process
there are two forms of basic media: 1) that between the
change agent and the adopters, and 2) communicators among
the adopters themselves (intra-group communication).(59) In
attempting to introduce innovations, the basic media have
two advantages: 1) they allow a two-way exchange of ideas
(feedback), and 2) they are best capable of persuading individuals to change strongly held attitudes.(60)

   Edward T. Hall lists ten kinds of human activity which he
calls Primary Message Systems (PMS) only one of which involves language.(61) All the other Primary Message Systems
are non-linguistic forms of the communication process. This
emphasizes the important place of non-verbal communication.

Non-Verbal Communication

   This discussion of non-verbal communication will merely
seek to point out in a very brief way the most significant
types of non-verbal communication which are likely to affect
the communication of religious innovations in the Arab world.

   Gestures. Many Arab gestures have a far more precise
meaning than is customarily assigned to gestures in North
America.(62) Two false explanations have been advanced for
the Arab's more overt use of gestures: 1) they use gestures
to save breath in the hot summer sun, and 2) they use gestures more because their language is deficient and they
would be unable to communicate their messages unless they
used gestures.(63) Gestic action on the part of the Arab
takes many forms and may be analyzed on many levels including
the cultural, linguistic, psychological, and social. The
author highly recommends Barakat's article for anyone who
intends to do extensive work among the Arabs. After an ex-

tensive analysis of cultural and linguistic gestures he lists
descriptions of two hundred and forty-seven different gestures most of which are illustrated with photographs.(64)

   Proxemic behavior. Hall coined the term "proxemics" as
"the study of how man unconsciously structures microspace--
the distance between men in the conduct of daily transactions,
the organization of space in his houses and buildings, and
ultimately the layout of his towns."(65) Watson and Graves
conducted an empirical study of Arab and American proxemic
behavior to test pragmatically Hall's system for the notation of proxemic behavior.(66) Highly significant Arab-
American differences emerged with the Arabs confronting each
other more directly, moving closer together, more apt to
touch each other while talking, looking each other more
squarely in the eye, and conversing in louder tones.(67)
Hall's discussion of proxemic behavior in the Arab world is
highly recommended for anyone who intends to do extensive
work among the Arabs.(68)

   Clothing. Muslims are often critical of western dress.
Marah recommends that male missionaries should not wear
shorts when going to Muslims, and says that women who wear
short skirts will be very embarassed when sitting on mats
with Muslim women.(69) Gulick points out some differences
between Arab and western views of erotic stimulation.

   Modern Muslim men seem to be stimulated by the
   exposure of women's upper arms but not by the
   exposure of their bosoms. Western men's reactions
   are approximately the reverse. Many western men
   seem to feel that women wearing slacks are either
   uninteresting or definitely unattractive. Many
   Muslim (and Christian) Lebanese men are so stimulated
   by such women that they seem to assume that they
   are whores. To Muslim men (and women), belly dan-
   cers are good family entertainment, suitable for
   wedding parties if one can afford them, and usually
   to be seen in Arabic cinema comedies. To many
   Westerners, they have the forbidden, indecent aura
   of nightclub strippers.(70)

Speaker-Audience Setting

   Probably more has been written about the speaker-audience
setting than any other of the communication settings (private face-to-face, small group, and mass media).(71) Martin
points out several important characteristics of this channel

of communication: 1) the opportunity for feedback is very
slight, 2) the majority of the audience will already agree
with the speaker's position, and 3) large numbers of people
can be reached through this setting.(72) This discussion
will consider the sermon and the lecture (the most common
examples) as well as summer camps.

Sermons. Nida points out that the sermon has become such
an important part of Protestant religious communication that
the two tend to be equated.(73) However, it is questionable
just how much communication the average sermon actually effects. The sermon is only one means of communication and is
often not the most effective. In the Middle East, the worship of the churches of Christ has been very western in form
and thus centered around the sermon. Gospel meetings have
been tried on various occasions, but have not proven to be
a successful means of reaching the Arab people or even con-
victing them of truth.(74) Making a decision by responding
to an invitation song is a form of decision making that is
foreign to Arab society. Another disadvantage that the sermon has is that very few Muslims will entertain the thought
of going to a Christian place of worship and listening to a
sermon.(75) Many Muslims will go to listen to a lecture if
it is not located in a Christian place of worship.

Lectures. Lectures might be a viable alternative for initial presentations of the Gospel to Arabs, and especially
Muslims. But the religious worker must realize how much he
can effectively hope to accomplish with this channel of communication. It can effectively introduce the knowledge of
an innovation but will rarely provide the means to convince
them to adopt it.(76) Therefore, lectures may be useful in
the knowledge function of the innovation-decision process,
but not in the persuasion function. The lecture can serve
as a useful means of introducing the Christian message, to
be supplemented by other forms of communication.

Summer camps. Summer camps have turned out to be one of
the most effective methods of evangelism in the Middle East.
Bible correspondence course students were invited to attend
a summer camp which would last from one to two weeks. Each
morning they would study the Bible and in the afternoon they
participated in different forms of recreation.(77) Huffard
gives four reasons why the summer camps were successful:
1) the young people had very little recreation, 2) none of
the young people had studied the Bible in a serious way, 3)
they were away from their family group pressures, and 4) they
were given the opportunity to see Christianity practiced as
well as taught.(78)

The speaker-audience setting and the extending media are
most conducive to fulfilling the knowledge function in the
innovation-decision process. The persuasion function can
best be accomplished through communication with small groups.

Small Groups

In all three of the preceeding chapters it has been emphasized that Arab society is a group-oriented society, and
that important decisions are usually group decisions. Individuals rarely make decisions without consulting with their
family. It is recommended that the religious communicator
follow the natural lines of interaction and decision making
in Arab society. This means that the evangelist will aim
for group decisions rather than individual decisions. This
study indicates that the evangelist will be most effective
if he communicates the persuasive part of the Christian message to small groups. The question arises: What groups
should be addressed?

Doob points out that basic media may be evaluated according to their versatility. What kinds of information can the
medium transmit? The previous discussion of hospitality
indicated that Arabs do not normally discuss their differences in the home, and especially not religion (p. 17).
Therefore, the medium of home Bible studies might not be
versatile enough to use as an effective channel for communicating religious innovations.(79)

The religious communicator is now confronted with a
dilemma. The nuclear family is the decision making unit in
Arab society and yet the nature of Arab hospitality forbids
the discussion of religious differences with one's guests.
Huffard indicates that although religion should not be mentioned during the very first visits, that it is proper to
discuss religion after an initial acquaintance has been
made, but it should not be in a formal way at all.(80) Although this may be true, a tension exists which needs to be
solved. A possible solution seems to lie in teaching the
family as a group in a geographical location separate from
the home of either the teacher or the prospects.

This could be done by bringing several family groups
together for a weekly Bible study session some evening during the week. In light of the fact that two strong categories of identity in Arab culture are religion and language, the evangelist would be wise to respect these categories. More effective communication could take place if

the families brought together were from the same religious
and linguistic background. This would be much more conducive to small group discussion. Rather than calling for
individual decisions the evangelist would be wise to call
for a group decision of each family unit.

Another potentially effective small group setting would
be among university students. Since university campuses are
focal points for Transitionals, campus evangelism would be
an effective approach.(81) This area of receptivity is
quite large since the student body in the Middle East is
379,000, and this number is increasing at an annual rate of
twenty-five percent.(82) Since the young Transitional Arab
is taking over the opinion leadership in many parts of the
Middle East (see p. 58), campus evangelism would be a very
important part of an effective evangelistic approach to the
Middle East.

There is one negative factor associated with campus evangelism. Because of the increasing number of graduates who
cannot find employment a good number strive to emigrate to
the industrialized countries of the West, and the number of
emigrants has been rising at a steady pace. Eighty percent
of all Jordanian and Egyptial students never return home.(83)
There is the chance therfore, of converting a large number
of students who would then emigrate, thus not contributing
to the growth of the church in the Arab world.

THE SITE

There are certain places where people go to get information. The crucial question is: Where can the Christian
message be communicated most effectively? It has been noted
that there are certain difficulties in attempting to discuss
religion in the home (p. 17). Huffard concluded in his thesis that because Arab hospitality did not allow for the discussion of important ideas, home Bible studies would be
self-defeating.(84) Although, there is some difficulty in
attempting to meet in Arab homes, the option should not be
entirely eliminated as an opportunity for teaching. Huffard
notes that after the first visit one is often freer to exchange ideas, and says that he is often asked questions about
the church.(85) Answering these probes are good teaching
opportunities. An organized and systematic presentation
(such as filmstrips) or even open Bible study would not be
as effective. But effective teaching could take place by
frequent unscheduled visits in the homes and by exposing oneself to questions and turning these into teaching opportuni-

ties.(86) One center of information seeking in the Middle East is the coffeehouse or cafe. Male social life goes on outside the home usually in the coffee houses where friends meet to chat, discuss politics, and transact business.(87) The coffeehouse is available to younger and more educated groups who feel uncomfortable in the traditional hierarchy based largely on age and wealth. It resembles the general store of the rural United States or the pub in Britain. It is the forum for discussion and decision on village social and economic matters and political issues.(88) If this is the place where the men (decision makers) of the community get their information, why not make the Gospel available there? Could not free literature be made available there? Could it not be a place for getting to know the men in the community and locating the opinion leaders?(89)

Another way of spreading information is through the use of the reading rooms which have been used successfully by various groups.(90) Ideally a reading room would be set up along a busy street with a glass front. It could be stocked with books, pamphlets, and tracts. Evangelists for the churches of Christ have not yet tried reading rooms as an evangelistic tool in the Middle East. Other religious groups have found them to be a very successful method. This approach could serve a very useful purpose in reaching the Transitional Arab not only through the channel of the printed page but also through personal contact. Reading rooms would overcome the disadvantage mentioned earlier of discussing religion in the homes. If individuals had questions they could be given a specific book to read or could talk personally with the religious worker in an atmosphere outside the home. Such an approach would require a greater investment of personnel and finances, but the return would probably be well worth the investment.

Peursem, in discussing evangelism in the Middle East, recommends that the place where the church meets is important.(91) It must be of easy access so as to guarantee an audience. An upstairs room is wholly inadequate, because few men and even fewer women are likely to come upstairs unless they receive an urgent invitation from the evangelist.(92)

CONCLUSION

The study of communication channels in the innovation-decision process lead to the following conclusions:

1. A combination of extending media and basic media channels is the most effective way of reaching people with the Christian message and persuading them to accept it.(93)

2. Extending media channels are relatively more important at the persuasion function in the innovation-decision process.(94)

3. If the probability of adoption is to be maximized, communication channels must be utilized in an ideal time sequence, progressing from extending media to basic media. (95)

4. Using a communication channel that is inappropriate to a given function in the innovation-decision process will result in a later adoption of the religious innovation.(96)

5. Extending media are relatively more important than basic media for reaching the innovators and opinion leaders. (97)

6. The effects of extending media channels can be increased when followed by small group discussion.(98)

7. By incorporating the advantages of each type of channel into a single propelling force, the religious communicator can reach a greater percentage of the Arab people and better persuade them to accept Christianity.

Therefore, the correspondence courses and newspapers can best be used to locate areas of receptivity. Lectures, tracts, and reading rooms can best be used to increase the knowledge of the Christian message. Summer camps and small group sessions can best be used to persuade the Transitional Arab to accept Christianity. Once persuasion has been successful the religious worker should call for a group decision to be made by the family unit rather than on an individual basis.

It is important to consider, not only the channels one can use in communicating a message, but also the specific goals which the communication of that message is intended to achieve. In chapter six the goal of cross-cultural Christian communication will be examined in the context of Arab culture. Unless the goal is well thought out the end result may be very different from what the evangelist intended.

6

The Goal

The Christian message can change people, but to teach that message without sufficient understanding of the motivations, cultural themes, social structure, and world view of those being converted, may produce results that are greatly different from those intended. Therefore, it is necessary to correlate an understanding of Arab culture with valid principles of evangelism in order to produce a valid and workable evangelistic approach to the Transitional Arab.

In the following chapters a basic familiarity with church growth principles will be assumed and periodically reference will be made to significant material that has been written on principles of evangelism that are being used. Slate has pointed out that New Testament evangelism involves at least three goals:

1. to internationalize the message
2. to facilitate a valid decision
3. to work for persistence of obedience.(1)

This chapter is concerned with the second and third goals mentioned above. The first goal will be dealt with extensively in chapter seven.

Doob states that a clear-cut distinction needs to be made between the conscious goal of the communicator and the goal which he in fact achieves.(2) Goals are never easy to determine even when the communicator is present. Evangelists are acutely aware of their intended goals, but they must decide

the extent to which modifications in the ritual they advocate
are desirable or necessary in order to achieve essentially
spiritual ends.(3) An attempt will be made here to isolate
those variables which the evangelist must be aware of in order to insure a valid decision. Tillich makes an important
distinction concerning the goal of Christian communication.

> The question cannot be: how do we communicate
> the Gospel so that others will accept it? For
> this there is no method. To communicate the
> Gospel means putting it before the people so they
> are able to decide for or against it. The Christian
> Gospel is a matter of decision. It is to be accepted
> or rejected. All that we who communicate this
> Gospel can do is to make possible a genuine decision.
> (4)

Tippett says that the basic problem is how to communicate
the essential supracultural core of the gospel to individuals
in other cultures without having it contaminated by forms of
expression which are foreign to the indigenous population.(5)
He contends that upon examining the churches in modern day
mission fields, one frequently finds one of two situations.
First, they may be thoroughly western in form, teaching, and
values and be completely unrelated to the cultural ethos. Or
second, they may have syncretistic worship which is more animistic than Christian.(6) In presenting the Gospel message
to Transitional Arabs the former is more likely to be the
probelm encountered. When Christianity fails to become indigenous it usually fails to recognize and provide ways of
dealing with the basic felt needs of the society. The universal human problems will all have their peculiar formations in
different cultures. No religion can be indigenous unless it
comes to grips with these universal problems in their cul-
tural-bound forms.(7)

CHRISTIANIZATION OR WESTERNIZATION

In 1932 MacDonald discussed what is still an important
issue in evangelism in the Middle East. He posed the question: "Are the missionaries of the future to be missionaries
of Christ or missionaries of the Christian civilization of
the West."(8) Similarly, Sa'adah, of the American University
of Beirut affirmed that the Christian churches and the Christian theology which prevail in the Arab world are completely
alien and strange to the Arab mind.(9) Charistianity has
never had a legitimate opportunity to pass through the Arab
mind. The situation described by Sa'adah in 1939 is still

very much the same in the Arab world. Among both the churches
of Christ and other religious groups, Christianity is still
to a large extend disguised in foreign western attire. It is
this situation that makes it very difficult for the Arab to
make a valid decision. To facilitate a valid decision the
Christian message must be presented in a relevant way,
stripped of all useless western overhang (see chapter seven).
Kraemer has succintly stated the problem:

> The problem of adaptation is that of genuine
> translation of Christianity into indigenous terms
> so that its relevancy to their concrete situations
> becomes evident.(10)

He goes on to assert that in most cases Christianity is presented in the forms that have been developed in the West.
Most western missionaries are unable to separate themselves
from their cultural, mental, emotional, and social frame of
reference.(11) The missionary in the Arab world has never
been regarded as simply a Christian; he was always a western
Christian.(12)

In many cases it is not Christianity itself which is rejected so much as it is the manner or form in which that
message is presented. When this happens, the evangelist has
failed to present the Gospel in such a way as to facilitate
a valid decision. Kraft has devised a model which sheds
considerable light on the issue at hand.(13) Peter was a
Jew, and, though a Christian, understood Christianity in the
Hebrew cultural context. But it was Peter's task to communicate the Christian message which he received in Hebrew
dress and to which he responded in Hebrew terms, to Cornelius
who was a Roman, a member of another culture. Peter could
have assumed that Hebrew culture was a suitable vehicle of
God's communication. Before God communicated to Peter in a
dream, Peter likely assumed that conversion to Christianity
implied conversion to Judaism. But scripture indicates that
this is not what was expected of Cornelius. Diagram 10 illustrates the conversion process of Cornelius.

All traces of Hebrew culture were not eliminated from
Cornelius' conversion, but it was not necessary for each
convert to Christianity to embrace the culture in which
Christianity was born.(14) The first-century Judaizers were
advocating that Gentiles should be required to become Jews
to become Christians. Diagram 11 illustrates this view.

DIAGRAM 10
CHRISTIAN CONVERSION

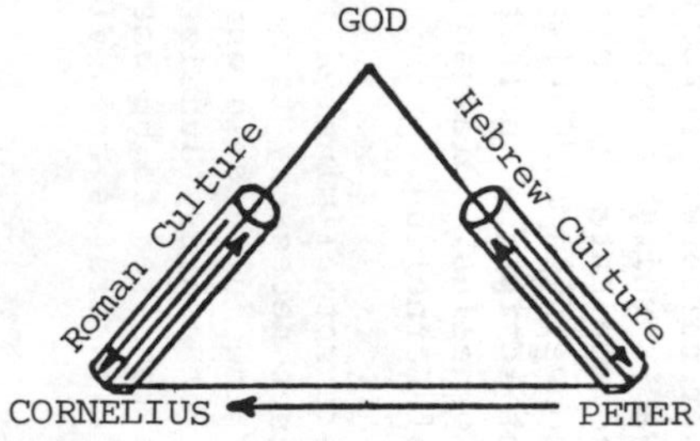

DIAGRAM 11
CULTURAL CONVERSION

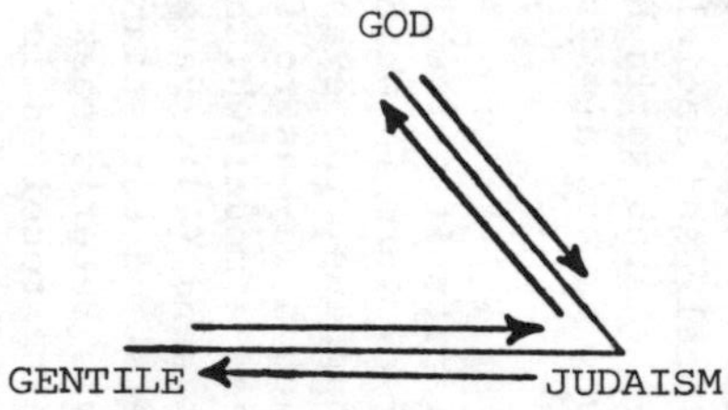

DIAGRAM 12
CULTURAL CONVERSION

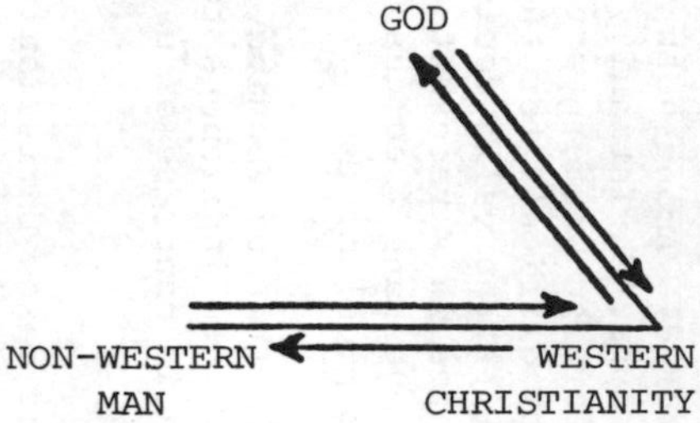

DIAGRAM Peter, in contact with God within Hebrew culture, has communicated the possibility and terms of such contact with God to Cornelius across cultural boundaries. Cornelius, upon hearing the message, responds to God (not merely to Peter), whereupon contact is established between God and Cornelius without the necessity of change of cultural allegiance on the part of the latter.

DIAGRAM God's revelation has come first to the Jew and only thence, through Judaism, to Gentiles (following the outside arrows). Conversion of Gentiles involves, therefore, first a conversion along the horizontal line to Judaism, then a response to God in terms of the same culture in which his revelation is couched. In other words, a Gentile must first become a Jew to become a Christian.

DIAGRAM God's message has been proclaimed to non-Western man through the instrumentality of Western Christianity. The non-Western convert is urged to respond to God by embracing that Western-style Christianity. "Conversion to Christianity" is, therefore, defined as conversion to the particular Western system of Christianity presented. The non-Western man must first become Westernized to become a Christian.

SOURCE: Charles H. Kraft, "Christian Conversion or Cultural Conversion," *Practical Anthropology* 10 (July-August 1963): 179-87.

In Acts 15, the council held in Jerusalem decided against
the teaching of the Judaizers. Unfortunately, many modern
missionaries, are, albeit inadvertently, promoting an approach
to Christianity which is similar to that of the Judaizing
teachers. They have merely substituted western culture for
Hebrew culture. Their attitudes are a primary hindrance to
effective cross-cultural communication of the Christian message.(15) A diagram of the message presented by such missionaries would be the same as diagram 11 but with different
labels (diagram 12).

Many western missionaries fail to recognize the fact that
western culture is but one of many usable by God. A correct
concept of conversion must be conceived in terms of bringing
about a relationship between the individual and the supracultural God. The forms used to respond to and worship that
God should be allowed to differ as much from western Christianity as their non-western culture differs from western
culture.(16)

Nida applies this same principle not just to the conversion process, but to the form in which the message is presented.(17) The process of communication can be broken down
simply into three variables: the source (S), the message (M),
and the receiver (R). In diagram 13 the traingle indicates
that communication takes place within the total cultural context. The contrast between the squares, circles, and triangles is an attempt to symbolize the basic difference between cultures. A close look reveals the fact that the message (M) reflects in many ways the structure of the culture
of which it is a part.(18) Therefore, a small triangle or
square around the M in the diagram symbolizes this relationship between the total cultural framework and the linguistic
form of the message.

Nida points out that "one of the most obvious contrasts in
any communication involving two languages is that the form of
△M̲ is not the form ☐M̲ ."(19) In diagram 13 the triangles
represent communication in Bible times, the squares the cor-
responding communication in English, and the circles the form
which the communication takes in the Arab world. Remember
that the goal is that the message be presented to the Arab
in a familiar form so that he can make a valid decision
regarding Christianity. In other words, Ⓡ should be able to
respond to Ⓜ within the context of his own culture in sub-
stantially the same manner as △R̲ responded to △M̲ within the
setting of Biblical culture. But in order to achieve this,
the form of the message in a circle culture will be differ-

ent from the form of the message in a square culture. These
differences are allowable because the aim is not a formal
equivalence, but a functional one.(20)

DIAGRAM 13

THE FORM OF CHRISTIANITY

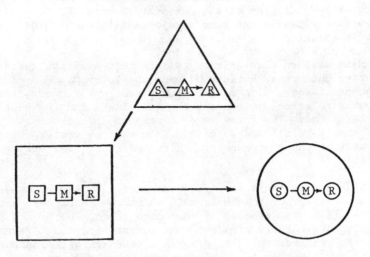

SOURCE: Eugene A. Nida, *Message and Mission*
(Pasadena: William Carey Library, 1960),
p. 47.

   Luzbetak proposed three levels of culture which evangelism must not interfere with or squelch: 1) form, 2) function,
and 3) underlying philosophy.(21) Form is the culture content
such as how one gets married; who is a good wife; what is or
is not beautiful; how to speak to God; and an infinite number of other answers to the what, when, where, and how of
coping with the various aspects of life. Function refers to
the way the elements of culture are related to one another
and form a system of solutions to human problems. Underlying philosophy is the third and deepest level of culture
which is the set of premises, attitudes, and motives behind
the system spoken of above.

THE EVANGELIST

   According to Doob's theoretical structure there is a vital
interrelationship between the goal and the communicator. (22)
Therefore, it is relevant to discuss the role of the evan-

gelist at this stage of the study, because the evangelist is
the communicator of the religious innovations. The evangelist is a change agent, which may be defined as "a professional
who influences innovation-decisions in a direction deemed
desirable by a change agency."(23) The role of the evangelist
as a change agent is illustrated in diagram 14. It shows
that the change agent functions as a communication link between two or more social systems. There is often a social
or cultural chasm between the system (or culture) represented
by the agent of change (evangelist) and the client's system
(or culture).(24) This chasm or gap creates role conflict
and problems in communication. This is discussed more thoroughly below under the heading "identification."

Rogers and Shoemaker isolate seven roles by which a change
agent introduces an innovation. An evangelist could increase
his effectiveness by utilizing these in his evangelistic
strategy.

> The change agent often fills seven roles in the
> change process: (1) he develops a need for change
> on the part of his clients, (2) establishes a
> change relationship with them, (3) diagnoses their
> problem, (4) creates intent to change in his clients,
> (5) translates this intent into action, (6) stabi-
> lizes change and prevents discontinuances, and (7)
> achieves a terminal relationship with his clients.(25)

The following generalizations demonstrate how the role of
the evangelist is interrelated with the other aspects of the
innovation-decision process.

> Change agent success is positively related to:
> (1) the extent of change agent effort, (2) his client-
> orientation, rather than change-agency orientation,
> (3) the degree to which his program is compatible
> with client's needs, (4) the change agent's empathy
> with clients, (5) his homophily with clients, (6)
> the extent he works through opinion leaders, (7)
> his credibility in the eyes of his clients, and
> (8) his efforts in increasing his clients' ability
> to evaluate innovations.(26)

These generalizations on the role of the change agent in
the innovation-decision process provide theoretical evidence
that the evangelist will be more successful if he properly
identifies with the local people, if he makes Christianity
relevant to their felt needs, and if he utilizes the proper
opinion leaders.

DIAGRAM 14

ROLE OF THE CHANGE AGENT

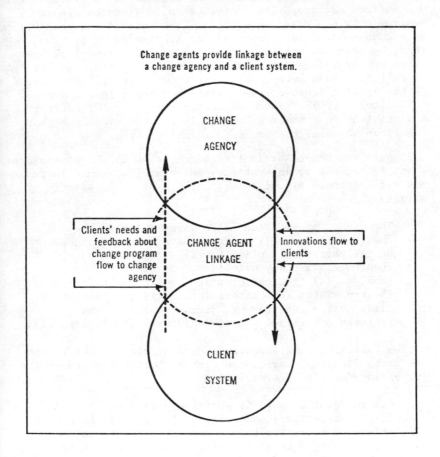

SOURCE: Everett M. Rogers and F. Floyd Shoemaker
Communication of Innovations, 2nd ed. (New York:
Free Press, 1971), p. 228.

Capabilities

The capabilities of an evangelist include his resources,
past experience, motive to communicate, and his preparation.
Stennett emphasizes three special areas of preparation for
the missionary confronting the Muslim: 1) a knowledge of
Islam, 2) a knowledge of Arabic, and 3) the ability to make

concessions in customs.(27) The importance of learning the
language cannot be overemphasized.(28) Even though many of
the local people might be able to speak English, it is still
necessary to learn the local language because this is the
language of the heart. Not knowing the local language is a
severe handicap in communication.

Millions of men live in two worlds: 1) that of our inti-
mates who speak our own language, and 2) the language of
trade or business.(29) The trade language is not regarded
as adequate for things that really matter. Men fight, make
love, and mourn in their mother tongue (the language of the
heart). The Bible gives two examples of the use of the
language of the heart for effective communication. The Lord
spoke to Paul in the Hebrew language, the language he had
learned at his mother's knee.(30) Paul had been educated
in Greek, but God did not only want to transmit information,
he wanted to move Paul to action, and so he used the language of his heart. On the day of Pentecost, in order to
convert the various Jewish peoples who had been raised in
languages other than Hebrew, the Holy Spirit used the languages of their birth.(31) McGavran argues that it makes
a great deal of difference whether the Gospel is proclaimed
in the standard language or in the language of the heart.(32)
While it is possible to convert men to Christ through a
secondary language, the evangelist who speaks to people in
a language other than what they speak in their homes should
never deceive himself that the standard language is "just
as good" as the heart language as a vehicle for the Gospel.
(33)

Experienced missionaries in the Middle East have seen
the necessity of learning the language thoroughly.(34) If
one does not learn the language he will forever remain an
outsider, and his working capacity will be reduced by at
least fifty percent.(35) Imagine a Muslim who could only
speak Arabic trying to convert people to Islam in New York,
relying on translators whose qualities he is unable to
check. Only when the evangelist is able to talk to the
people on all subjects concerning their lives, to read their
books, and understand their way of thinking, will he be able
to exercise a permanent influence on them. Without learning
their language he is little more than a curiosity to them.
(36)

Marsh claims that "God has made it impossible to communicate the Gospel effectively to Muslims without knowing their
language."(37) He says that eternity alone will reveal the

immense amount of harm that has been done in Muslim lands
by well-meaning but misguided individuals.

> No man or woman called to permanent work among
> them (Muslims) should presume to attempt to work
> without learning the language, and learning it
> well. This is the sine qua non of Muslim evan-
> gelization.(38)

Learning the language is more than just learning words
with which to communicate, it is learning the culture of the
Arab people. One cannot fully understand Arab culture without a thorough knowledge of Arabic. Unless a man understands
the subtle cues that are implicit in language, tone, gestures,
and expression, he will not only consistently misinterpret
what is said to him, but he may offend irretrievably without
knowing how or why.(39)

Identification

Probably no subject relating to the role of the evangelist is more debated than that of identification. The apostle
Paul chose as his missionary motto: "all things to all men."
(40) The problem arises over just how the evangelist is to
go about becoming "all things to all men." How Paul put
this into practice is really astounding.

> He had Timothy circumcised because his mother
> was Jewish and this was necessary to win the
> Jews where he was known. But Titus, who was
> thoroughly Greek was not required to be circumcised
> because nobody really expected it among the Greeks
> where the law was not observed.(41)

In addition to this, Paul stopped using the Hebrew form of
his name (Saul), and Silas probably switched to the Latin
form (Sylvanus).(42) Even though Paul was flexible, he did
not permit the Jews to force their customs on those of another culture (the Gentiles).(43) The way the early church
dealt with this problem is very helpful in learning how to
deal with the problem today. Nida has emphasized the importance of this problem by pointing out that where evangelism
has been unsuccessful one always finds that the evangelist
has failed in identification and communication.(44)

The problem can be briefly stated as follows. Some have
advocated total physical identification with the local
people, which could include dressing exactly like the

nationals and living on the same economic level with them.
Reyburn describes how he tried to identify in the Andes of
Ecuador. He dressed like them, worked with them, talked
like them, and ate like them. Yet with all this he was
still limited in being able to identify. Finally one day an
Indian put his arm around Reyburn and said, "We call you
rich landowner because you were not born of an Indian mother."
(45)

Van Ess, a former missionary to the Arabs, confirms that
such total physical identification is impossible.

> For one reason or another a foreigner will try
> to wear native clothing. If he imagines that by
> doing so he can pass for an Arab, given of course
> the Arab's complexion, he is deceiving only himself.
> An Arab will spot any one of a dozen mistakes he is
> bound to make. I neither know of or have heard of
> any foreigner who could pass for an Arab for any
> length of time. It simply cannot be done. All
> tales told of T. E. Lawrence's skill in that re-
> spect are pure fiction.(46)

The reason for the impossibility is that no matter how hard
man tries it is impossible for him to divest himself of his
own culture. Most of culture lies hidden and is outside
voluntary control; in fact the process of enculturation is
so thorough and subtle that even one's emotional reactions
and muscular movements reflect one's cultural conditioning.
(47) If it is the case that one cannot completely rid himself of his cultural influence, then how can one legitimately
become all things to all men? In resolving this problem one
must keep in mind the second goal of evangelism and pose the
question: What role is necessary to facilitate a valid decision from the Transitional Arab?

Various answers have been given to this question.
Loewen, after comparing the advantages of missionaries
leading an insider's role as compared to an outsider's role,
concludes that the attainment of "identification" leading
to an insider's role may yield some short term advantages
but is often fraught with significant long term hazards.(48)
This is because once the alien has assumed one or two inside
roles, he will gradually be held responsible for more inside
roles. In addition, he will emit many non-insider cues,
which will cause people to question his integrity.(49)

Kietzman poses the question: How indigenous can a missionary become? He concludes that it is not within the
power of the evangelist to demonstrate by his life how the
practices of a native culture are to be "transvaluated."
This is the job of the native Christian. Therefore, the
task of the evangelist is to make the message and not himself culturally relevant. He says that to follow a parti-
cipative role in the culture is often dangerous.(50) Elsewhere Kietzman says that the role of the evangelist is that
of a catalyst, a source of new ideas and new information.(51)

Hall and Whyte affirm that if one tries to conform completely the Arab would find his behavior confusing and in-
sincere, and would suspect his motives.(52) Obviously such
circumstances would not be conducive to obtaining a valid
decision for Christ. The role the evangelist assumes has a
tremendous effect on the message he seeks to communicate.

Badeau states that the evangelist in the Arab world is
always regarded as a double character: as a Christian and
as a Westerner. He goes on to say that the tensions and
contacts between western and eastern are probably more
influential and basic to the missionary role than the tensions between Muslim and Christian.(53) This emphasizes
the difficulty that the evangelist has in communicating
the Christian message without the western cultural overhang.
In Jenning's discussion of Islamic culture, he points out
that the Arab lower classes and villagers categorize most
American missionaries as upper class people with considerable
wealth. This class identification has both advantages and
disadvantages for missionary efforts. It fosters rapport
with the indigenous upper class, which means you are associated with those characteristically most receptive to western ideas. The disadvantage is that he is sometimes linked
with those who have traditionally exploited the lower classes
and rural people.(54) However, since it is the Transitionals
who are most receptive to innovations, the evangelist should
assume the role which is most conducive to presenting a relevant message to them.

Nida concedes that identification can only be partial,
but if communication is to be effective, identification
should be as extensive as possible. Nida gives six basic
ingredients of effective identificaiton.

    1. One must recognize that he is identifying with
        specific persons, not with a generalization or
        a type...

2. The very process of obtaining partial identification is possible only if one recognizes the
   inherent limitations...
3. It is necessary that we first fully recognize
   our own motivations...
4. The next requirement for identification is to
   know others. To do so, one very effective tool
   is a familiarity with the field of anthropology
   and the techniques whereby customs and cultures
   different from our own can be understood...
5. Identification means also participation in the
   lives of people...
6. Another requirement is that we be willing to expose ourselves to being known...
7. The indispensable ingredient in identification
   is a genuine love for people...(55)

Diagram 15 illustrates the possible forms of adjustment
to a new culture. One who adjusts in a healthy way to the
culture jolts he encounters will go the way of empathy and
identification. But one who reacts in a blind and unrea-
soned way will go into culture shock. The diagram shows
that the culture-shocked person tries to escape from a dis-
agreeable cultural environment in two ways: he either goes
native or goes anti-native. Going native results from a
neurotic longing for security and an exaggerated hunger for
belonging and leads to indiscriminate acceptance of all local ways and values. The American evangelist who goes anti-
native beomes more and more unflinching in his determination
to remain at all times a true blue-blooded American. The
local people must become like him rather than his becoming
like them.(56)

Rogers and Shoemaker note that change agent success is
positively related to his client orientation. Client orientation refers to empathy and emotional identification.
Rogers and Shoemaker give three reasons for this principle.
Client oriented change agents are more likely 1) to be feedback minded, 2) to have close rapport and high credibility
in the eyes of the people, and 3) to base their innovations
on the felt needs of the society.(57)

When Paul identified with the Gentiles in order to be
fruitful among them, he found that he was rejected by his
own "Christian" brothers. It did not matter that he was
successful, because he was accused of joining them.(58)
Nevertheless, for the evangelist to be successful in communicating religious innovations to Transitional Arabs he

must become as an Arab to the Arabs in order to win Arabs,
and he must become as a Muslim to the Muslims in order to
win Muslims. Nida summarizes effectively the significance
of identification:

> Identification with the people is not attained by
> wearing a breechcloth, eating manioc and termites,
> or dwelling in a grass hut; what really counts is
> having a mind which can understand, hands which
> join with others in a common task, and a heart
> which responds to other's joys and sorrows.(59)

DIAGRAM 15

FORMS OF ADJUSTMENT

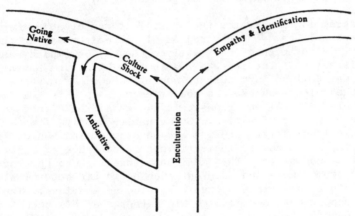

A diagrammatic sketch of possible forms of adjustment to a new cultural environment.

SOURCE: Louis J. Luzbetak, *The Church
and Cultures* (Pasadena: William Carey
Library, 1970), p. 97.

CONVERSION: A VALID DECISION

Conversion relates directly to the second goal stated at
the beginning of this chapter: to facilitate a valid decision. In order to convert people to Christ in such a way
that they make a valid decision it is necessary to recall
that the evangelist must aim not to westernize the people

but to bring about a direct interaction between the non-
western people and God, without the necessity of allegiance
of the convert to the culture of the evangelist.(60) In order for this to be done effectively, the decisions for Christ
must be made following the normal decision-making process of
the culture.(61) Directly relevant to this is the previous
discussion of the prominent role of the family in Arab culture and the sociological restrictions. As pointed out
earlier, the primary barriers are sociological and not theological. Therefore, one must ask, what are the valid alternatives open to the evangelist in trying to overcome the
sociological restrictions?

Overcoming the Sociological Restrictions

From the very beginning of the Protestant efforts to
reach Muslims, the sociological barriers seemed to make it
virtually impossible to convert Muslims to Christianity.
It was the concensus of Protestant missionaries during the
early period that the greatest handicap against which the
Christian evangelist has to strive is the power of group
solidarity.(62) Therefore, a great deal of effort was involved in trying to discover valid alternatives to extracting
an individual from his social and political groups when he
becomes a Christian. One proposal was that those Muslims
who were secret believers in Christ be allowed to remain in
their social groups without publicly professing themselves
as Christians.(63) The idea was that he would remain a
loyal member of the Muslim community and thus the leaven
would be kept in the lump. However, this approach brought
many adverse criticisms. It was rejected by the majority of
the missioanries to Islam including Zwemer and Wilson.(64)
In addition, it is an unbiblical alternative since forming
Christians into local churches is an inherent part of evangelism (see p. 122).

It remains a fact that the process of extracting individuals from their setting in Arab communities does not
build a church, but on the contrary it builds barriers
against the spreading of the Gospel.(65) In spite of this,
most Protestant missionaries and those of the churches of
Christ have emphasized the right of the individual to make
his own religious choices. This is not a basic Arab conception, because (as has been noted) Arab society and Islam
do not recognize the right of the individual to make his own
religious decisions. Farsoun points out that Protestant
missionary education was barely successful in converting
people to Protestantism, because Protestant values were

construed to be antithetical to familism. He says that
Protestant education did not accomplish more than to introduce certain subversive (to familism) values such as "indi-
vidualism." Conversion seems to have been more a function
of economic factors than of ideological or belief change.(66)

     At the International Congress on World Evangelization at
Lausanne, Switzerland the idea of a type of halfway house
for Muslim converts was recommended.(67)   Several experiments
are under way with the use of "Fraternities of New Believers"
which would include a culturally attractive form of worship
with a view of minimizing the societal dislocation for the
new convert. Although the author has seen nothing else discussing such an approach, it would appear to deserve some
investigation for the possibilities that it might hold.

     The previous study of cultural themes and social struc-
ture indicated that the degree of people-consciousness in
the Arab extended family is strong (pp. 40-43). People
consciousness is an aspect of social structure that has a
tremendous influence on when, how, and to what extend the
Christian message will flow through that segment of the
society.(68)   Those who have a high people-consciousness
will resist the Gospel primarily because to them becoming a
Christian means "joining another people."

     They refuse Christ not for religious reasons, not because
they love their sins, but precisely because they love their
brethren. Therefore, McGavran concludes that whenever becoming a Christian is considered racial rather than a religious decision, the growth of the church will be exceedingly
slow.(69)   The main problem for the evangelist is how to
present Christ so that men can truly follow him without
having to forsake their kin. McGavran proposes that that
the solution is to enable men and women to become Christians
in groups while still remaining members of their family and
kinship structure.(70)   The resistance of Arabs to the
Christian faith does not arise primarily from theological
considerations, but social. Their resistance arises primarily from the fear that "becoming a Christian will separate me from my people." A great turn of Muslims can be
expected as soon as ways are found for them to become Christian without renouncing their brethren. This can be seen in
the 1966 and 1967 conversion of perhaps fifty thousand Muslims in Indonesia, where in one place twenty-five mosques
became twenty-five churches.(71)

The crucial role of the extended family obviously has a profound significance for the Christian evangelist who wishes to introduce religious innovations. What seems to be the best possible solution to overcoming the sociological barriers in bringing Arabs to Christ is the concept of group conversions, people movements, or multi-individual conversions as it is variously called. Usually it is futile to ask a person to make a decision on his own. He will feel compelled to consult his family.(72) To ask for an individual decision would threaten the family solidarity to such an extent that most Westerners do not comprehend all the ramifications. A husband and wife team that would aim for a multi-individual group decision would have much greater chances for success. A few have recommended this approach for the Muslim world only in passing, but the author has found no well-researched strategy applying this concept to the Arab world.(73) The matter needs to be investigated further.

Multi-individual Conversions

It is beyond the scope of this study to present a defense of the validity of multi-individual conversions. That has been successfully done elsewhere.(74) But it is the author's intention here to inquire whether such an approach to conversion is valid and relevant to Arab culture.

The dominant role of the family is emphasized by the fact that the participation of the individual in all larger social groupings is not on an individual basis but through his family.(75) The most important instrument through which religion exercises its hold on the individual is the Middle Eastern family. Since this family system itself is a religious institution, sanctioned and supported by religion, family and religion mutually strengthen each other.(76) Westernization has had a tendency to break the hold of the family on the individual, and when the individual has extricated himself from the hold of his family, he has also left behind an intrinsically religious atmosphere.(77) Thus when western evangelists attempt to convert individuals one at a time by extricating them from their families they are actually contributing to a decline in the religiosity of the Arab, because in Arab society family and religion strengthen each other.

What is a multi-individual conversion? McGavran says that it is a people movement but not a mass movement, which suggests an entirely erroneous idea that large masses of

people enter the church without making a valid decision for,
Christ.(78) A multi-individual conversion is not merely a
case of large numbers becoming Christians, but it consists
of a series of small groups coming to a decision.

> A people movement results from the joint decision
> of a number of individuals--whether five or five
> hundred--all from the same people, which enables
> them to become Christians without social disloca-
> tions, while remaining in full contact with their
> non-Christian relatives, thus enabling other groups
> of that people, across the years, after suitable
> instruction, to come to similar decisions and form
> Christian churches made up exclusively of members
> of that people.(79)

Tippett proposes that the process of conversion can be
schematized in terms of periods and points of time using
the following diagram to illustrate the structure of the
process:

DIAGRAM 16

THE PROCESS OF CONVERSION

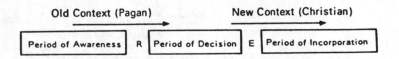

SOURCE: A. R. Tippett, Verdict Theology in
Missionary Theory (Pasadena: William Carey
Library, 1973), p. 123.

The period of awareness would correspond to the knowledge
function in the innovation-decision process. Although at
first the meaning of the Gospel may not be clear, at the
point of realization (R) it suddenly becomes relevant. Only
when it becomes relevant does it then become a recognizable
option for the group, which initiates the long or short
period of decision. In the case of group or multi-individual
decisions it may involve long discussions spread over a year
or more. Ultimately they are brought to the point of encounter (E), which must be followed by some act of incorporation (baptism) whereby the decision-making is consummated.

I want to stress that this is a process and that the
evangelist, whether a missionary or a national, needs
to bring the group along step by step, so that the
period of decision-making is brought to a head in
a clear-cut encounter, a definite verdict for Christ,
and the following incorporation is not left incom-
plete.(80)

Power Encounter

Tippett argues for the necessity of a power encounter.(81)
In the non-Christian religions there are certain elements
which may be described as stepping stones to the Gospel.
But there are other elements which are in diametric opposition to Christianity. It is at these points where the power
encounter is necessary.(82) Among Transitional Arabs there
is still the influence of the animistic superstitions (see
pp. 24-29). Therefore, Tippett's approach to the process of
conversion is useful in the Middle Eastern context.

The Diffusion Effect

The religious worker must realize that he will not see
immediate results from his work and that it will sometimes
take several years for the seed that is sown to bear fruit.
In the innovation process this concept is called the diffusion effect. The diffusion effect. The diffusion effect is
the cumulatively increasing degree of influence upon an individual to adopt or reject an innovation.(83) There is a
complex but important interrelationship between the rate of
knowledge about an innovation and its rate of adoption.
When the level of information is very low, adoption of the
innovation is very unlikely for any given individual. But
as the level of information increases past a certain thresh-
hold, adoption is more likely to occur. This relationship
is illustrated in diagram 17 where the rate of adoption is
plotted over the rate of awareness-knowledge. The diagram
demonstrates that the diffusion effect is positive but not
linear and direct. In other words as the rate of awareness-
knowledge of the innovation increases up to about twenty or
thirty percent, there is almost no adoption. Then once this
threshold point is passed, each additional percentage of
awareness-knowledge is associated with several percentage
increases in the rate of adoption. Therefore, Rogers and
Shoemaker conclude that until an individual has a certain
minimum level of information and influence from his cultural
environment, he is unlikely to become an adopter. But once
this threshold is passed, adoption of the idea is further

DIAGRAM 17

THE DIFFUSION EFFECT

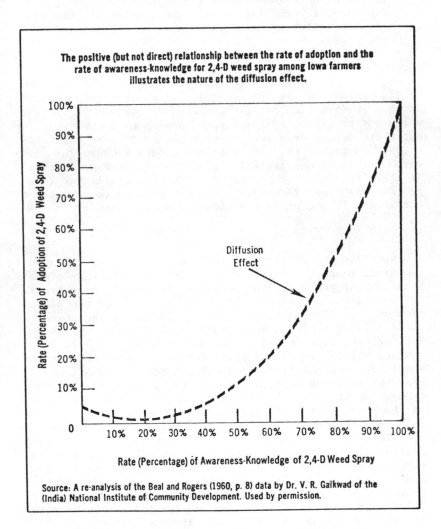

The positive (but not direct) relationship between the rate of adoption and the rate of awareness-knowledge for 2,4-D weed spray among Iowa farmers illustrates the nature of the diffusion effect.

Rate (Percentage) of Adoption of 2,4-D Weed Spray

Diffusion
Effect

Rate (Percentage) of Awareness-Knowledge of 2,4-D Weed Spray

Source: A re-analysis of the Beal and Rogers (1960, p. 8) data by Dr. V. R. Gaïkwad of the (India) National Institute of Community Development. Used by permission.

SOURCE: Everett M. Rogers and F. Floyd Shoemaker, *Communication of Innovations*, 2nd ed. (New York: Free Press, 1971), p. 162

increased by each additional input of knowledge and influence. Further, the threshold seems to occur at about the point where the opinion leaders begin to favor the innovation.(84) Until at least a threshold of information and influence is reached, little adoption occurs. Evangelists need to know approximately where this threshold point is and then plan their strategies of change accordingly.

THE LOCAL CHURCH

Of the three goals stated at the beginning of this chapter, this section on the local church is primarily concerned with the third: to work for persistence of obedience. Slate has argued that responsible evangelistic strategy must include as a deliberate objective the establishment of churches as functional units of Christians.(85) He gives three reasons for this: 1) the church is a supportive group which provides fellowship, worship, and appropriate discipline, which are necessary for the persistence of faith, 2) a church group is required for effective self-propagation and it therefore becomes a means of further evangelization and not merely the result of evangelizing, and 3) the church is necessary for a demonstration of Christian relationships. Therefore, starting churches offers the greatest possibility to reach the world responsibly, produce valid decisions, and stabilize new converts so that they will remain faithful.

It is beyond the scope of this study to give a thorough discussion of indigenous church principles. The primary concern will be to determine how these principles are relevant to the evangelization of the Arab world. Many think that it is self-evident that a church which is "self-governing, self-supporting, and self-propagating" is by definition an indigenous church. In Elkin's study of the church-sponsored missions of the churches of Christ he discovered that one could make the "three-self" formula the goal of the missionary and result with a church which failed to honor Christ.(86) It might become the end instead of the means to an end. Smalley argues that the criteria of "self-governing, self-supporting, and self-propagating" are not necessarily diagnostic of an indigenous movement.(87) It might be very easy to have a self-governing church which is not indigenous. On the other hand, if the church makes its own decisions as to how its funds shall be used this church may be considered indigenous, even though funds are provided by an outside source.(88) What then is an indigenous church? Consider the following definitions:

It is a group of believers who live out their life,
including their socialized Christian activity, in
the patterns of the local society, and for whom any
transformation of that society comes out of their
felt needs.(89)

Indigenization consists essentially in the full
employment of local indigenous forms of communication, methods of transmission, and communicators,
as these means can be prepared and trained.(90)

The "three-self" formula is an inadequate concept of
indigeneity, and Kraft proposes an alternate approach.(91)
He applies a linguistic model to the indigenous theory. A
church that is merely a "literal" (formal correspondence)
rendering of the forms of one church will always be foreign
and insensitive to the local culture and the needs of the
people.(92) However, an indigenous (or dynamic equivalence)
church is the kind that produces the same kind of impact on
its own society as the early church produced upon the original hearers. A dynamically equivalent church will use
familiar, meaningful, and indigenous forms adapting them and
filling them with Christian content.(93) Table 8 illustrates
the alternatives available if one does not establish a dynamically equivalent church by using the anthropological
formulation of form and meaning.

TABLE 8

DYNAMIC EQUIVALENCE CHURCHES

Form	Meaning	Results
Foreign form	Foreign meaning	Foreign dominated church
Indigenous form	Indigenous meaning	Nativistic church
Foreign form	Indigenous meaning	Syncretism
Indigenous form	Christian meaning	Dynamically equivalent

SOURCE: Philip Slate, class notes, Fall 1976, Harding
Graduate School of Religion; drawn from C. H. Kraft.

According to the above conception a dynamically equivalent church 1) conveys to its members truly Christian
meanings, 2) functions within its own society in the name

of Christ, meeting the felt needs of that society, and 3) is couched in cultural forms that are as nearly indigenous as possible.(94)

The process of winning converts to Christianity and help-ing them to develop an indigenous church is difficult in any field. In the Arab world it is exceptionally hard for rea-sons that were enumerated in chapter four. Watt has stated that if Christianity is really to take root among the Arabs and become a strong plant, it must produce a theology, thought out in the Arabic language, which is genuinely Chris-tian and at the same time relevant to the Arab mentality.(95) For the most part this has not been accomplished in the Mid-dle East and the result has been a foreign dominated church.

Gerlach and Hine have identified five key factors in move-ments that successfully diffuse their innovations:

1. A segmented, usually polycephalous, cellular organi-zation
2. Face-to-face recruitment using pre-existing social relationships
3. Personal commitment generated by an act or experience
4. An ideology which forms the basis for conceptual uni-fication of a segmented network of groups
5. Real or perceived opposition from the society(96)

Upon examination one discovers each of these factors to de-scribe the nature of the first century church. The church does not have a central head, recruits through personal con-tact (basic media), accepts committed members through baptism, has a unifying belief in God's word, and has real opposition. Therefore, the church as described in the New Testament is most conducive to successful evangelism and church growth.

Indigenous Worship

Elkins discovered that the worship which most missionaries introduced was nearly identical to western worship forms.

> It has western songs; four-part harmony; non-confrontational seating arrangements...; primary emphasis on the sermon; typically American meeting times and length of service; a similar homiletic form and content; multi-cupped western made com-munion ware; a brief Lord's Supper on Sunday mornings; extemporaneous prayers by one person at a time; and one scripture reading by a member of the congre-gation.(97)

Most of the characteristics of western forms of worship do not attract the Muslim at all and are not relevant to the Arab mind.(98) Gulick has argued that the mosque is a marvelous adaptation to the needs of the people living at high densities and often in a state of acute social tension. (99) This raises the question whether it would be wise to offer the Arab people an approach to worship which is radically different from what most Westerners are used to.

At Lausanne it was recommended that worship forms be modified to be more familiar for the convert. Prayer five times a day could be retained. Fasting as taught in the Bible could be accepted. Scripture memorization and recital could act as substitutes for Koranic readings. Removal of one's shoes and bowing for prayer could act as a further point of non-compromising identification with the convert's background.(100) Formal prayer is the most important act of worship in Islam. A Muslim prays not only with his lips but with his whole body.(101) Could not Muslim converts be encouraged to maintain a similar form of prayer as a Christian?

Although translated western hymns seem to be the rule rather than the exception among churches in the Arab world, would not a more indigenous hymnody be more relevant to the Arab? This of course is a whole study within itself.(102)

The time of worship also needs to be relevant to the local situation. In many Arab countries Sunday is a work day and the traditional times of assembly would be inconvenient for many Arabs. Worship needs to be adapted to the Arab's concept of time. The western concept of time demands that the worship period begin and end at an exact specified time. If the sermon or the announcements are too long the church members become irritated. However, in regard to the Arab's concept of time it is the writer's judgment that the very thing that would irritate the western church members would make worship in the Arab world more conducive and relevant to their way of life. Of course, the specific arrangements would need to be worked out differently in each situation, but the following proposal may have merit in places that have not become thoroughly westernized.

A gathering could take place on Sunday morning or evening for the purpose of worship, observing the Lord's Supper, and teaching. A specific time to begin would not be necessary. If, as in most Arab countries, Sunday was a work day, the members of the church could begin to gather at a particular place after getting off work. As each member arrived at the

place or worship he would immidiately begin a period of private meditation, scripture reading, or prayer. As the group
became larger, various forms of corporate worship could begin with spontaneous singing, prayer, scripture reading, and
exhortations interspersed by quiet periods of meditations.
It might take an hour or more for the whole fellowship of
Christians in that community to assemble. When all had arrived, the Lord's Supper could then be observed. This could
be followed by a period of teaching and exhortation. A
thirty-minute sermon would not be necessary every week.

The above is merely a probe and not a statement of what
would have to take place for worship to be relevant to the
Arab. Another very important aspect of the indigenous church
is its leadership.

Indigenous Leadership

> The success or failure of the Christian religion to
> win the hearts of men in every nation will not depend
> ultimately upon the work of the American missionaries,
> but will depend upon the type of native preachers who
> assume the responsibility of evangelizing their own
> people.(103)

Elkins points out that when leadership training is provided by churches of Christ on the mission field it is usually
not directed toward encouraging the development of elders,
but toward the training of preachers. Such training seems
to contradict the indigenous theory.(104) There are three
aspects of indigenous leadership: the selection, the support, and the training of local leaders.

About eighty percent of the missionaries of the churches
of Christ who responded to Howell's questionnaire reported
that the congregations in their area did not select their own
ministers.(105) Elkin's study indicated that congregations
appointed elders in only six of the sixty-six countries
where missionaries were working.(106) Such practice is not
conducive to indigenous church principles.

Concerning the support of local leaders it is generally
agreed that the method of paying native evangelists with
foreign funds will not establish indigenous churches.(107)
Howell's study indicated that seventy-five percent of the
missionaries do not feel that the native churches will be in
a position to support their evangelist within the next ten
years, that fifty-nine percent of the native preachers re-

ceive a better salary than the average member, and seventy-
two percent of the missionaries replying do not feel that the
local church would pay a salary as high as the American
church.(108)

Various methods have been tried in training local leaders.
One method was bringing local leaders to North America for
their training, but it is generally agreed that this is one
of the poorest ways of training local leaders. Recall that
the greatest majority of Arab students who went to the West
never returned home (p. 100). Howell reported that ninety
percent of the missionaries responding to his questionnaire
felt that the local men should not be brought to North
America for training.

The Middle East Bible Training College in Beirut was an
attempt to train leaders for the local churches without
taking them out of Arab culture. The students came to the
school and did part-time study with the missionaries as well
as part-time study at one of the universities in Beirut.
Huffard points out two problems that were encountered:
1) the students showed signs of frustration in adjusting to
a different environment (because they moved from a Transitional society to a modern city), and 2) there were strong
cross-cultural differences between the students and the
faculty.(109) One contributing factor was that the faculty
did not know Arabic well enough to teach in Arabic, and
therefore relied on translators.

The author believes that these two problems point to two
requirements of a successful leadership training program in
the Arab world: 1) the training must be done entirely in
the local language (Arabic), and 2) it is best not to move
the student to a different geographical location to receive
the training. Both of these requirements can be met through
a theological education by extension program. Theological
education by extension is a new concept of instruction which
has been developed and applied to mission work by various
authors in the field of church growth.(110) It involves
taking the training to the individual rather than bringing
the individual to the training. It can be used in evangelistic work, strengthening new Christians, and training local
church leaders. The procedure involves programmed instruction materials along with cassette tapes in many cases. This
approach is recommended as a viable alternative to training
local leaders through a localized school such as the Middle
East Bible Training College which was tried previously.

Ethnic Unit Churches

One requirement of indigenous churches is that they be
culturally meaningful to the local people. Recall in the
previous analysis of social structure that there are territorial expressions of language, religious sect, and kinship
(pp. 40-56). Members of the same religious sect tend to
live in the same geographical area, even in the cities of
the Middle East. The result is that very little interpersonal communication takes place among members of the different religious sects. Obviously, such communication is absolutely necessary before Christians in one group will ever
attempt to evangelize those in another group. Therefore, in
the foreseeable future it seems unreasonable to expect converted Greek Orthodox and Maronites to make serious efforts
to reach any sect of Muslims with the Christian message.
Neither does it seem reasonable to expect converts from one
of the Christian sects to do a great deal about communicating
the message among the other Christian sects. The sectarian
social structure in the Arab world is just not conducive to
that type of communication.

The implication of the territorial identity of Middle
Easterners is that the evangelist must find the receptive
homogenous units or subcultures of the city and then begin
extensive efforts to plant churches in those areas of the
city. The city is the logical center for evangelism in the
Middle East. There are three reasons why the major thrusts
of evangelism should be located in the cities: 1) innovations radiate from cities to villages, 2) most Transitionals
live in the cities, and 3) the cities have a disproportionate
influence on the rest of the population.

In his excellent discussion of the social mosaic of Lebanon, Halim Barakat notes that Christians and Muslims in
Lebanon have differing attitudes toward the West.(111) The
Lebanese Christians, especially the Maronites, have a very
favorable attitude toward Western influence. The Lebanese
Muslims, on the other hand, are more pro-Arab and they have
feared and mistrusted the West. Since promises made to the
Arab world during World War I were soon broken, and instead
of helping to unite the Arab world, the West has contributed
to the tragedies caused by the introduction of the Zionist
State of Israel, their mistrust has not been without reason.
Therefore, allowing for exceptions, innovations which have
the ear marks of being western will be more readily accepted
by Lebanese Christians than by Lebanese Muslims.

This theory may be applied to religious innovations to
indicate that the very form of Christianity which might appeal most to one group would by the same token not appeal to
the other group. The form of New Testament Christianity
that would most likely appeal to the Christian sects in Lebanon would be different in many respects to the form of Christianity which would most likely appeal to the Muslim. The
problem of a Muslim convert's having to worship in a congregation of a different ethnic group from his own has been a
much discussed problem and presents a major barrier to the
conversion of Muslims.(112) Not only are there significant
cultural differences between Muslims and other ethnic groups
but their religious language is entirely different from that
of Christianity even though both groups may speak the same
language. The Muslim worships God in an entirely different
way from most Arab Christian groups. Among the non-Muslim
minorities are several different ethnic groups that are divided along sectarian and linguistic lines (see p. 45).
Since the various religious sects are geographically and
socially isolated in Middle Eastern cities, and since there
are indications that different forms of Christianity appeal
to these various sects, an effective evangelistic strategy
would not force converts from these various ethnic units to
worship together.

McGavran argues that the establishment of ethnic unit
churches would allow churches to grow much more rapidly.(113)
To the extent that the ethnic or homogeneous units of people
tend to live to themselves in separate districts of the city
it would seem wise to start separate churches in each district. This would allow each congregation to be much more
culturally meaningful to the members. Since the Transitionals are regarded as the most receptive in the Middle
East, it becomes the task of the evangelist to locate the
geographical regions in the city where these receptive
groups tend to live.

Recall Gulick's distinction between religion and sect
(p. 44). The primary reason for loyalty to these sects is
cultural and not religious or theological, and the sectarian
(cultural) concerns seem to be far more important than religious ones. If this is the case, then the barriers to
change may not be as great for religious innovations as one
might think. The barriers to overcome in relation to the
religious sects would tend to be primarily cultural rather
than religious or theological. If this is the case, an
effective evangelistic strategy would aim for the multi-
individual conversion of nuclear families or even extended

families in a way that they could maintain the cultural and social support of the sect to which they belonged.

As noted earlier (p. 54), one exception to the tendency for religious sects to cluster together in their own quarter of the city is that of the Greek Orthodox. For the most part the missionaries of the churches of Christ and Protestant groups have not started ethnic unit churches in the Middle East. Most of their conversions have come from the Greek Orthodox Church.(114) One reason why more converts came from the Greek Orthodox was precisely because the evangelists have not attempted to start ethnic unit churches. The logical conclusion seems to be that by not starting ethnic unit churches, church growth has been hindered unnecessarily. Therefore, by starting ethnic unit churches each cultural group would be allowed to worship God in a culturally meaningful way, a greater receptiveness to the Gospel would be found, and the persistence of faith would be greatly increased. In this kind of situation the first business of the church is not to fuse the various populations of the metropolis into one people. The establishment of congregations whose members worship God in their own dialect and in forms that are relevant to them should be the aim.(115)

CONTEXTUALIZATION

Contextualization is a term which expresses a deeper concept than indigenization ever does. It means "making concepts or ideals relevant in a given situation...It is an effort to express the never changing Word of God in ever changing modes for relevance."(116) Since the Gospel message is inspired but the manner of its expression is not, contextualization of the modes of expression is not only right but necessary. A crucial question in the contextualization of the Gospel to the local culture is: How far can one go in adapting (or accomodating) before one has gone too far? Below are three short lists of features from the culture and religion of the Arabs: one of biblically supported items; one of neutral items which can be maintained; and one of items which are contrary to biblical principles.

Biblically Supported Items

1. Honor to parents
2. Hospitality
3. Strict sex regulations
4. Giving to the poor
5. Prohibitions against drunkenness
6. Fasting
7. Loyalty

Neutral Items Which Can Be Maintained

1. Types of clothing
2. Sitting on the floor
3. Ways of greeting one another
4. Ways of making decisions
5. Removing one's shoes before entering a place of worship
6. Circumcision
7. Bowing prostrate when praying
8. Ways of getting married
9. Religious gatherings on Friday

Items Which Are Contrary to Biblical Principles

1. Polygamy
2. Animistic superstitions
3. Belief in Mohammad as a prophet of God
4. Maintaining honor at any price
5. Fatalistic practices

Obviously some of the above features apply more to Muslims
than to Arab Christians, but such a classification is an example of how contextualization would apply to Arab society.

CONCLUSION

It is crucial for the evangelist to know exactly what his
goal is. This chapter has emphasized two goals that are
crucial to New Testament evangelism: 1) to facilitate a
valid decision, and 2) to work for persistence of obedience.
A valid decision cannot be achieved if the evangelist does
not identify meaningfully with the local people and if he
does not use the natural decision making processes of the
local culture. The evidence indicates that multi-individual
group decisions are most relevant to the Transitional Arab.
Unless the local church is relevant to the Transitional Arab,
persistence of obedience will be very difficult. The conclusion of this study is that ethnic unit churches would be most
relevant to the Transitional Arab. In order for the Christian way of life to be effectively contextualized in Arab society
it is necessary for the evangelist to have thought through
those aspects of the local culture to which accomodation can
be made.

A third necessary goal of New Testament evangelism is to
internationalize the message. Before Christianity can be

communicated to the Transitional Arab in a relevant manner, it must be stripped of its foreign characteristics. This is the subject of the following chapter.

7

A Relevant Message
for the Transitional Arab

Most former missionaries (both Protestant and members of
the churches of Christ) have assumed that they knew what
their message was. When seeking to convert others, the missionary preached the form of Christian truth which had converted him. He was not especially interested in adapting
himself to what his hearers already knew and felt.(1)   The
evangelist tends to come to the mission field with his pre-
conceived ideas and opinions of what the local people need.
But unless the evangelist develops close interrelationships
with the local people he will never really understand what
is involved in the communication of the word of God and he
will never really know the needs of those he has come to
teach.(2) Without an intimate acquaintance with the local
people the message will be largely irrelevant to the listener.
The Christian message most often communicated in the Middle
East is unmistakably western. C.S. Lewis may be an excellent
protagonist of the Christian faith in England, but it remains
unproved that in direct translation he is effective in the
Arab world.(3)   Traditional western theology often appears
incomprehensible and irrelevant to the modern Arab. Recall
from chapter six that the goal is a dynamically equivalent
response. To communicate a message that will produce a
dynamically equivalent response demands that the message be
put in a different form in order to be relevant to the cultural context.

> The essential importance of the real cultural con-
> text in which communication takes place is that
> only in terms of this setting does any message have
> any significance.(4)

Two principles are involved in communicating a dynamically equivalent message: 1) the communicator must select from the revelation features which are culturally relevant, and 2) he must find certain cultural parallels which will make such a message significant within the immediate context of people's lives.(5)

The western form of the Christian message which emphasizes the doctrinal differences between Islam and Christianity, is a form that most readily antagonizes the Muslim. It emphasizes those features which he is most likely to resent-- especially the deity of Christ, the crucifixion, the inspiration of scripture, and the trinity. The historic consequence of this approach was that it became a head-on collision with the Muslim. This period is known as the great "Muslim Controversy."(6)

Addison says that when the disadvantages of the method of controversy were seen that the manner of presentation was changed. Missionaries simplified their message and began to attempt the discovery of points of contact in order to lead the individual from the known to the unknown.(7) Missionaries to the Middle East agreed that the doctrines which antagonize Muslims the most should not be communicated in the initial stages and that one should begin with features of Christianity which were most appealing to the Muslim.

THE MOST APPEALING FEATURES OF CHRISTIANITY

One should never be surprised at the doctrine or the aspect of Christianity which seems to appeal most to any individual Muslim. He must begin where he can. Therefore, fixed and easy methods should be avoided. MacDonald knew a man who became a "Christian" with a real grasp of Christian doctrine who began by being impressed with the historical continuity of the books of Samuel and Kings.(8) Below are listed those features of Christianity which are most appealing to the Arab and especially the Muslim.(9)

1. The unity of God
2. The divine omnipotence coupled with divine goodness
3. The use of miracles by Christ and his apostles
4. The Christian doctrine of the future life
5. The purity and nobility of the moral ideals set forth in the life and teachings of Jesus
6. The lives of the prophets and their teaching
7. The personal religion of the psalms
8. The parables of Christ

9. The conviction that ethical interests are supreme in all God's dealings with men
10. To proclaim God as a God of character and Jesus as the apostle of character-redemption
11. Christian institutions for the relief of suffering
12. The simple worship of Christians
13. Secret Christian prayer, public prayer, and family prayer
14. Ethical freedom and spirituality of Christianity
15. The visual example of free strong Christian womanhood
16. That Christ came to fulfill the highest aspirations of every religion
17. The function of Christ as a mediator
18. The possession of and reliance upon a book of revelation

PERCEIVED ATTRIBUTES OF THE MESSAGE

Paul and Barnabas cured the cripple at Lystra after preaching with the intention of praising the name of God. The people took them to be Greek gods anthropomorphized and began to worship them--the very last thing that Paul and Barnabas wanted.(10) The problem here is a problem of meaning. An entirely different meaning was perceived by the people than what was intended. Evidence is available from anthropological writings that changes occur in the meaning of an innovation in the diffusion process.(11) Tippett suggests three factors from anthropology which can affect the meaning of a communication: 1) the world view of the listeners (acceptor end), 2) the image of the evangelist in the eyes of his audience (the advocate end), and 3) the evangelist's conceptualization of his message (the message itself). (12)

The evangelist must remember that what really matters is the attributes of an innovation as perceived by the potential adopters. It is here that the anthropological distinction between form and meaning is relevant. "Form" refers to the objects or behaviors that can be experienced by an observer; and "meaning" is an implicit and subjective association of the trait within the culture.(13) A particular form associated with Christianity in North American culture could have a totally different meaning in Arab culture. Therefore, it is necessary that the evangelist pay attention to the actual meaning that is communicated to the audience. Rogers and Shoemaker suggest five general characteristics by which any innovation may be described to show how individual's perceptions can determine the meaning of a communication.(14)

1. *Relative Advantage.* Relative advantage is the degree to which an innovation is perceived as being better than the idea it supersedes.(15) It is positively related to the rate of adoption. One of the subdimensions of relative advantage is the immediacy of the reward.(16) The more immediate the reward the more rapidly the innovation will be adopted. Therefore, the evangelist should emphasize not only the reward of heaven but the present advantages of becoming a member of the family of God.

2. *Compatibility.* Compatibility is the degree to which an innovation is perceived as consistent with the existing value, past experiences, and needs of the receivers.(17) It is positively related to the rate of adoption. A thorough discussion of formulating a Christian message compatible with the values and felt needs of the Arab is presented below.

3. *Complexity.* Complexity is the degree to which an innovation is perceived as relatively difficult to understand and use.(18) It is negatively related to its rate of adoption. This is evident in that the simple worship of Christians is an appealing factor for Muslims, but when doctrines are presented which are complicated and difficult to understand the Muslim is repelled.

4. *Trialability.* Trialability is the degree to which an innovation may be experimented with on a limited basis.(19) At first glance, Christianity would seem to be at a disadvantage, since one can hardly become a Christian on a trial basis. However, potential converts can be exposed to the dynamics of Christianity by means of worship services, interaction in the homes of Christians, and observing everyday behavior.

5. *Observability.* Observability is the degree to which the results of an innovation are visible to others.(20) It is positively related to its rate of adoption. This is very closely related to the characteristic of trialability. This characteristic is crucial in the Middle East since most Arabs have a misconception of what a true Christian really is. The example of the Christian life is an absolute necessity for effective evangelization in the Middle East.

These five characteristics may be used in predicting the rate of adoption of an innovation. Rate of adoption is the relative speed with which an innovation is adopted by members of a society. There are other variables which influence the rate of adoption such as 1) the type of innovation-decision,

2) the nature of communication channels used to diffuse the
innovation at various functions in the innovation-decision
process, 3) the nature of the social structure, and 4) the
extend of the change agent's promotion efforts.(21) An adapted paradigm of the variables determining the rate of adoption of innovations from Rogers and Shoemaker appears in
diagram 18.

The functions of the innovation-decision process are also
important here because the receiver's perceptions of the
attributes of an innovation may vary on the basis of these
functions.(22)

1. At the *knowledge* stage, the innovation's complexity
    and compatibility should be most important.
2. At the *persuasion* stage, the innovation's relative
    advantage and observability should be most important
3. At the *decision* stage, the innovation's trialability
    should be most important.(23)

The perceived attributes of an innovation determine the
meaning it will have to the local people. If the Transitional Arab perceives Christianity to mean something which
is relevant to him he will more likely accept Christianity.
But Christianity only becomes relevant when the message is
related to the felt needs of the people. Watt says that the
future of the Christian church will depend on its success in
providing a faith which will meet the personal needs of the
people.(24) Nida states:

    A careful and systematic study of any culture can
    reveal numerous ways in which any mission program
    can be more effectively oriented to meet the needs
    of the people and to bring them in a more meaning-
    ful way the life-transforming significance of the
    Good News in Jesus Christ.(25)

Christianity cannot satisfy all the felt needs of the
people without becoming distorted. Therefore, a distinction
needs to be made between satisfying the felt needs and making
Christianity relevant to the felt needs; the first is not
feasible, the second is. An awareness of the felt needs
helps the evangelist understand where the people are. Many
religious workers go to a new culture and teach accurately
biblical subjects which are not perceived by the receptors
as being related to their needs in any way, but they ignore
other subjects which would make Christianity much more relevant and important to the local people. If there are aspects

DIAGRAM 18

A PARADIGM OF VARIABLES DETERMINING THE RATE OF ADOPTION OF INNOVATIONS

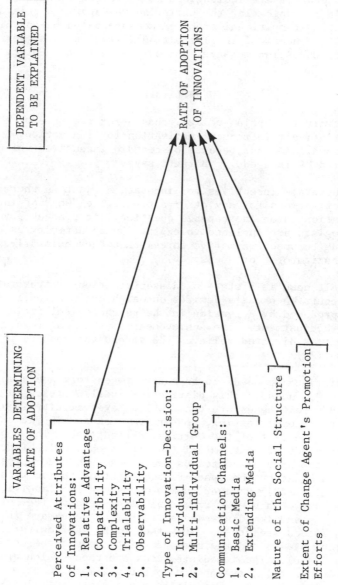

VARIABLES DETERMINING
RATE OF ADOPTION

DEPENDENT VARIABLE
TO BE EXPLAINED

Perceived Attributes
of Innovations:
1. Relative Advantage
2. Compatibility
3. Complexity
4. Trialability
5. Observability

Type of Innovation-Decision:
1. Individual
2. Multi-individual Group

Communication Channels:
1. Basic Media
2. Extending Media

Nature of the Social Structure

Extent of Change Agent's Promotion
Efforts

RATE OF ADOPTION
OF INNOVATIONS

SOURCE: Everett M. Rogers and F. Floyd Shoemaker, *Communication of Innovations*, 2nd ed. (New York: Free Press, 1971), p. 158.

of the gospel which have more initial meaning to the local
people, the evangelist should begin there. The felt needs
in this chapter are indications of where the evangelist might
begin in communicating the Christian message in a relevant
way to the Transitional Arab. A message based on and directed
to the felt needs of the Transitional Arab is in no way a
complete Christian message, but only an effective place to
begin.

                        THE FELT NEEDS

   Contrary to popular belief, change for the sake of change
is a relatively infrequent motivation for innovation. Change
and innovation occur because of certain incentives which may
be called "felt needs." Barnett says:

     There are incentives for innovation, just as there are
     motivations for any other action...The "why" of inno-
     vation is an inescapable question...At present psycho-
     logists are inclined to explain human activity as being
     due to specific motive forces that they call drives,
     instigators, or needs.(26)

   A felt need is a state of dissatisfaction or frustration
that occurs when one's desires outweigh one's actualities.(27)
It is produced by a tension in the psychological field which
seeks readjustment. The achievement of the goal towards
which it is directed relieves the stress and results in satisfaction.(28)

   A distinction needs to be made between felt needs and
other human needs. This distinction is illustrated in diagram 19. Felt needs are those which have validity in a particular cultural setting, and are represented in the diagram
by the space left of the vertical dotted line. The opposite
of felt needs are subliminal (unfelt) needs, which function
outside the area of conscious awareness, and are represented
in the diagram by the space to the right of the vertical
dotted line.(29) However, human needs can be classified in
another way when viewed from a biblical perspective--ulti-
mate needs and immediate needs. Ultimate needs are the needs
of man as God sees them. They tend to be supracultural and
universal needs, and the message which meets these needs is
called Gospel. The immediate needs are those which are physical and earthly, as opposed to the ultimate needs which are
spiritual in nature. The ultimate needs are not always immediately felt by men. For instance, some men may not feel
they need to overcome sin. Diagram 19 illustrates that some

ultimate needs are felt and others are unfelt or subliminal. There are occasions when a subliminal or unfelt need could become a felt need, and therefore the vertical dotted line in the diagram is not stationary but movable. However, there is never any exchange between ultimate needs and immediate needs. Since ultimate needs are spiritual and immediate needs are physical, they are inherently different and one can never become the other. This is communicated by the solid horizontal line in the diagram which is stationary and does not move.

DIAGRAM 19

THE NEEDS OF MAN

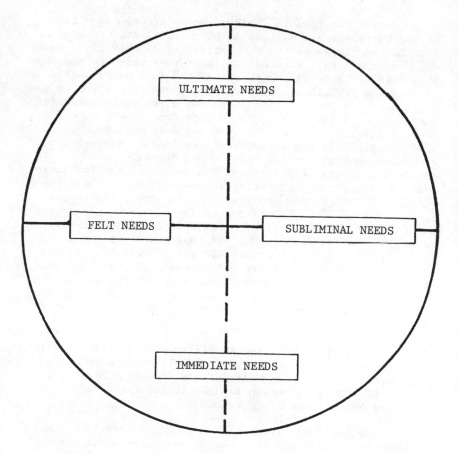

The Anthropological Basis

It is a well established fact that many innovations have not taken place because of a failure to deal with the felt needs of the local people.(30) This occurs because the change agents speak to needs which the people do not feel they have.

> Change projects not based on the client's felt needs
> often go awry or produce unexpected consequences...
> Change agents must have knowledge of their clients'
> needs, attitudes, and beliefs, their social norms
> and leadership structure, if programs of change are
> to be tailored to fit the clients.(31)

A crucial question is whether the felt need comes first or the awareness of the innovation comes first. Some argue that the awareness of the innovation comes first since some-one cannot actively seek out an innovation which he does not know exists. But others argue that the felt need comes first since individuals will seldom expose themselves to mes-sages about an innovation unless they first feel a need for the innovation.(32) What can be concluded? Does a need precede knowledge of an innovation or does knowledge of an innovation create a need for that new idea? Perhaps this is a chicken-or-egg problem. Rogers and Shoemaker say that it can work both ways depending on the nature of the innovation.(33) Sayigh's study of entrepreneurs of Lebanon poses the question: Can the opinion leader or innovator ignite the first spark and thus create a need for change in the society and thus set the innovation in motion? The answer is nega-tive.(34) In spite of the exceptional qualities of the in-novators, the fact that Lebanon is well developed, and the fact that the innovators are well placed, they are not the decisive factor in generating the desire for change. Sayigh submits that the starting point for the innovation process lies in the needs produced by physical and social dissatis-faction.(35)

The necessity of locating the felt needs of a society is clear enough. Innovations based on felt needs have good potential for acceptance. If such is lacking a need will have to be generated, which is usually not easy.(36) There are three basic types of felt needs.

1. A *demonstrated* felt need is one in which the people have demonstrated their interest to the extent that they have attempted to solve the problem by their own efforts without any outside assistance.

2. A *solicited* felt need is one for which the people solicit assistance from the change agent.

3. An *ascertained* felt need is one which, although already existing when the change agent arrives, is only latent within the group and must be ascertained by both the innovator and the recipient.(37)

Clearly a generated need is different from all of the above in that it refers to something which was not even recognized as a problem before the change agent arrived. An evangelist would be generating (or creating) a need when trying to teach a society that they are guilty of sin when they do not have a concept of sin.

How does an evangelist discover what the felt needs are of the local people? He must have communication channels established so that he can obtain relevant information. He must have a high degree of empathy and rapport with the people in order to assess their needs accurately. Such techniques as informal probing, local informants, and surveys are sometimes used to determine the felt needs.(38) The felt needs listed in this study were compiled on the basis of library research, and therefore will need to be tested on the field before they can be accepted as totally valid.

It is anthropologically sound to adapt innovations to meet the felt needs of the society. But is it biblically sound to adapt the Christian message to relate it to the felt needs of the society? That is the issue in the following section.

The Biblical Basis

Can a message directed toward the felt needs of the Transitional Arab be properly called a part of the Gospel? In response to this consider the following. First, as noted earlier the previous emphasis on controversy with its stress on doctrinal issues has proven to be ineffective in the Middle East. The evangelist must not suppose that he has presented Christianity to Muslims when he has exhausted all the issues on which the two faiths differ. Christianity must be explained not only in terms of what divides the creeds, but in terms of what confronts the person (felt needs). The evangelist must not speak at Islam but to the Muslim. The difference is expressed in the following question: When the evangelist strives to take the Arab where

and how he is, does the evangelist determine the "where"
and the "how" primarily in terms of the Arab's doctrinal
background, or of his personal hopes, fears, and yearnings.
(39)

Most of the essential truths of the Christian faith cannot be understood by a Muslim on the first hearing. He is
not prepared emotionally, mentally or spiritually for their
reception. Much preliminary teaching is indispensable to a
right attitude towards them.(40) If this is the case, what
should be the content of the preliminary teaching? The
author submits that it should be that part of the biblical
message which appeals to the felt needs of the Transitional
Arab.

Second, Jesus adapted his message to the specific needs
of the people. For one person salvation meant freedom from
fear; for another a deeper faith; for a third, the conquest
of pride; and for a fourth, the abandonment of ambition or
of worldly wealth.(41)   Christ did not approach people by
confronting them with a theological question. Instead he
began to deal with the problems that they had by healing
the sick, making the blind to see, and the lame to walk.
He met them where they were. The Bible presents one unchanging message for all mankind. But in the Middle East
one must not conceive of one exclusive formulation of that
unchanging message.

Third, a Christian message not directed at the felt needs
of the people can result in reversion, syncretism and heresy.
Tippett says that just because people become Christians does
not mean their felt needs cease to exist. If these needs
are not met by a relevant message and functional substitutes,
the people will be forced to revert to the old ways of meeting those needs.

> This is another way in which Christianity has often
> become syncretistic--by failing to meet the basic
> felt needs of the society. These long-standing needs
> often arise from the environment or physical condi-
> tion of the converts and continue after conversion,
> and Christianity is effective only as it meets the
> needs of its adherent.(42)

Therefore, it can be questioned whether a message that only
communicates the basic Christian doctrines is a full Gospel.
If full Gospel is defined as purely doctrinal then in many
cases it can produce heresy and very unstable Christians.

But if full Gospel includes a message directed at the felt
needs it immediately becomes relevant to the local people.
Recall the previous distinction in Middle Eastern religion
between the great tradition (doctrinal and intellectual level)
and the little tradition (animistic superstitious level). A
message directed only at the great tradition does not deal
with all the aspects of religion in the Middle East. Gulick's
list of four features of religious behavior which recur in
different sects (p. 22) indicate that most Arabs who are
internally committed to religious beliefs are more intensely
committed emotionally to the superstitious rituals than to
any formalized theological doctrine. This fact has important
implications on what to stress when trying to convert others.
They must not only be converted on the intellectual level,
but on the emotional level as well, which affects their daily
behavior.

Fourth, a message directed at the felt needs provides a
springboard for dealing with the ultimate needs of man as
God sees them. In many cases there is a close relationship
between the felt needs of Arabs and the ultimate needs of
man in terms of biblical revelation. In terms of felt needs
the Arab asks how he can obtain the approval of his family.
The ultimate question he needs to learn to ask is how he can
overcome sin and live a life pleasing to God. The best way
to bring him to see his ultimate needs in relation to God is
to begin with his felt needs.

Fifth, a decision to become a Christian based on felt
need does not necessarily produce a weak Christian. The
problem of motivation is a very real problem in the Middle
East. Some will decide to become Christians through a love
of money rather than a love of Christ. They will have no
belief in Christ, no guilt of sin, and they will get what
they can from the missionary and when they can get no more
they will cease claiming to be Christians. Every evangelist
needs to beware of such people. On the other hand it is
necessary for the evangelist to be cautious lest his suspi-
cions hinder those who are groping their way toward salvation.(43)

> Our Lord took men whose chief motivation for three
> years was that of sharing in His glory when he drove
> the Romans into the sea--and turned them into apostles.
> (44)

Pickett found four kinds of motives for becoming Christians:
spiritual, secular, social, and natal.(45) It was very

surprising that there was very little difference in the
Christian attainment of those who came from spiritual, secular, and social motives. Obviously the more spiritual the
motive the better, but the evidence indicates that post-
conversion instruction had more to do with Christian maturity
than the motives which brought them to Christ.(46) The
author does not wish to be misunderstood to say that any
motive which causes someone to decide to become a Christian
is acceptable. Simon the sorcerer was rebuked because he
had a complete misunderstanding of the nature of the Gospel,
due to his wrong motivation.(47) It is possible that a person would develop a genuine interest in Christianity and
possibly even state that he wants to follow Jesus in response
to a message directed at his felt needs. The question
arises: At what point should the interested follower be
baptized? How much should he know before baptism? This will
depend on the individual situation and on how much the felt
needs and ultimate needs overlap. It is valid to argue that
one should not be baptized until he sees that act as meeting
his ultimate needs in relation to God.

     From these lines of argument it seems evident that a mes-
sage related to the felt needs of the Transitional Arab is
biblically sound, and can properly be called a part of the
Gospel. Felt needs move people to accept innovations, and
a need that is felt is necessarily relevant to the culture.
(48) Therefore, the Christian message which is related to
the felt needs is necessarily a relevant message. Such an
approach does not imply the proclamation of a partial Gospel,
but the beginning at a relevant rather than an irrelevant
point.

The Felt Needs

     At some point it becomes necessary to tabulate the felt
needs of the Transitional Arabs. Here an attempt is made to
extract such needs from the earlier analysis of Middle Eastern
Arab culture. Obviously, one specific group will not necessarily have all of these needs; and some of them will be more
characteristic of Muslim Arabs than Christian Arabs. Suggestions will be offered on how the biblical message can meet
these needs and for possible functional substitutes. The
tabulated needs may be grouped into the following categories:
1) universal needs (1-2), 2) needs based on cultural themes
(3-11), 3) needs based on Islam (12-16), and 4) needs produced by westernization (17-18)

1. *Need to solve basic human problems.* The Christian
message should speak to the basic sorrows and yearnings of
human beings. It is sometimes assumed that the Muslim mind,
with its tendency to submission and its capacity to be un-
emotional, is impervious to these emotions. But many Arab
writers have attempted to deal with the situations of common
life, of sickness, pain, fear, poverty, and death.(49)

2. *Need to solve urgent social and communal problems.*
Some have claimed that since Islam lacks a sense of sin that
this precludes its discovery of the salvation offered by
Christ. Cragg suggests that the consciousness of social
evils might be a means to the awareness of personal evils to
be cleansed.(50)

3. *Need to reconcile modern thought with religion.* The
Christian message needs to be addressed to those who begin
to doubt because of the impact of modern scientific thought.
A translation of western works will not do, the message must
be geared to the Arab mind.

4. *Need for community.* This felt need can be labeled
in various ways: the need for group solidarity, for family
approval, for protection and privacy of the family, and for
intimate social contact with the extended family. This is
one of the most widespread felt needs of Arab society, and
is expressed even in the most modern sections of Arab cities.
(51) This need is derived from the previous discussion of
the dominance of the family and kinship in Arab society. In
the Middle East it is a cultural theme that people participate in most larger social units through the extended family.
The Arab's sense of community occurs within the membership
of sect and kinship group.(52) The group solidarity of Arab
culture has been regarded as the greatest restriction to
evangelism in the Middle East, and leads Speight to conclude
that the institutional expression of a body of Muslims de-
siring to follow Christ is an impossibility.(53) There are
bases for disagreeing with this conclusion and arguing that
a Christian message directed at this felt nebd can successfully establish a fellowship of Christians even from among
Muslims. Goldsmith contends that Christianizing the community is a response to a Muslim felt need.(54) Christians
usually stress the benefits of salvation for the individual,
but Muslims may be more aware of the needs of society.
Goldmsith tells of a Muslim convert who became convicted of
the truth of the claims of Christ not because of personal
need but because he was deeply conscious of the needs of
his people as a race. He felt that the Christian faith

could be the one power that could change his people's national characteristics and attitudes.(55)

> The Old Testament teaches that God works in whole
> peoples and the Old Testament is the introduction
> to the New. Could it therefore be right that such
> community movement could be the prelude to the salva-
> tion of individuals? Might it therefore be right to
> *start* our Christian witness in such societies with
> a message of what Christ can do for a whole society
> rather than just for the individual believer?
>
> If we are to permeate a whole society with Chris-
> tian truth, and if we are to appeal to the felt needs
> of a society, it of course assumes a deep understand-
> ing of that society and its inner workings. This
> will require Christians...who are willing to stay a
> long time in that country, learn the language and
> culture, make close friends and develop an in-depth
> empathy with the workings and feelings of that so-
> ciety...The short-term Christian worker will only
> be able to communicate with the fringes of society.
> (56)

Goldsmith's statement is confirmed by the experience of
several of the missionaries of the churches of Christ. The
average time spent in the Middle East by missionaries of the
churches of Christ is three years. That explains why in many
cases only social marginals have been reached. Only those
who are willing to devote a major portion of their lives to
the work will become acquainted with the culture well enough
to communicate a really relevant Christian message to the
Transitional Arab.

Another suggestion for making Christianity relevant to
this felt need is the label for the fellowship of believers.
In the New Testament there are a large number of images and
names by which the church is called.(57) Many of these
would likely be more relevant than the term "church of
Christ." Would not the biblical image "the family of God"
be more relevant to the Arab?

5. *Need for honor*. The implications of the cultural
theme of honor for the evangelistic worker are obvious. No
one can stay on good terms with an Arab if he attacks or
even so much as slights his honor. The way that honor is
expressed in certain types of Arab behavior will obviously
need to be corrected through Christian teaching, although

the evangelist must always be on his guard to insure that he
does not infringe on another's honor.

One reason why the method of controversy has been so unsuccessful in the Middle East is because it has conflicted
with the Arab's felt need to maintain his honor. Rather
than confronting the Arab with Christianity in such a way
that he must admit that he is wrong, why not appeal to what
is the honorable thing to do? Rather than emphasizing the
necessity of becoming a Christian it would be honorable to
obey God's will. Just as Paul took pagan terms and filled
them with new Christian meaning, so the evangelist can fill
the Arab's concept of honor with Christian meaning by teaching that it is God's will that a Christian honor God, Christ,
his parents, the aged, and the church leaders.(58) In addition the evangelist can point out God's ways of obtaining
honor is through wisdom, graciousness, humility, peaceable-
ness, righteousness, mercy, honoring God, and serving Christ.
(59)

6. *Need to show hospitality.* Arab hospitality is a
theme that should be utilized by Christianity. Arab Chris-
tains should be urged to do what they do in the name of
Christ. Knowledge of the nature of Arab hospitality will
enrich one's understanding of the Arab way of life, and it
will help one to establish a bond of friendship and sympathy
with the Arab people. The Arab's concept of hospitality can
also be filled with Christian meaning. The evangelist should
be sure to emphasize the duty of the Christian to show hospitality, since this will be very meaningful to the Arab.(60)
The hospitality that Lot showed to the angels and the parable
of the friend at midnight become much more meaningful to the
Arab and the evangelist does well to take advantage of this.
(61) The Arab can comprehend the many examples of hospitality in the Bible much better than can the average Westerner.
(62)

7. *Need for an all encompassing religion.* In contrast
to the West, Middle Eastern religion affects all aspects of
life. In order for Christianity to become a viable alternative for the Arab it must fulfill this function. If New
Testament Christianity is to become indigenous in the Arab
world, it will of necessity need to fulfill the normative
and psychological functions of Middle Eastern religion. If
it is true that the main differences between Islam and
western Christianity lie in their normative and psychological
functions, the logical implication is that the point of initial encounter is not needed so much on the doctrinal level

as on the functional level. Protestant evangelistic efforts
have for nearly two hundred years presented good doctrinal
arguments for the superior nature of Christianity and have
failed to reach a significant number of Muslims. Therefore,
until the proponents of New Testament Christianity can learn
to present it in such a way that it is free of all western
trappings and able to fulfill the normative and psychological
functions necessary, the New Testament church will never be
successfully planted in the Arab world.

Luzbetak suggests three criteria for determining how thoroughly the message has become a part of the local way of
life: 1) the number of linkages between the missionary's
message and the native life-way; 2) the degree of consistency;
and 3) extent of reciprocity between the two.(63)

   8. *Need for protection from the evil eye and spirits.*
There is little advantage to be gained by denying the existence of the evil spirits. Not only does such a denial reflect a glaring disregard for the needs of the people, but
it indicates how the western missionary has been led to disregard the obvious New Testament message concerning the power
of Jesus over evil spirits.(64) There are a number of passages in the New Testament which demonstrate Jesus's power
over the evil spirits, but passages denying the existence
of evil spirits are rather scarce.(65) If the Christian
message is not adapted to meet this need the Arab will continue to meet it through his animistic practices.

   9. *Need for blessings.* There are apparently certain
blessings that one can obtain through visits to shrines of
the saints (see p. 27). The evangelist would do well to
stress all the spiritual blessings one receives from becoming a member of the family of God.

   10. *Need for freedom from sickness.* Some Arabs believe
that sickness can be caused by the evil eye, spirits, the
devil, and jinn. Their animistic practices are designed to
protect the Arab from sickness from such sources. Again the
evangelist does well not to deny that such forces can cause
sickness, but instead he should point to a better way. The
western missionary tends to think of disease in terms of
germs and medicine. But for the Arab the most relevant approach is a practical application of James 5:14, and to urge
that God can heal disease better than his animistic practices.

   11. *Need for freedom from guilt.* It was noted earlier
that some Arabs will visit saint's shrines to prove their

innocence of any crime (p. 27). Although a false concept of
sin may be involved, it is not necessary to correct that
concept of sin in order to appeal to this felt need. In
other words, whatever type of guilt they might feel, a Christian message can be directed at that felt need. But it will
be necessary in time to teach the correct biblical concept
of sin and guilt, but it is not necessary to begin one's
teaching at this point in order to gain a hearing.

   12. *Need to surrender to God's will.* Watt says that
Christianity will never really take root among the Arabs
unless it incorporates whatever is good among the religious
perceptions of the Arabs; and these are found in developed
form chiefly among the Muslims.(66) Surrender to God's will
is the very essence of Islam and should be incorporated into
the Christian message where appropriate.

   13. *Need to be thankful.* The spirit of gratitude has
deep meaning in Islam. An important part of the Muslim
ritual prayer is repetition of the phrase, "O the praise of
my great Lord," as many as ten times, depending on the circumstances.(67) Since the Muslim is accustomed to thinking
of himself in a relation of indebtedness to God for his
mercies and favors, it seem very important that the Christian message should be expressed in the same context. This
is not a concession to the Muslim, but it is an attempt to
communicate the Christian message in a manner that will be
relevant to the Muslim.

   14. *Need for inward spiritual vitality.* Earlier missionaries argued that the legalistic and mechanical forms of
worship of the Muslim have deprived him of this need for
spiritual vitality.(68) However, Muslims have been judged
severely and often unjustly by not considering the spiritual
aspects of Islam.(69) The regular ritual of prayer is often
followed by a period during which private devotions may be
offered according to individual inclination or the teaching
of the different religious societies.(70) Gulick argues
that Islam is not fundamentally defective in providing for
this need, but that the mosque is a marvelous adaptation to
the needs of the people.(71) Therefore, if Christianity is
to be relevant to the Muslim it must appeal to this felt
need, which would probably demand a form of worship different from what most Westerners are accustomed.

   15. *Need to overcome the fear of death.* Because of the
Muslim concept of salvation by works, the Muslim fears death.
He cannot have confidence in his salvation if he must earn

it. The Christian can argue that as a member of the family
of God one does not have to fear death.

16. *Need for a mediator between God and man.* One of the
supreme difficulties of Islam is that God is so exalted and
powerful that in his presence man is but a slave too degraded
to look even into the face of his master. There is an awful
gulf that separates man and God. A number of sects have
arisen in an attempt to provide some way in which man may
come nearer to God. The Muslim seems to have a felt need
for a mediator between themselves and God and a message
which tells them of the existence of such a mediator would
be highly relevant to the Muslim.(72) Barton says that
there is hardly another aspect of Christianity more suited
to the Muslim.(73)

17. *Need for individual freedom.* This need is produced
by westernization. As the Arab becomes more modern this
need produces more tension. Some felt needs may conflict
with instead of reinforcing or complementing other felt
needs.(74) An Arab's need for individual freedom would conflict with the need for intimate relations with the extended
family. When the evangelist appeals for an individual decision he is appealing to this felt need. But since this need
conflicts with the more dominant need for a close relationship with the extended family, those who respond to such an
appeal tend to be social marginals rather than opinion leaders. Social marginals do not help build a respected congregation in the community.

18. *Need for an education.* This need is also produced
by westernization. A large percentage of the Protestant effort in the Middle East has been devoted to educational missions and from the educational point of view much progress
was made. For the most part this approach converted very
few to Protestantism. It would seem better to accent a non-
conversion education program, where education is needed.

Using the Felt Need Approach

This section consists of some suggestions for using these
felt needs effectively. There are indications that individuals should not be asked personal questions as to whether
they participate in animistic superstitious practices. Many
of those who do sincerely believe and practice such superstitions would not admit it to a Westerner.(75)

There is evidence that the emotional needs met by the
animistic rituals are still felt needs.(76) It is reasonable
to assume that although modernizing Arabs have dropped some
traditional animistic practices, the emotional felt needs
still exist and are not being met.

The evangelist might do well to set forth the need and
then describe various ways that men have dealt with that
need. These illustrations could be taken not only from Arab
culture, but from other cultures as well, showing in each
case how they are unsatisfactory in meeting the felt need.
Then the evangelist could present the biblical alternative,
demonstrating its superiority over the other ways mentioned.

Diagram 20 illustrates how to use the felt need approach.
When the evangelist begins to communicate the Christian
message he relates it only to those needs the Transitional
Arab feels he has. These felt needs are represented in the
diagram by the area to the left of the vertical dotted line.
However, the purpose of Christian teaching is to bring all
men to see the needs that they have as God sees them. These
ultimate needs are represented by the area above the solid
horizontal line. Although it is best to begin with the felt
needs the evangelist will gradually begin to teach the Transitional Arab about the ultimate needs which may still be
subliminal or unfelt. These become generated needs as indicated on the diagram. Gradually more and more emphasis
should be placed on the ultimate needs, this movement being
illustrated by the arrows and the shaded area in diagram 20
indicating the emphasis of Christian teaching. This does
not mean that the immediate physical needs will cease to be
met by Christianity. Christian fellowship and brotherly
love should automatically take care of those needs. But the
emphasis in teaching should gradually reveal the needs that
man has in his relationship to God.

Three advantages to the felt need approach should be
noted. First, it allows innovations to be introduced gradually. Patai affirms:

> A change that if sprung upon the people precipately
> would meet with the determined resistance can be-
> come acceptable without any noticeable repercussion
> if protracted over a number of years.(77)

If the evangelist introduces Christianity using the felt
need approach it will take him longer to communicate the
complete gamut of the Christian message, but it will have

the advantage of being introduced gradually. Second, the
felt need approach avoids the initial emphasis on those doctrines which lead to premature controversy. Third, it will
make Christianity more relevant to the Transitional Arab.

DIAGRAM 20

THE FELT NEED APPROACH

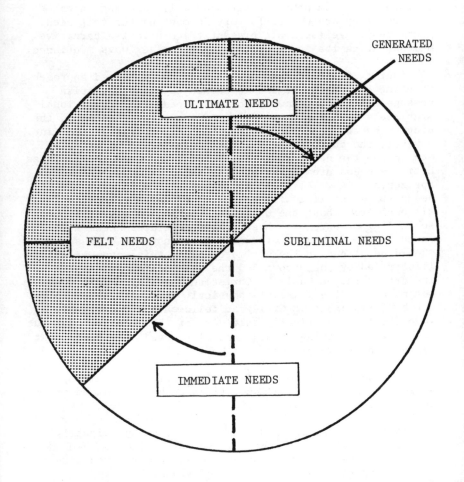

The Ultimate Needs

It is essential to relate the felt needs of the people to
the ultimate needs, such as the problem of sin. But even
when the evangelist reaches this stage a North American correspondence course or a Jule Miller filmstrip will not
achieve effective communication. The ultimate needs must be
presented in terms that the Arab mind can comprehend. An
illustration of an effective approach in communicating a
doctrinal issue to a Muslim is Hargreaves sample conversation
with a Muslim. (78)

THE STYLE OF THE MESSAGE

It has been estimated that the most literate and well-
informed people rarely understand one another more than
eighty percent of the time. (79) If this applies to people
of the same cultural background, it is fair to assume that
less than half of what is said between people of widely different backgrounds is understood in the way intended. (80)
This fact stresses the importance of finding styles with
which to communicate the message in the most meaningful way.

Poetry and Proverbs

The frequent poetic passages in the Old Testament usually
do not impress the Westerner nearly as much as they do the
Arab, whose life is filled with poetic expression. It is
integrated into Arab life to such a degree that vendors
praise their wares in rhymed ditties recited to special tunes.
(81) McCurry states that he "cannot too strongly recommend
their use as an effective means of communicating our message."
(82)

Figures of Speech

Figures of speech are expressions with meanings which are
not precisely the sum total of the meanings of the words
which make up the phrases. In communicating the biblical
message there is the tendency to preserve these figures even
if they mean something quite different from what was intended.
"He lifted up his eyes" means in Turkish only that he picked
his eyes up off the table. (83) One who communicates effectively in other languages must make use of indigenous figures
of speech. The evangelist can use the Arab's concept of nature to his advantage if he has an understanding of the rural
culture which dominates the Bible. The bulk of the narrative
in the Bible is couched in rural metaphors and concepts. (84)

The Arab who begins to read the Bible soon finds himself at
home in textual descriptions, allusions, and figures of
speech used to explain Christian concepts. Many of Jesus's
parables are based on an understanding of nature. Carl P.
Matheny, the author's father, advertized a Bible study course
with the question, "Would you like to know more of the book
the Middle East gave the world?" If in such an introductory
course the evangelist will emphasize the close parallels the
Bible has with the Middle Eastern concept of nature, the
relevance of the Bible to the Middle Easterner will become
even more striking. To neglect to bring out the Bible's
emphasis on nature will serve only to obscure and confuse
the Christian message.

Illustrations

   "If it is rational discourse you're looking for--do not
go East, young man. Not anyway to that region known, variously, as the Near or Middle East."(85) In approaching
Arabs, the evangelist has often failed to comprehend the
methods of thought and the mind set of the Arab. The western evangelist has attempted to convince them by using the
same arguments he would use at home. But frequently an illustration is vastly more persuasive than a syllogism, and
is more likely to secure his assent and win his allegiance.
(86) There are many similarities between the Semitic mind
of the first century and the Semitic mind of the twentieth
century. Therefore the parables of Christ become very relevant to the Arab.(87)

Islamicized Parables

   Goldsmith proposes that Islamicized parables can be used
to teach basic biblical concepts of the nature of God, man
and sin.(88) The Muslim cannot get angry with such para-
bolic teaching because Christ or the Bible is not even mentioned in the initial stages.

Pointed Questions

   Goldsmith suggests this as another style which avoids the
method of controversy. One can ask the question of how one
is to get rid of the evil in one's life in order that one
may be acceptable in heaven. Muslims will give different
answers and some will not be willing to face the problem, but
others will become deeply concerned with the whole issue.(89)
This style of teaching can be used to stimulate thought
about a felt need or to generate a need, and afford an opportunity for approval.

Overassertion

In an article on the effect of the Arabic language on
psychology of the Arabs, Shouby has argued that "Arabs are
forced to overassert and exaggerate in almost all types of
communication" if they do not wish to be misunderstood."(90)
He believes that the language is so filled with techniques
for exaggeration that any statement which is merely matter-
of-fact will be taken to imply the contrary.

> English cannot be translated into Arabic literally
> without losing a part of its meaning. Those who
> read the same paragraph in both English and Arabic
> will get more meaning from the English version (when
> the Arabic is a literal translation) because, among
> other things, a great deal of the meaning is lost in
> the Arabic version if no devices of assertion and
> exaggeration are added. It is significant to note
> that even Arabs whose English is inferior to their
> Arabic often prefer to read serious matter in English.
> One reason is the failure of the Arabic translation
> to put enough emphasis in the way of exaggeration
> and overassertion to convey to the reader what is
> stated simply in English.(91)

Prothro tested this evaluation empirically and concluded
that Arab students were more prone to overassertion than are
American students.(92) This difference would seem to be of
considerable importance to anyone interested in written communication between Arabs and Americans, especially the writ-
ing of religious tracts and correspondence courses. An
American who is interested in communicating with a literate
Arab should note that a statement which seems to be a firm
assertion to the American may sound weak and even doubtful
to the Arabs who read it.(93)

Therefore, the style which the evangelist uses in presenting the Christian message can greatly affect the meaning
which the Arab attributes to that message. If he assigns an
unintended meaning to the Christian message, then a valid
decision is very difficult to achieve.

CONCLUSION

The thesis of this chapter is that in order for the Christian message to be relevant to the Transitional Arab it must
be related to their felt needs. The evangelist cannot stop
with their felt needs. It is absolutely necessary that he

lead them to an understanding of their ultimate needs as God
sees them. The felt-need approach can increase the chances
of establishing a mature fellowship of believers and decrease
the chances of reversion.

8

Conclusion

The purpose of this study has been to construct an evangelistic strategy to reach the Transitional Arabs, who are considered to be the most receptive segment of Middle Eastern society. Transitionals are those who have moved from the village to the city during their life time and are in the process of becoming modern. This study is restricted by all the limitations of library research, and the proposed evangelistic strategy will have to be tested on the field before its validity can be totally demonstrated. But the research indicates the following:

1. The areas of Arab culture which are most significant to evangelism are primarily cultural themes and social structure.
2. The most effective work can be done by the evangelist who goes to the Middle East on a long term basis. The chances for making a significant contribution to the growth of the church in the Middle East on a short term (three years or less) basis are very slim.
3. It is essential that the evangelist learn the Arabic language thoroughly and study Arab culture.
4. If Christianity is to be relevant to the Arab it must divest itself of its foreign western characteristics.
5. In attempting to diffuse an initial awareness of Christianity the religious worker must use the channels of communication that are most conducive to that purpose (the knowledge function). The various extending media are most conducive to this purpose.

6. When attempting to persuade to bring about a valid
decision the evangelist must use the channels that are most
conducive to that function: interpersonal communication and
the use of small groups (basic media).

7. The decision making process must be a culturally relevant way of making decisions: multi-individual group decisions of the nuclear family or the extended family depending
on the circumstances.

8. When the religious worker is ready to form churches
he must respect the categories of identity of the Arab people.
Where different ethnic and sectarian units tend to cluster
in specific areas of the city, it is recommended that the
evangelist respect those lines of division and form ethnic
unit churches in the different areas of the city. This will
allow each group to worship their Lord in a culturally relevant way.

9. The time of assembly for worship should not conflict
with the Arab's concept of time. This may imply having the
major Sunday service in the evenings where Sunday is a work
day. It may also mean that the evangelist should not insist
on "starting formal worship" at a prearranged time.

10. The primary restrictions to evangelism in the Middle
East are sociological and not theological (or doctrinal).

11. An encounter must take place at both the intellectual
level (great tradition) and at that emotional or behavioral
level (little tradition). If this does not occur the chances
for reversion are much greater.

12. The initial Christian message must be related to the
felt needs of the Transitional Arab. By doing this he will
perceive Christianity as being relevant to his way of life.

13. The evangelist must strive as soon as possible to
teach the ultimate needs that each man has in the eyes of
God according to his word.

14. The message must be communicated in a style that is
conducive to the Arab's mode of perception.

The research assembled and sifted here indicates that if
the above evangelistic strategy is followed the chances for
successful evangelism in the Middle East will be much greater,
more souls will be won to the Christian way of life, and
Christianity will be more relevant to the Arab people.

Appendixes

Appendix 1

A Sample Message
Directed at a Felt Need

Below is a message directed at the felt need of honor.
This is an example of how the felt needs can be used in
making the Christian message relevant to the Transitional
Arab.

WHAT IS HONORABLE?

All men want to have the honor of their friends and family. Everyone wants to be regarded as honorable. There are
many things that men will do to build up their honor. Some
will have a large family with many sons to build up their
honor. Others will sacrifice many things in order to get a
good education. Still others will go on a pilgrimage in order to increase their honor. Some people will even kill
people they love in order to maintain the honor of the family.

Many people consider only what other people think about
them. Many people will be very concerned about what society
thinks is honorable, but they are not very concerned about
what God thinks is honorable. It is very important for
every man to be honorable not only in terms of what society
wants but also in terms of God's will. If man's life is not
honorable in God's eyes, then it does not matter a great
deal what other people think about him.

Is your life honorable in God's eyes? God's will says:
"To the King of ages, immortal, invisible, the only God, be
honor and glory for ever and ever, Amen." (1 Tim. 1:17)
This means that if your life is to be honorable in God's

eyes, you must first honor God. God deserves more honor
than any man. Do you think it would be possible to honor
God without obeying his will? No, of course not.

All of this means that if you are to do what is honorable,
you must first honor God. And if you honor God you must
obey his will. Therefore, it is very important to know what
God's will is. God's will says the following things about
honor:

1. If you honor your father and mother you will live
    long on the earth (Eph. 6:2-3).
2. Younger men should honor all older men and women
    (I Tim. 5:1-3).
3. God said that if anyone does not honor Jesus Christ
    then he does not honor God (John 5:23). Therefore,
    it is very important to honor Christ.
4. God also says that men should honor those who are
    leaders in the family of God (Phil. 2:29).
5. If your life is to be truly honorable in God's eyes
    you must obey all of God's will. God has revealed
    his will to man in what is known as the Bible.

God's will, as revealed in the Bible, points out many ways
that you can obtain honor.

1. If a man becomes wise he becomes honorable (Prov. 3:16).
2. A woman who is gracious gets honor (Prov. 11:16)
3. A humble man is an honorable man (Prov. 15:33). This
    is something that is very difficult for many to accept
    because it is not easy to be humble. Yet God says
    that we must be humble to be honorable.
4. An honorable man is not one who is always fighting but
    one who is peaceable and gentle (Prov. 20:3).
5. The man who is righteous and kind will find honor
    (Prov. 21:21).
6. The man who honors God will be honored by God (I Sam
    2:30).
7. God's will also says that if a man will serve Christ,
    then God will honor him (John 12:26).

Therefore, how can you live a life of honor? The answer
is by obeying God's will and by serving Christ. The scriptures tell you how to do this. Those who do what the Bible
says, and who serve Christ are members of the family of God.
If you would like to become a member of the family of God,
you need to study God's will, the Bible, which tells you how.

Appendix 2

Questionnaire
From Field Notes

In the summer of 1975 the author spent six weeks in the Middle East with a group led by Carl P. Matheny. The group spent three weeks in Lebanon, one week in Egypt, a week and a half in Jordan, and three days in Israel. A questionnaire was prepared, designed to evaluate the effectiveness of various teaching methods in Arab culture. It was translated into Arabic after arriving in the Middle East. It consisted of three parts: 1) background of the respondent, 2) teaching methods, and 3) Bible knowledge. Appendix 2 will inlcude only the first part of this questionnaire, since it is the only part that is relevant to the thesis. (see p. 21). There were fifty-seven respondents, distributed as follows: in Lebanon mostly Christians, in Jordan Christians and non-Christians, and in Egypt a few Christians and a large number of non-Christian high school students.

BACKGROUND QUESTIONNAIRE

1. Your religious background is:
   a. Maronite   e. Assyrian   i. Presbyterian
   b. Muslim   f. Armenian   j. Coptic
   c. Greek Orthodox   g. Baptist   k. Druze
   d. Roman Catholic   h. Lutheran   l. Methodist
                                        m. Other

2. Who taught you most of what you know about religion?

3. Your present education level is:
   a. 0-5 years   c. attended university
   b. 6-12 years   d. graduated from university

4. Your marital status:
   a. single   c. widowed
   b. married   d. divorced

5. Where did you spend most of your life before age 20?
   a. village   c. other
   b. city

6. Where would you rather live if you had a choice?
   a. Lebanon   d. Syria   g. other
   b. Europe   e. Jordan
   c. America   f. Egypt

7. Who is the most influential in the majority of the
   religious decisions you make?
   a. friends   d. teacher   g. priest
   b. family   e. wife/husband h. grandfather
   c. father   f. political   i. boss
                      leader

8. How often do you listen to the radio?
   a. almost every day   c. once a week
   h. 2 or 3 days a week   d. less than once a week.

9. What do you like to listen to most on the radio?
   a. news   e. religious speeches
   b. reading of the Koran f. western music
   c. Arabic music   g. regular programs
   d. political speeches h. other

10. How often do you read a newspaper?
    a. almost every day   c. once a week
    b. 2 or 3 days a week d. less than once a week

11. How often do you go to the movies?
    a. once or more a week   c. 3 or 4 times a year
    b. once or twice a month d. less than 3 times a year

12. How often do you watch television?
    a. almost every day   c. once a week
    b. 2 or 3 days a week d. less than once a week

13. What kind of literature do you prefer?
    a. magazines   c. history   e. newspapers
    b. novels   d. religious material f. other

14. How do you spend your leisure time?
    a. reading   c. movies and television e. other
    b. sports   d. visiting

Appendix 3

Additional
Sources of Information

RELIGIOUS ORGANIZATIONS THAT HAVE MATERIALS OF INTEREST TO
THE RELIGIOUS WORKER IN THE MIDDLE EAST

1. American Bible Society, 1865 Broadway, New York, NY 10023.

2. Baptist Publications, P.O. Box 2026, Beirut, Lebanon.
    They produce several correspondence courses, tracts,
    children's literature, and some books.

3. Fellowship of Faith for Muslims, 205 Yonge St., Room 25,
    Toronto, Ontario, Canada M5B 1N2. Their catalog con-
    tains a wealth of material on Islam and the Middle East.

4. Gospel Recordings, Inc., 122 Glendale Blvd., Los Angeles,
    CA 90026. Religious messages in Arabic available on
    records and cassettes and cardboard record players are
    available free.

5. Middle East Christian Outreach, P.O. Box 1742, Aberdeen,
    SD 57401. They publish a free bi-monthly magazine,
    Crossroads.

6. Moody Institute of Science, 12000 E. Washington Blvd.,
    Whittier, CA 90606. The Film Catalog: Overseas Edition
    lists a number of "Sermons From Science Films" available
    in Arabic.

7. National Council of Churches publishes "SWASIA," a bi-
    weekly publication summarizing news of southwest Asia

and North Africa including summaries of radio broadcasts.
Write: SWASIA, P.O. Box 29060, Washington, D.C. 20017.

8. North Africa Mission, 239 Fairfield Ave., Upper Darby,
    PA 19082. They publish "Cross & Crescent" three times
    a year.

9. Radio School of the Bible, 151 bis, Avenue de Monteliver,
    13012 Marseille, France. They have correspondence
    courses and a newspaper in French and Arabic, as well as
    over 500 radio sermons on cassette. A research library
    of materials in French, English, and Arabic is available
    to anyone who cares to spend time in Marseille.

10. Scripture Gift Mission, Inc., Radstock House, 3 Eccleston
    St., London SW1S 9LZ, England. They have publications
    in English, French, and Arabic consisting primarily of
    compilations of passages of Scripture on various sub-
    jects, and thus would be useable by any religious group.

GENERAL INFORMATION ON THE MIDDLE EAST

One can obtain an abundance of free material and some good
material for sale from the following sources.

1. Americans for Middle East Understanding, 475 Riverside
    Drive, Room 771, New York, NY 10027. They publish a
    free newsletter, "The Link," and offer books on the
    Middle East at a discount.

2. American Friends of the Middle East, 1717 Massachusetts
    Ave., NW, Suite 100, Washington D.C. 20036. They have
    items for sale on the Middle East.

3. American Jewish Alternatives to Zionism, 133 East 73rd
    Street, Suite 505, New York, NY 10021.

4. American Near East Refugee Aid, 900 Woodward Bldg., 733
    15th Street, NW, Washington, D.C. 20005. They publish
    an interesting newsletter.

5. Arab Information Center, 747 Third Ave., New York, NY
    10017. They publish "Arab Perspectives" which is a
    well done monthly magazine.

6. Aramco Corporation, 1345 Avenue of the Americas, New York,
    NY 10019. They publish "Aramco World Magazine" free of
    charge.

7. Association of Arab-American University Graduates, Inc., P.O. Box 7391, North End Station, Detroit, MI 48202. They promote knowledge and understanding of the Arab World through papers, books, and bibliographies.

8. Council for the Advancement of Arab-British Understanding, 21 Collingham Road, London SW5 ONU, England.

9. Egyptian Government Tourist Office, 630 Fifth Ave., New York, NY 10020.

10. Israel Government Tourist Office, Suite 635, 805 Peachtree Street NE, Atlanta, GA 30308.

11. Jordan Information Bureau, 1701 K. Street NW, Washington, D.C. 20006. They publish a free quarterly magazine, *Jordan*.

12. Lebanon Tourist Office, 405 Park Ave., New York, NY 10022.

13. Middle East Airlines, 680 Fifth Ave., New York, NY 10019.

14. Middle East Institute, 1761 N. Street NW, Washington, D.C. 20036. They publish *The Middle East Journal* quarterly.

15. *MidEast Markets* is published by Chase World Information Corporation, 1 World Trade Center, Suite 4627, New York, NY 10048.

16. Middle East Studies Association, New York University, Washington Square, New York, NY 10003.

17. *The Muslim World* is published by the World Muslim Congress, P.O. Box 5030, Karachi-2, Pakistan.

18. *The Muslim World* is published quarterly by the Duncan Black MacDonald Center at the Hartford Seminary Foundation. Address: The Muslim World, 55 Elizabeth St., Hartford, CN 06105.

19. *The News Circle*, P.O. Box 74637, Los Angeles, CA 90004, is a monthly newspaper on Arab-American affairs.

20. Turkish Tourism Office, 500 Fifth Ave., New York, NY 10020.

21. University of California Extension Media Center, Berkeley, CA 94720, have for sale 100 tapes on the Middle East.

ARABIC LANGUAGE STUDY OPPORTUNITIES IN THE UNITED STATES

1. Columbia University, Middle East Institute, International Affairs Building, 420 West 118th St., New York, NY 10027.

2. Dropsie University, Dept. of Arabic and Islamic Studies, Broad and York Streets, Philadelphia, PA 19132.

3. Harvard University, Center for Middle Eastern Studies, 1737 Cambridge Street, Cambridge, MA 02138.

4. Indiana University, Department of Near Eastern Languages, Bloomington, IN 47401.

5. John Hopkins University, School of Advanced International Studies, 1740 Massachusetts Ave., NW, Washington D.C. 20036. They offer a summer program in Arabic and Arab Studies in cooperation with Georgetown University.

6. The Middle East Institute, 1761 N Street NW, Washington, D.C. 20036. They have a regular language training program in the spring, summer, or fall.

7. Princeton University, Program in Near Eastern Studies, Jones Hall, Princeton, NJ 08540.

8. University of California, Gustave E. Von Grunebaum Center for Near Eastern Studies, 405 Hilgard Ave., Los Angeles, CA 90024.

9. University of Michigan, Center for Near Eastern and North African Studies, 144 Lane Hall, Ann Arbor, MI 48104. In addition to the courses available on campus, a fully programmed course with tapes designed for self-instruction is available.

10. University of Texas at Austin, Center for Middle Eastern Studies, Austin, TX 78712.

11. University of Utah, Middle East Center, Salt Lake City, UT 84112.

12. University of Wisconsin, University Extension, 432 North Lake Street, Madison, WI 53706. They offer Arabic by correspondence course as university credit courses.

Notes

CHAPTER 1

[1] Raphael Patai, *Society, Culture and Change in the Middle East*, 3rd ed. (Philadelphia: University of Pennsylvania Press, 1969), p. 383.

[2] Kenneth Cragg, "The Arab World and the Christian Debt," *International Review of Missions* 42 (April 1953):159.

[3] L. Bevan Jones, *The People of the Mosque* (London: S. C. M. Press, 1932), p. 321.

[4] Conrad M. Arensberg and Arthur H. Niehoff, *Introducing Social Change*, 2nd ed. (Chicago: Aldine Publishing Co., 1971), p. 7.

[5] Louis J. Luzbetak, *The Church and Cultures: An Applied Anthropology for the Religious Worker* (South Pasadena: William Carey Library, 1970), p. 204.

[6] Homer G. Barnett, *Innovation: The Basis of Cultural Change* (New York: McGraw-Hill, 1953), p. 7.

[7] The concept of restoring New Testament Christianity is most relevant in the West among denominational groups. But although the restoration concept is not meaningful to the Muslim since he has never been a Christian, it is meaningful to members of the Eastern churches.

[8]Everett M. Rogers and F. Floyd Shoemaker, *Communication of Innovations: A Cross-Cultural Approach*, 2nd ed. (New York: Free Press, 1971), p. 11.

[9]Leonard W. Doob, *Communication in Africa* (New Haven: Yale University Press, 1961), p. 9.

[10]Rogers, *Innovations*, p. 12.

[11]Ibid., p. 13.

[12]Rogers, *Modernization Among Peasants: The Impact of Communication* (New York: Holt, Rinehart, and Winston, 1969), p. 48.

[13]James T. Addison, *The Christian Approach to the Moslem: A Historical Study* (New York: Columbia University Press, 1942; reprint ed., New York: A. M. S. Press, 1966), p. 283.

[14]John Gulick divides the Middle East into nine cultural-ecological sub-regions, of which the fertile crescent is one, *The Middle East: An Anthropological Perspective* (Pacific Palisades, California: Goodyear Publishing Company, 1976), p. 5.

[15]Evertt W. Huffard, "An Agenda for the Evangelization of Egypt, Jordan, and Lebanon with Specific Reference to the Effect of Modernization on Receptivity," (M.A. thesis, Harding Graduate School of Religion, 1973), p. 13.

[16]Luzbetak, "Toward an Applied Missionary Anthropoligy," *Practical Anthropology* 10 (September-October 1963):201.

[17]*The Passing of Traditional Society: Modernizing in the Middle East* (New York: Free Press, 1958), p. 71.

[18]Lerner, *Traditional Society*, p. 50.

[19]Ibid., p. 91.

[20]The Christian groups tend to be more modernized and open to innovations than do the Muslims, Herant Katchadourian, "A Comparative Study of Mental Illness Among the Christians and Moslems of Lebanon," *International Journal of Social Psychiatry* 20 (Spring-Summer 1974):57.

[21]Huffard, "Agenda for Evangelization," p. 88. This was based on an analysis of 23 converts in Egypt, 130 in Jordan, and 22 in Lebanon.

22 Ibid., p. 88.

23 Ibid., p. 89.

24 "Linguistic Models for Religious Behavior," *Practical Anthropology* 19 (January-February 1972):13-26.

25 David J. Hesselgrave, "Dimensions of Cross-Cultural Communication," *Practical Anthropology* 19 (January February 1972):1-12; Edward T. Hall, *The Silent Language* (Garden City, New York: Doubleday, Anchor Books, 1959), p. 38; Arthur H. Niehoff, ed. *A Casebook of Social Change* (Chicago: Aldine Publishing Co., 1966), p. 12; Doob, *Communication.*

26 Doob, *Communication*, pp. 4-5.

27 Ibid., p. 11.

28 Ibid., p. 16.

29 Doob's variables are indicated by number according to which chapter they are dealt with in this thesis: chapter two (8), chapter three (5), chapter four (6, 9), chapter five (3, 4, 5, 12), chapter six (1, 2, 10, 11), chapter seven (7, 9).

30 Doob, *Communication*, p. 6.

31 Harold A. Fisher, "Communicating the Christian Message: A Study of Some Essentials in Christian Communication with Special Reference to Conveying the Gospel Message to Muslims," (STM thesis, San Francisco Theological Seminary, 1959).

32 Ibid., pp. 159-61.

33 Hendrik Kraemer, "Islamic Culture and Missionary Adequacy," *Muslim World* 50 (October 1960):250-51.

CHAPTER 2

1 *Patterns of Culture* (New York: New American Library, 1934).

[2]Luzbetak, *Church and Cultures*, p. 157; and Robert B. Taylor, *Introduction to Cultural Anthropology* (Boston: Allyn and Bacon, 1973), p. 44.

[3]Morris E. Opler, "Themes as Dynamic Forces in Culture," *American Jorunal of Sociology* 51 (November 1945):198.

[4]Ibid., p. 200.

[5]Ibid., p. 201.

[6]Sania Hamady, *Temperament and Character of Arabs* (New York: Twayne Publishers, 1960); Joe E. Pierce, *Understanding the Middle East* (Rutland, Vermont: Charles E. Tuttle, 1971); Morroe Berger, *The Arab World Today* (Garden City, New York: Doubleday, Anchor Books, 1962), chapter 5.

[7]Luzbetak, "Missionary Anthropology," p. 206.

[8]William L. Wonderly and Eugene A. Nida, "Cultural Differences and the Communication of Christian Values," *Practical Anthropology* 10 (November-December 1963):242.

[9]The American University, *Area Handbook for Syria* (Washington: U. S. Government Printing Office, 1965), p. 86.

[10]Julian Pitt-Rivers, "Honour and Social Status," in *Honour and Shame: The Values of Mediterranean Society*, ed. Jean G. Peristiany (Chicago: University of Chicago Press, 1966), p. 21.

[11]Ahmed M. Abou-Zeid, "Honour and Shame Among the Bedouins of Egypt," in Peristiany, *Honour and Shame*, p. 245.

[12]Patai, *The Arab Mind* (New York: Charles Scribner's Sons, 1973), p. 90.

[13]American University, *Syria*, p. 88.

[14]Pierce, *Middle East*, p. 50, quoting Fulinain, *The Marsh Arab* (Philadelphia: J. P. Lippincott, 1928), p. 73.

[15]Patai, *Arab Mind*, p. 113.

[16]William A. Darity, "Some Sociocultural Factors in the Administration of Technical Assistance and Training in Health," *Human Organization* 24 (Spring 1965):81.

[17]Although this figure is accurate for the entire Middle East according to John Gulick, *Middle East*, p. 57, it should be noted that in the countries of primary concern to this study (Lebanon, Jordan, and Egypt) urbanization is estimated to be as high as sixty percent.

[18]Judith R. Williams, *The Youth of Haouch El Harimi: A Lebanese Village* (Cambridge: Harvard University Press, 1968), p. 124.

[19]So potent is the prestige attached to a university degree among the literate that many thousands prefer to expend time, money, effort—and endure the subsequent deprivation of unemployment and under-employment—rather than settle for free technical education offered by the Ministry of Education, Lerner, *Traditional Society*, p. 238.

[20]Patai, *Arab Mind*, p. 103.

[21]Ibid., p. 105.

[22]Ibid., p. 91.

[23]American University, *Area Handbook for Lebanon*, 2nd ed. (Washington: U. S. Government Printing Office, 1974), p. 139.

[24]Berger, *Arab World*, pp. 160-61.

[25]Richard T. Antoun, "Anthropology," in *The Study of the Middle East: Research and Scholarship in the Humanities and Social Sciences*, ed. Leonard Binder (New York: John Wiley and Sons, 1976), p. 180.

[26]Ibid.

[27]Exod. 22:21; 23:9; Lev. 19:33; Deut. 10:18; 24:17.

[28]Pierce, *Middle East*, p. 153.

[29]Patai, *Arab Mind*, p. 86. The importance of hospitality as a cultural theme is illustrated by a recent issue of *Anthropological Quarterly*, which was devoted to visiting patterns in Eastern Mediterranean communities, 47 (January 1974).

[30]Berger, *Arab World*, p. 142

[31]Berger, *Arab World*, p. 142.

[32]Hamady, *Arabs*, p. 79.

[33]Berger, *Arab World*, p. 49.

[34]Dorothy L. Van Ess, "Arab Customs," *Practical Anthropology* 6 (September-October 1959):221.

[35]Hamady, *Arabs*, p. 79.

[36]"Arab Customs," pp. 221-22.

[37]Hamady, *Arabs*, p. 82.

[38]American University, *Lebanon*, p. 138.

[39]Fathi S. Yousef, "Cross-cultural Communication: Aspects of Contrastive Social Values Between North Americans and Middle Easterners," *Human Organization* 33 (Winter 1974): 385.

[40]Amal Vinogradov, "Visiting Patterns and Social Dynamics in Eastern Mediterranean Communities: Introduction," *Anthropological Quarterly* 47 (January 1974):7.

[41]Patai, *Middle East*, chapter 4; American University, *Lebanon*, chapter 7; Gulick, "The Arab Levant," in *The Central Middle East*, ed. Louise E. Sweet (New Haven: Human Relations Area Files Press, 1971), pp. 103-10; Hamady, *Arabs*, pp. 87-96; George J. Jennings, "Islamic Culture and Christian Missions," *Practical Anthropology* 18 (May-June 1971):133-36.

[42]John Elder, "Family Life in Shi'ah Islam," *Muslim World* 18 (July 1928):250-55; Ilse Lichtenstadter, "An Arab Egyptian Family," *Middle Eastern Journal* 6 (Autumn 1952): 379-99; Dorthy F. Beck, "The Changing Moslem Family of the Middle East," *Marriage and Family Living* 19 (November 1957): 340-47; John H. Chamberlayne, "The Family in Islam," *Numen* 15 (May 1968):119-41; and H. S. Karmi, "The Family as a Developing Social Group in Islam," *Asian Affairs* 62 (Febuary 1975):61-68.

[43]Patai, *Middle East*, p. 84.

[44]Hamady, *Arabs*, p. 87; and Pierce, *Middle East*, p. 61.

[45]American University, *Lebanon*, p. 4.

[46] Levon H. Melikian and Lutfy N. Diab, "Group Affiliations of University Students in the Arab Middle East," *Journal of Social Psychology* 49 (May 1959):145-59; Aida K. Tomeh, "The Impact of Reference Groups on the Educational and Occupational Aspirations of Women College Students," *Journal of Marriage and the Family* 30 (February 1968): 102-10.

[47] Melikian, "Group Affiliations," p. 155.

[48] Tomeh, "Reference Groups," p. 104.

[49] More details on the nature of this survey and a copy of the questionnaire appear in appendix 2.

[50] Jennings, "Islamic Culture," p. 141.

[51] Charles J. Adams, "Islamic Religious Tradition," in Binder, *Middle East*, p. 29.

[52] Patai, *Arab Mind*, p. 144, quoting Rebecca West, *Black Lamb and Gray Falcon* (New York: Viking Press, 1943), p. 298.

[53] Patai, *Arab Mind*, p. 146.

[54] Gulick, "Arab Levant," p. 131.

[55] Rogers, *Modernization*, p. 273.

[56] Gulick, *Middle East*, p. 235.

[57] Gulick, *Middle East*, p. 235, quoting Ali. A. Paydarfar, *Social Change in a Southern Province of Iran* (Chapel Hill: University of North Carolina, Institute for Research in Social Sciences, Comparative Urban Studies, Monograph no. 1, 1974), p. 124.

[58] Lerner, *Traditional Society*, pp. 86-100.

[59] Gulick, *Middle East*, p. 236, quoting Paul J. Magnarella, *Tradition and Change in a Turkish Town* (New York: John Wiley and Sons, 1974), p. 156.

[60] Rogers, *Modernization*, p. 290.

[61] Patai, *Middle East*, pp. 301-2; and Pierce, *Middle East*, p. 108.

[62]Pierce, *Middle East*, p. 108, quoting Hamed Ammar, *Growing Up in an Egyptian Village* (London: Routledge and Kegan Paul, 1954), p. 193.

[63]Pierce, *Middle East*, pp. 108-9.

[64]Patai, *Arab Mind*, p. 147.

[65]Pierce, *Middle East*, p. 86.

[66]Hamady, *Arabs*, p. 185.

[67]Ibid.

[68]Eugene A. Nida, *Religion Across Cultures: A Study in the Communication of Christian Faith* (New York: Harper and Row, 1968), p. 40.

[69]Samuel M. Zwemer, *The Influence of Animism on Islam* (New York: Macmillan, 1920); H. A. R. Gibb, "The Structure of Religious Thought in Islam, I: The Animistic Substrate," *Muslim World* 38 (January 1948):17-28; Emile Dermenghem, *Le Culte Des Saints Dans L'Islam Maghrebin* (Paris: Gallimard, 1954): Rudolph Kriss and Hubert Kriss-Heinrich, *Volksglaube im Bereich des Islams*, 2 vols. (Wiesbaden: Harrassowitz, 1960-62); Mounir Chamoun, *Les Superstitions Au Liban: Aspects Sociologuques* (Beirut: Dar el-Machreq Editeours, 1973): Bess A. Donaldson, *The Wild Rue: A Study of Muhammadan Magic and Folklore in Iran* (New York: Arno Press, 1973); Ernest Gellner, *Saints of the Atlas* (Chicago: University of Chicago Press, 1969); Michael Gilsenan, *Saint and Sufi in Modern Egypt: An Essay in the Sociology of Religion* (Oxford: Clarendon Press, 1973); and Edward Westermack, *Pagan Survivals in Mohammedan Civilization* (Amsterdam, Netherlands:Philo Press, 1973).

[70]Patai, *Arab Mind*, p. 145.

[71]Ibid.; and Patai, *Middle East*, p. 330.

[72]Patai, *Arab Mind*, p. 154.

[73]Gulick, *Middle East*, p. 46.

[74]Ibid.; and Hamady, *Arabs*, p. 172.

[75]Gulick, *Middle East*, p. 46.

[76]Pierce, *Middle East*, p. 93; and Hamady, *Arabs*, p. 171.

[77]Gulick, *Middle East*, p. 46; Pierce, *Middle East*, p. 94; and Hamady, *Arabs*, p. 173.

[78]Pierce, *Middle East*, p. 95; Hamady, *Arabs*, p. 172; and Marie K. Khayat and Margaret C. Keatinge, *Lebanon: Land of the Cedars* (Beirut: Khayats, 1960), p. 144.

[79]Gulick, *Middle East*, p. 47.

[80]Hamady, *Arabs*, p. 175.

[81]Gulick, *Middle East*, p. 180.

[82]Abdulla M. Lutfiyya, *Baytin: A Jordanian Village* (London: Mouton, 1966), p. 71.

[83]Pierce, *Middle East*, p. 107.

[84]Gulick, *Social Structure and Culture Change in a Lebanese Village* (New York: Wnner-Gren Foundation for Anthropological Research, 1955), p. 93.

[85]Lutfiyya, *Baytin*, p. 74; Hamady, *Arabs*, p. 164.

[86]Lutfiyya, *Baytin*, p. 74; Gulick, *Lebanese Village*, p. 93; and Hamady, *Arabs*, p. 168.

[87]Elizabeth W. Fernea, *Guests of the Sheik* (Garden City, New York: Doubleday, Anchor Books, 1965), pp. 216-48.

[88]Gulick, *Middle East*, p. 127.

[89]Gulick, *Middle East*, p. 189.

[90]Hamady, *Arabs*, p. 167.

[91]Pierce, *Middle East*, p. 94; and Khayat, *Lebanon*, p. 144.

[92]Gulick, *Lebanese Village*, p. 94.

[93]Gulick, *Middle East*, p. 47.

[94]Darity, "Technical Assistance," p. 80.

[95] Patai, *Arab Mind*, p. 154.

[96] Ibid.

[97] Don M. McCurry, "Cross-Cultural Models for Muslim Evangelism," *Missiology* 4 (April 1976):281.

[98] Wonderly, "Christian Values," p. 247.

[99] Luzbetak, *Church and Cultures*, p. 88.

[100] Patai, *Arab Mind*, p. 65.

[101] Edward T. Hall and William F. Shyte, "Intercultural Communication: A Guide to Men of Action," *Practical Anthropology* 10 (September–October 1963):221–23.

[102] Hamady, *Arabs*, p. 216.

[103] Phil Parshall, *The Fortress and the Fire: Jesus Christ and the Challenge of Islam* (Bombay: Gospel Literature Service, 1975), p. 95.

[104] Patai, *Arab Mind*, p. 66.

[105] Hall, *Silent Language*, p. 19.

[106] Ibid., p. 151.

[107] Patai, *Arab Mind*, p. 241.

[108] Arensberg, *Social Change*, p. 169.

[109] Hall, *Silent Language*, p. 157.

[110] Ibid., p. 2.

[111] Ibid., p. 4.

[112] Yousef, "Cross-cultural Communication," p. 386.

[113] Huffard, personal letter, March 25, 1977.

[114] Arensberg, *Social Change*, p. 219.

[115] Hall, "Intercultural Communication," p. 223.

[116] Hall, "Intercultural Communication," p. 223.

[117] Hall, *Silent Language*, p. 158.

[118] Ibid., p. 6.

[119] Westerners become very irritated over the amount of time it takes to conduct almost any kind of business, such as having to go to four different individuals to change money in a bank; but such things are not a nuisance to Arabs.

[120] Patai, *Arab Mind*, p. 66.

[121] 2 Cor. 6:2.

[122] Jennings, "Cultural Features Important to Missionaries in Lebanese Villages," *Practical Anthropology* 19 (March-April 1972):65.

[123] Hamady, *Arabs*, p. 73.

[124] Carleton S. Coon, *Caravan: The Story of the Middle East*, rev. ed. (New York: Holt, Rinehart, and Winston, 1958), p. 6.

[125] Patai, *Arab Mind*, p. 231.

[126] Gulick, "Old Values and New Institutions in a Lebanese Arab City," *Human Organization* 24 (Spring 1965): 52.

[127] Hamady, *Arabs*, p. 74.

[128] Hall, *Silent Language*, p. 107.

[129] Ibid., p. 127.

[130] Ibid., p. 128.

[131] Fuad I. Khuri, "The Etiquette of Bargaining in the Middle East," *American Anthropologist* 70 (August 1968):701.

[132] Hall, *Silent Language*, p. 128.

[133] Anne H. Fuller, *Buarij: Portrait of a Lebanese Muslim Village* (Cambridge: Harvard University Press, 1961), p. 20.

[134] Ibid., pp. 22-26.

[135] Fuller, *Buarij*, p. 25.

[136] Gulick, *Middle East*, p. 224.

CHAPTER 3

[1] Taylor, *Cultural Anthropology*, p. 243.

[2] Rogers, *Innovations*, p. 29; Arensberg, *Social Change*, p. 149; Ina C. Brown, *Understanding Other Cultures* (Englewood Cliffs, New Jersey: Prentice-Hall, 1963), p. 48.

[3] Luzbetak, *Church and Cultures*, p. 299.

[4] Donald A. McGavran, *Understanding Church Growth* (Grand Rapids: Eerdmans, 1970), p. 183.

[5] Nida, *Message and Mission* (New York: Harper and Row, 1960; reprint ed., Pasadena: William Carey Library, 1972), p. 130.

[6] American University, *Lebanon*, p. 59; Gulick, *Middle East*, p. 35.

[7] Ibid. Lerner's threefold classification of Traditionals, Transitionals, and Moderns falls into the category of vertical structure, Lerner, *Traditional Society*.

[8] Halim Barakat, "Social and Political Integration in Lebanon: A Case of Social Mosaic," *Middle East Journal* 27 (Summer 1973):309; Gulick, "Lebanese City," p. 51; and American University, *Lebanon*, p. 123.

[9] Melikian, "Group Affiliations," pp. 145-59.

[10] Barakat, "Social Integration," p. 310, citing Habib Hamman, "A Measure of Alienation in a University Setting," (M.A. thesis, American University of Beirut, 1969).

[11] Arensberg, *Social Change*, p. 48.

[12] Gulick, *Middle East*, p. 42.

[13]McGavran, *Church Growth*, p. 190.

[14]Gulick, "Arab Levant," p. 104.

[15]Ibid., p. 105.

[16]Churchill's survey of nearly 2,000 homes in Beirut revealed only two cases of polygamy, *The City of Beirut: A Socio-Economic Survey* (Beirut: Dar el-Kitab, 1954), p. 5.

[17]Gulick, "Arab Levant," p. 105; Lebanese City," p. 51. For a more thorough discussion of the kinship structure in the city see Fuad I. Khuri, *From Village to Suburb: Order and Change in Greater Beirut* (Chicago: University of Chicago Press, 1975), pp. 102-20.

[18]Gulick, "Arab Levant," pp. 109-10; Gulick, *Middle East*, pp. 128-31. The reason the prevalence of nuclear families has been obscured is probably because the earlier observers were greatly impressed with the fact that the extended family is deinitely a functional unit even in the urban milieu.

[19]Samih K. Farsoun, "Family Structure and Society in Modern Lebanon," in *Peoples and Cultures of the Middle East*, 2 vols., ed. Louise E. Sweet (Garden City, New York: Doubleday, Natural History Press, 1970), 2:270.

[20]Pierce, *Middle East*, pp. 63-64.

[21]An example of the function of the extended family in the decision making process is the marriage custom. Marriage is a family affair rather than a personal affair. Even in the most modernized Muslim countries, marriages of middle class urban men and women are still family sponsored even when they are not entirely arranged. Although a number of students are beginning to challenge the traditional norms of mate selection, the family is still highly involved. See Janet Abu-Lughod and Lucy Amin, "Egyptian Marriage Advertisements: Microcosm of a Changing Society," *Marriage and Family Living* 23 (May 1961):127; and J. Henry Korson, "Student Attitudes Toward Mate Selection in a Muslim Society: Pakistan," *Journal of Marriage and the Family* 31 (February 1969):165.

[22]*Human Organization* 24 (Spring 1965):59-64.

[23]Ibid., p. 59.

[24] Williams, "Extended Family, " p. 61.

[25] Ibid., p. 64.

[26] Ibid.

[27] Gulick, "Arab Levant," p. 105.

[28] Samih K. and Karen Farsoun, "Class and Patterns of Association among Kinsmen in Contemporary Lebanon," *Anthropological Quarterly* 47 (January 1974):103.

[29] Ibid., p. 104. Of sixteen calls made or received per day twelve were to or from kinsmen. Automobiles in Beirut are most frequently filled with an assortment of relatives going along for a ride or a visit.

[30] E. Terry Prothro and Melikian, "Social Distance and Social Change in the Near East," *Sociology and Social Research* 37 (September 1952):10.

[31] Reuben Levy, *The Social Structure of Islam* (New York: Cambridge University Press, 1962): and Edwin E. Calverley, "The Fundamental Structure of Islam," *Muslim World* 29 (July 1939):364-84.

[32] Gulick, *Middle East*, p. 164.

[33] Ibid.

[34] Gulick, *Middle East*, p. 169.

[35] Ibid., p. 170.

[36] Katchadourian, "Christians and Moslems," p. 56. His introduction to the religious structure of Lebanon is excellent.

[37] Gulick, *Middle East*, p. 171; and Prothro and Melikian, "Generalized Ethnic Attitudes in the Arab Near East," *Sociology and Social Research* 37 (July 1953):379.

[38] Hassan Saab, "Communication Between Christianity and Islam," *Middle East Journal* 19 (Winter 1964):51.

[39] Barakat, "Social Integration," p. 312.

[40] Barakat, "Social Integration," p. 315.

[41] Gulick, *Middle East*, pp. 171–73.

[42] Ibid. Please note that the words "religious" and "sectarian" are being used as defined on p. 77.

[43] Gulick, *Middle East*, pp. 173–95.

[44] Gulick, *Middle East*, p. 196.

[45] Ibid., p. 197.

[46] Nida, *Customs and Cultures: Anthropology for Christian Missions* (New York: Harper and Row, 1954; reprint ed., Pasadena: William Carey Library, 1975), p. 211.

[47] Patai, *Arab Mind*, pp. 41–72. Patai's chapter on language of the Arabs provides significant insight which is essential for the effective evangelist.

[48] Gulick, *Middle East*, p. 36.

[49] Hamady, *Arabs*, p. 19; American University, *Lebanon*, p. 51; American University, *Area Handbook for the Hashemite Kingdom of Jordan*, 2nd ed. (Washington: U.S. Government Printing Office, 1974), p. 75; and Anwar G. Chejne, "Arabic: Its Significance and Place in Arab-Muslim Society," *Middle East Journal* 19 (Autumn 1965):456.

[50] Gulick, "Arab Levant," p. 135.

[51] For more extensive treatment of language in the Middle East, one can go to the following sources: Patai, *Arab Mind*, pp. 41–72; Chejne, "Arabic," pp. 447–70; Eli Shouby, "The Influence of the Arabic Language on Arab Psychology," *Middle East Journal* 5 (Summer 1951):284–302; T. M. Johnstone, "The Languages of the Middle East," in *Peoples and Cultures of the Middle East*, 2 vols., ed. Louise E. Sweet (Garden City, New York: Natural History Press, 1970), 1:114–23; and Jabra I. Jabra, "Arab Language and Culture," in *The Middle East: A Handbook*, ed. Michael Adams (New York: Praeger Publishers, 1971), pp. 174–78.

[52] American University, *Lebanon*, p. 52.

[53] Richard G. Hovannisian, "The Ebb and Flow of the Armenian Minority in the Arab Middle East," *Middle East Journal* 28 (Winter 1974):19. For additional information on Armenians see Arpi Hamalian, "The Shirkets: Visiting

Patterns of Armenians in Lebanon," *Anthropological Quarterly*
47 (January 1974):71-92.

[54]American University, *Lebanon*, p. 54.

[55]Ibid., p. 57.

[56]Gulick, *Middle East*, p. 155.

[57]Gulick, "Arab Levant," p. 104.

[58]American University, *Jordan*, p. 86.

[59]Gulick, *Middle East*, p. 132.

[60]American University, *Jordan*, p. 90.

[61]American University, *Lebanon*, p. 75.

[62]Gulick, "Arab Levant," p. 105. For additional infor-
mation on women in the Middle East see the following: Patai,
Middle East, pp. 115-34; Doreen Ingrams, "The Position of
Women in Middle Eastern Arab Society," in Adams, *Middle East*,
pp. 526-31; Ibrahim Abdulla Muhyi, "Women in the Arab Middle
East," in *The Modern Middle East*, ed. Richard H. Nolte (New
York: Atherton Press, 1963), pp. 124-40; and Baer, *Arab
East*, pp. 34-57.

[63]McCurry, "Muslim Evangelism," p. 281.

[64]Gulick, *Middle East*, p. 45.

[65]Gulick, "Arab Levant," p. 113.

[66]See especially the two studies by Farsoun, "Family
Structure," and "Patterns of Association."

[67]*Middle East and North Africa, 1976-77*, 23rd ed.
(London: Europa Publications, 1976), p. 15. The population
of Tehran is 3.5 million, Baghdad is 2.5 million, Beirut is
one million, and Casablanca is one million.

[68]Bulick, *Middle East*, p. 57.

[69]American University, *Lebanon*, p. 46; Khuri, *Greater
Beirut*, p. 6; American University, *Jordan*, p. 55; John I.
Clark and W. B. Fisher, eds., *Population of the Middle East
and North Africa* (New York: Africana Publishing Corporation

1972), pp. 136, 193; Donald N. Wilber, *United Arab Republic, Egypt: Its People, Its Society, Its Culture* (New Haven: Human Relation Area Files Press, 1969), p. 4; Peter Beaumont, Gerald H. Blake, and J. Malcolm Wagstaff, *The Middle East: A Geographical Study* (New York: John Wiley and Sons, 1976), p. 205.

[70]There are a number of sources that discuss urbanization in the Middle East: Gulick, *Middle East*, pp. 101–40; Beaumont, *Middle East*, pp. 189–221; Patai, *Middle East*, pp. 303–21; Coon, *Caravan*, pp. 226–59; F. Benet, "The Ideology of Islamic Urbanization," in *Urbanism and Urbanization*, ed. Nels Anderson (Leiden: E. J. Brill, 1964), pp. 111–26; Morroe Berger, ed., *The New Metropolis in the Arab World* (New Delhi: Allied Publishers, 1963); Leon Carl Brown, *From Madina to Metropolis, Heritage and Change in the Near East City* (Princeton: Darwin Press, 1973); Philip K. Hitti, *Capital Cities of Arab Islam* (Minneapolis: University of Minnesota Press, 1973); and Ira M. Lapidus, *Middle Eastern Cities* (Berkeley: University of California Press, 1969).

[71]Gulick, *Middle East*, p. 123.

[72]The quarters of Beirut are inhabited as follows: Minet el-Hosn: Muslim; Saifi: Maronite; Medawar: Kurdish Muslim; Achrafiyeh: Maronite; Mazraa: Muslim; Mousseitbeh: Muslim; Ras Beirut and Ain al-Mreisseh: mixed.

[73]American University, *Lebanon*, p. 70; Gulick, *Middle East*, pp. 117, 123, 138; Barakat, "Social Integration," p. 312; and Gulick, "Lebanese City," p. 50.

[74]Farsoun, "Patterns of Association," p. 102.

[75]Khuri, "A Comparative Study of Migration Patterns in Two Lebanese Villages," *Human Organization* 26 (Winter 1967): 213.

[76]*Rand McNally Illustrated Atlas of the Middle East* (Chicago: Rand McNally, 1975), p. 28; and Gulick, *Middle East*, p. 105.

[77]Gulick, *Middle East*, p. 123; and Khuri, *Greater Beirut*, p. 6.

[78]American University, *Lebanon*, p. 63.

[79]The categories in table 6 were drawn from the follow-
ing sources: Gulick, *Middle East*, p. 133, citing James A.
Bill, *The Politics of Iran: Groups, Social, and Political
Aspects of Popular Religion* (Columbus, Ohio: Merill, 1972),
p. 8; Patai, *Middle East*, pp. 377-81; Hamady, *Arabs*, pp.
127-51; Sydney N. Fisher, ed., *Social Forces in the Middle
East* (Ithaca, New York: Cornell University Press, 1955;
reprint ed., New York: Greenwood Press, 1968), p. ix; and
William E. Hazen and Mohammed Mughisudden, eds., *Middle
Eastern Subcultures* Lexington, Massachusetts: Lexington
Books, 1975), p. viii.

[80]Huffard, "Agenda for Evangelization," p. 5.

[81]Lerner, *Traditional Society*, p. 222.

[82]Ibid.

[83]Ibid., p. 223.

[84]Rogers, *Innovations*, p. 35.

[85]Arensberg, *Social Change*, p. 136.

[86]Niehoff, *Social Change*, p. 31.

[87]Paul F. Lazarfeld, Bernard Berelson, and Hazel
Gaudet, *The People's Choice: How the Voter Makes up His Mind
in a Presidential Campaign*, 2nd ed. (New York: Columbia
University Press, 1948).

[88]Rogers, *Innovations*, p. 208.

[89]Rogers, *Innovations*, p. 209.

[90]Lerner, *Traditional Society*, pp. 185, 399; and Iliya
Harik, *The Political Mobilization of Peasants* (Bloomington:
Indiana University Press, 1974), p. 156.

[91]Lerner, *Traditional Society*, p. 185.

[92]Rogers, *Innovations*, pp. 200-43; and Rogers,
Modernization, pp. 219-41.

[93]Rogers, *Innovations*, p. 243.

[94]Lerner, *Traditional Society*, p. 246.

[95] Bruce M. Borthwick, "The Islamic Sermon as a Channel of Political Communication," *Middle East Journal* 21 (Summer 1967):312. Opinion leaders are also crucial in the rural areas, J. Mayone Stycos, "Patterns of Communication in a Rural Greek Village," *Public Opinion Quarterly* 16 (Spring 1952):58-70.

[96] Rogers, *Innovations*, p. 212.

[97] Ibid., p. 210.

[98] Khuri, "The Changing Class Structure in Lebanon," *Middle East Journal* 23 (Winter 1969):43.

[99] Rogers, *Innovations*, p. 224.

[100] Ibis., p. 223.

[101] Lerner. *Traditional Society*, p. 224.

[102] Harik, *Political Mobilization*, p. 156.

[103] Rogers, *Innovations*, p. 218.

[104] Harik, *Political Mobilization*, p. 153.

[105] Ibid., p. 155.

[106] Rogers, *Innovations*, p. 218.

[107] Borthwick, "Islamic Sermon," p. 312.

[108] Ibrahim Abu-Lughod, "The Mass Media and Egyptian Village Life," *Social Forces* 42 (October 1963):103.

[109] C. Ernest Dawn, "Arab Islam in the Modern Age," *Middle East Journal* 19 (Autumn 1965):445.

[110] Khuri, "Migration Patterns," p. 211.

[111] Rogers, *Innovations*, p. 219.

[112] Khuri, "Class Structure," p. 37.

[113] Yusif A. Sayigh, *Entrepreneurs of Lebanon* (Cambridge: Harvard University Press, 1962), p. xii.

[114] Rogers, *Innovations*, p. 219.

[115]Harik, *Political Mobilization*, p. 156.

[116]Lerner, *Traditional Society*, p. 196.

[117]Sayigh, *Entrepreneurs*, pp. 21, 69.

[118]Rogers, *Innovations*, p. 219.

[119]Rogers, *Modernization*, p. 229.

[120]Ibid., p. 230.

[121]Rogers, *Innovations*, p. 220.

[122]Rogers, *Modernization*, p. 231.

[123]Ibid., p. 227.

[124]Nida, *Message and Mission*, pp. 110, 132.

[125]Ibid., p. 113.

CHAPTER 4

[1]Thomas J. P. Warren, "The Problem of the Convert From Islam," *Muslim World* 8 (April 1918):149; Kraemer, *The Christian Message in a Non-Christian World*, 3rd ed. (Grand Rapids: Kregel Publications, 1956), pp. 353-55.

[2]Kraemer, *Christian Message*, p. 355.

[3]Warren Webster, "Why Do So Few Muslims Become Christians?" *Report of 1966 Conference: Committee of Evangelical Missionaries to Islam* (Hackensack, New Jersey: n.p., 1966), p. 57.

[4]McGavran, *Church Growth*, p. 191; and McCurry, "Muslim Evangelism," p. 268.

[5]McCurry, "Muslim Evangelism," p. 268.

[6]Two exceptions would include: Parshall, *Fortress and Fire*; and Charles R. Marsh, *Share Your Faith With a Muslim* (Chicago: Moody Press, 1975). But even these do not give a thorough treatment of the sociological restrictions to evangelism.

[7]Frank E. Keay, "The Challenge of Islam," *Christianity Today* 3 (December 22, 1958):11.

[8]Kraemer, *Christian Message*, p. 357; Elmer H. Douglas, "Christian Witness in the World of Islam," *South East Asia Journal of Theology* 8 (April 1967):14.

[9]S. A. Morrison, "Missions to Muslims," *International Review of Missions* 27 (October 1938):612; and William M. Miller, "The Presentation to Muslims of the Christian Doctrines of the Deity of Christ, the Trinity, the Atonement and the Inspiration of the Scriptures," in *International Missionary Council, Madras Series*, 6 vols. (New York: International Missionary Council, 1939), vol. 3: *Evangelism*, pp. 215-25.

[10]The evangelist attempting to deal with the theological differences between Islam and Christianity should become familiar with the various handbooks along with the following sources: Mohamed Al-Nowaihi, "The Religion of Islam: A Presentation to Christians," *International Review of Mission* 65 (April 1976):216-25; and Lawrence E. Browne, *The Quickening Word: A Theological Answer to the Challenge of Islam* (Cambridge: Heffer and Sons, 1955). The basic issues of the book are presented in his article, "Theological Problems in the Presentations of Christianity to Muslims," *Review and Expositor* 58 (January 1961):91-104.

[11]Zwemer, *The Moslem Doctrine of God* (New York: Young People's Missionary Movement, 1905), p. 7.

[12]J. N. D. Anderson, "Obstacles in the Muslim World," in *One Race, One Gospel, One Task: World Congress on Evangelism, Berlin 1966, Official Reference Volumes*, 2 vols., ed. Carl F. H. Henry and W. Stanley Mooneyham (Minneapolis, Minnesota: World Wide Publications, 1967), 1:283; R. C. Zaehner, *Christianity and Other Religions* (New York: Hawthorn Books, 1964), p. 106; and George K. Harris, *How to Lead Moslems to Christ* (Philadelphia: China Inland Mission, 1949), p. 59. This argument is based on three passages in the Koran: Surahs 4:167-70; 5:77, 116-17.

[13]Erich W. Bethmann, *Bridge to Islam* (London: George Allen and Unwin, 1953), p. 210.

[14]Edwin E. Calverley, "Christian Theology and the Qur'an," *Muslim World* 47 (October 1957):286. Lootfy Levonian devotes eighty pages to the differences in the Christian and Muslim conceptions of "Spirit" in *Studies in the Relationship Between Islam and Christianity: Psychological and Historical* (London: George Allen and Unwin, 1940), pp. 1-80.

[15]Nida, "Are We Really Monotheists?" in *Readings in Missionary Anthropology*, ed. William A. Smalley (South Pasadena: William Carey Library, 1974), p. 225. See also Cragg's discussion on interpreting the Christian doctrine of God to the Muslim, *The Call of the Minaret* (New York: Oxford University Press, 1956), pp. 304-18.

[16]In addition to the cited sources on the trinity see Zwemer, "The Doctrine of the Trinity," *Muslim World* 35 (January 1945):1-5; and W. H. T. Gairdner, "The Doctrine of the Unity in Trinity," *Muslim World* 1 (October 1911):381-407. Gairdner's article is very suggestive of material that could be used in a tract to give to Muslims.

[17]Bethmann, *Bridge to Islam*, p. 209. For a more thorough view of the Islamic view of Christ see Zwemer, "The Present Attitude of Educated Moslems toward Jesus Christ and the Scriptures," *International Review of Missions* 3 (October 1914):696-707; and Ishaw Musa Al-Husayni, "Christ in the Quran and in Modern Arabic Literature," *Muslim World* 50 (October 1960):297-302; Ernest Hahn, *Jesus in Islam: A Christian View* (Vaniyambadi, India: Concordia Press, 1975); Michael Hayek, *Le Christ De L'Islam* (Paris: Editions du Seuil, 1959); Zwemer, *The Moslem Christ* (Edinburgh: Oliphant, Anderson, and Ferrier, 1912); and Geoffrey Parrinder, *Jesus in the Qur'an* (New York: Barnes and Noble, 1965).

[18]Surah 19:38. J. Windrow Sweetman, *Islam and Christian Theology*, part I, vol. 1 (London: Lutterworth Press, 1945), p. 27.

[19]Zaehner, *Christianity*, p. 103.

[20]Cragg, *Minaret*, p. 295; and Stephen Neill, *Christian Faith and Other Faiths: The Christian Dialogue with Other Religions*, 2nd ed. (London: Oxford University Press, 1970), p. 67.

[21]Surahs 3:48 (55); 19:33; 4:157. Accad declares that it is legitimate to argue that Surah 4:152-57 can be interpreted to say that the Jews did not crucify Christ but God did, because it was in his plans according to Old Testament prophecy, Fuad Accad, "The Qur'an: A Bridge to Christian Faith," *Missiology* 4 (July 1976):340.

[22]Harris, *How to Lead Moslems*, p. 37.

[23]Livingston Bently, in "Christ and the Cross," *Muslim World* 41 (January 1951):5-10, presents the Christian message of Christ and the cross geared for the Muslim. Gairdner, in "The Essentiality of the Cross," *Muslim World* 23 (July 1933); 230-51, answers the Muslim objections to the crucifixion, which with adaptation could be used as a tract for Muslims.

[24]Annemarie Schimmel, "Islam," in *Historia Religionum: Handbook for the History of Religions*, ed. C. Jouco Bleeker and Geo Windengren (Leiden: E. J. Brill, 1971), p. 169.

[25]Anderson, "The Christian Message to Islam," *Christianity Today* 4 (December 22, 1958):218.

[26]Cragg, *Minaret*, p. 276.

[27]Zaehner, *Christianity*, p. 101; and Neill, *Other Faiths*, p. 53.

[28]Eric F. F. Bishop, "Impressions of the Bhamdun Conference, 1954," *Muslim World* 45 (January 1955):37-44.

[29]E. E. Elder, "The Development of the Muslim Doctrine of Sins and Their Forgiveness," *Muslim World* 29 (April 1939): 187.

[30]R. A. Blasdell, "The Muslim Attitude Toward Sin," *Muslim World* 31 (April 1941):145.

[31]Huffard, personal letter, March 25, 1977.

[32]Blasdell, "Sin," p. 146, recommends the book, *Hidayatu'l-Salikin fi Suluki Maslaki'l-Muttaqin* to cultivate a more intimate sense of sin among Muslims, but gives no further information.

[33]Watt, "The Missionary Task of the Church in Palestine and Syria," *International Review of Missions* 36 (April 1947): 160.

[34] Constance E. Padwick, "North African Reverie," *International Review of Missions* 27 (July 1938):346.

[35] Raymond Joyce expressed a great need for more study on terminology. He said that the Islam in Africa Project is working on a set of comparative studies of Muslim and Christian terms which should appear in book form soon. In addition, this matter of terminology was discussed considerably at the 1969 Beirut conference on Communicating the Gospel to Muslims. Raymond H. Joyce, "Literature for Muslims," paper presented at the Evangelical Alliance's Conference on the World of Islam Today, Great Britain, January 6-9, 1976. See also Henry G. Dorman, *Toward Understanding Islam* (New York: Bureau of Publications, Teachers College, Columbia University, 1948), pp. 126-31.

[36] Dorman, *Understanding Islam*, p. 127; David Brown, "The Christian Encounter with Islam," *Theology* 70 (January 1967):28; F. S. Khair-Ullah, "Linguistic Hang-Ups in Communicating with Muslims," *Missiology* 4 (July 1976):308; and Calverley, "Christian Theology," p. 285.

[37] Harold Spencer, "Humpty Dumpty," *International Review of Missions* 40 (April 1951):188.

[38] Percy Smith, "A Plea for the Use of Versions of Scripture and of Other Literature in the Vulgar Arabic," *Muslim World* 4 (January 1914):52-63; R. W. Kilgour, "Arabic Versions of the Bible," *Muslim World* 6 (October 1916):383-88; and Paul Erdman, "The Arabic Version of the Bible," *Muslim World* 27 (July 1937):218-36.

[39] "Evangelization Among Muslims Strategy Group Report," in *Let the Earth Hear His Voice*, ed. J. D. Douglas (Minneapolis: World Wide Publications, 1975), p. 826.

[40] Bishop, "Bhamdun Conference," p. 42.

[41] Watt, "The Use of the Word 'Allah' in English," *Muslim World* 43 (October 1953):245-47.

[42] Lootfy Levonian, "Islam and the Evangelical Churches in the Near East," *International Review of Misssions* 24 (July 1935):392; and James Barton, *The Christian Approach to Islam* (Boston: Pilgrim Press, 1918), p. 253.

[43] Morrison, "Missions to Muslims," p. 608.

44Morrison, "The Indigenous Churches and Muslim Evangelization," *International Review of Missions* 25 (July 1936): 306.

45Fisher, "The Christian Message," p. 107.

46Douglas, "Christian Witness," p. 12.

47John S. Badeau, *The Lands Between* (New York: Friendship Press, 1958), p. 126.

48Al-Nowaihi, "Religion of Islam," pp. 216–25.

49Smalley, "Respect and Ethnocentrism," in Smalley, *Missionary Anthropology*, p. 256.

50Parshall, *Fortress and the Fire*, p. 88.

51Ibid., chapter two.

52Marsh, *Share Your Faith*; and William M. Miller, *A Christian's Response to Islam* (Nutley, New Jersey: Presbyterian and Reformed Publishing Company, 1976).

53Jennings, "Islamic Culture," p. 143.

54Miller, *Christian Response*, p. 95.

55Parshall, *Fortress and the Fire*, pp. 29–37.

56Marston Speight, "Some Bases for A Christian Apologetic to Islam," *International Review of Missions* 54 (April 1965):203; J. Christy Wilson, "Evangelism for Mohammedans," *Muslim World* 36 (October 1946):294; and Wilson, *The Christian Message to Islam* (New York: Fleming H. Revell, 1950), p. 84.

57Riggs, "Shall we Try Unbeaten Paths in Working for Moslems," *Muslim World* 31 (April 1941):118; and Badeau, *The Lands Between*, p. 124.

58Martin Goldsmith, "Community and Controversy: Key Causes of Muslim Resistance," *Missiology* 4 (July 1976):319.

59"Evangelization Among Muslims," p. 826.

60Goldsmith, "Muslim Resistance," p. 317. The subject of using felt needs in the construction of the Christian message is presented in chapter seven.

[61]Pierce, *Middle East*, p. 112.

[62]Evertt W. Huffard, personal letter, January 24, 1977.

[63]Parshall, *Fortress and the Fire*, p. 100.

[64]C. George Fry, "Christianity's Greatest Challenge,"
Christianity Today 14 (November 7, 1969):113-16.

[65]Kraemer, *Christian Message*, p. 315; and Addison,
Christian Approach, p. 289.

[66]John D. C. Anderson, "The Missionary Approach to
Islam: Christian or 'Cultic'," *Missiology* 4 (July 1976):
285.

[67]Morrison, "Missions to Muslims," *International Review
of Missions* 27 (October 1938):609.

[68]"Evangelization Among Muslims," p. 826.

[69]R. Park Johnson, "Renewal of the Christian Mission to
Islam: Reflections on the Asmara Conference," *International
Review of Missions* 48 (October 1959):441.

[70]Miller, *Christian Response to Islam*, p. 97.

[71]Parshall, *Fortress and the Fire*, p. 101.

[72]George M. Foster, *Traditional Cultures: and the Impact
of Technological Change* (New York: Harper and Row, 1962),
p. 122.

[73]Barton, *Christian Approach*, p. 245.

[74]C. Philip Slate, "Modes of Perception: Cross-
Cultural Considerations," Fall 1974 (Typewritten).

[75]Slate, "Modes of Perception."; and Joyce, "Literature
for Muslims." See also Kenneth Bailey's dramatic presentation of the parable of the prodigal son, *The Cross and the
Prodigal* (St. Louis: Concordia Publishing House, 1973),
pp. 75-133.

[76]Duncan B. MacDonald, *The Religious Attitude and Life
in Islam* (Beirut: Khayats, 1909), p. 7.

[77]Levonian, *Islam and Christianity*.

[78]Levonian, "Muslim Evangelization: A Psychological Study," *International Review of Missions* 29 (April 1940): 237.

[79]Morrison, "Missions to Muslins," p. 611.

[80]Fry, "Christianity's Greatest Challenge," p. 115.

[81]Miller, *Christian Response to Islam*, p. 100.

[82]*Introducing Islam* (New York: Friendship Press, 1958), p. 55.

[83]Keay, "The Challenge of Islam," p. 11.

[84]R. H. Glover, *The Progress of World Wide Missions*, revised and enlarged by J. Herbert Kane (New York: Harper and Row, 1960), p. 214.

[85]Anderson, "Approach to Islam," p. 287; Nielsen, "Difficulties in Presenting the Gospel to Moslems," *Muslim World* 19 (January 1929):41; and Johnson, "Asmara Conference," p. 443.

[86]Kenneth Cragg, review of *Al-Tabshir Wa-l-Isti'mar Fi-l-Biladi-l 'Arabiyya* (Missions and Imperalism, Being an Account of Mission Work in the Arab World as a Medium of Cultural Expansion and a Preparation for Political Intervention), by Mustafa Khalidy and Omar A. Farrukh, in *International Review of Missions* 43 (January 1954):90-93.

[87]Badeau, *The Lands Between*, p. 104.

CHAPTER 5

[1]Niehoff, *Social Change*, p. 15.

[2]Rogers, *Innovations*, pp. 23-24.

[3]Kenneth E. Andersen, "Variant Views of the Communicative Act," in *Speech Communication*, eds. Howard H. Martin and Kenneth E. Andersen (Boston: Allyn and Bacon, 1968), p. 15.

[4]Allowing for variations, these basic categories are identified with different terms by different authors: oral system and media system, Lerner, *Traditional Society*, p. 55; personal and impersonal, Patai, *Middle East*, p. 367; and inter-personal and mass media, Rogers, *Innovations*, p. 252.

[5]Doob, *Communication*, p. 57.

[6]Rogers, *Innovations*, p. 24.

[7]Donald K. Smith, "Changing People's Minds," *Practical Anthropology* 18 (July-August 1971):168.

[8]Lerner, *Traditional Society*, p. 45.

[9]Rogers, *Innovations*, p. 100.

[10]James F. Engel, "The Audience for Christian Communication," in *Let the Earth Hear His Voice*, ed. J. D. Douglas (Minneapolis: World Wide Publications, 1975), p. 536.

[11]Doob, *Communication*, p. 97.

[12]Hazen, *Middle Eastern Subcultures*, p. 153.

[13]Hamid Mowlana, "Mass Media Systems and Communication Behaviour," in Adams, *Middle East*, p. 593.

[14]Frances E. Scott, *Dare and Persevere* (London: Lebanon Evangelical Mission, 1960), p. 136.

[15]Philip Butler, "Evangelism and the Media: A Theological Basis for Action," in Douglas, *Let the Earth Hear*, p. 530.

[16]Rogers, *Innovations*, p. 252.

[17]Lerner, *Traditional Society*, p. 232.

[18]Mowlana, "Mass Media Systems," pp. 594-95.

[19]Members of the Eastern Christian sects have never been exposed to the concept of restoring New Testament Christianity, in addition to the fact that Muslims have distorted concepts about the identity of Christ.

[20]Wilson, *Christian Message*, p. 95.

[21]Barton, *Christian Approach*, p. 283; and Knair-Ullah, "Evangelization Among Muslims," in Douglas, *Let the Earth Hear*, p. 822.

[22]Khair-Ullah, "Muslims," p. 821; and Wilson, *Christian Message*, pp. 50–53.

[23]Lerner, *Traditional Society*, p. 61.

[24]For additional information on the current status of evangelistic literature in the Arab world see the following: Joyce, "Literature for Muslims."; C. Richard Shumaker, ed., *Conference on Media in Islamic Culture* (Toronto: Fellowship of Faith for Muslims, 1974); *Report of the 1964 Conference: Committee of Evangelical Missionaries to Islam* (Hackensack, New Jersey: n.p., 1964), pp. 34–51; and *Report of the 1966 Conference: Committee of Evangelical Missionaries to Islam* (Hackensack, New Jersey: n.p., 1966), pp. 15–19, 42–46.

[25]Bethmann, *Bridge to Islam*, p. 208.

[26]Huffard, "Agenda for Evangelization," pp. 38, 51.

[27]Ibid., p. 59.

[28]Ibid., p. 36.

[29]Additional information on the material available from these religious groups is given in appendix 3.

[30]Robert Schneider, "Reaching Muslims Through Bible Correspondence Courses," in *1964 Conference*, pp. 36–40.

[31]Schneider, "Correspondence Courses," pp. 36–41.

[32]Huffard, "Agenda for Evangelization," p. 58.

[33]Two discussions of such literature in the journals are William N. Wysham, "The Use of Literature in Evangelism," *Muslim World* 27 (January 1937) : 56–64; and Fred F. Goodsell, "A New Venture of Faith: Communicating the Gospel to Muslims," *International Review of Missions* 43 (April 1954): 162–69.

[34]Hazen, *Middle Eastern Subcultures*, p. 154.

[35]Lerner, *Traditional Society*, p. 179.

[36]Huffard, "Agenda for Evangelization," p. 38.

[37]Hazen, *Middle Eastern Subcultures*, p. 155.

[38]Ibid., p. 156.

[39]He was the first American evangelist to write a column in Arabic for the newspapers, Huffard, "Agenda for Evangelization," p. 57.

[40]Wilson, *Christian Message*, p. 52.

[41]Mowlana, "Mass Media Systems," p. 592.

[42]Denys Saunders, "Visual Aids and the Communication of the Gospel, "*International Review of Missions* 45 (July 1956): 316; Matthew S. Ogawa and Vern Rossman, "Evangelism Through the Mass Media and Audio Visual Materials," *International Review of Missions* 50 (October 1961) : 417-29; and Hames C. Campbell, "Using Audiovisual Resources," in *Communication: Learning for Churchmen*, ed. B. F. Jackson (Nashville: Abingdon Press, 1968) , p. 240-43.

[43]Glover, *World Wide Missions*, p. 221; B. M. Madany, "Preparation of Radio Programs to Reach Muslims," in *1964 Conference*, p. 26; and Wesley Miller, "Demonstration of Media Solution," in Shumaker, *Media In Islamic Culture*, p. 124.

[44]Lerner, *Traditional Society*, pp. 175, 180, 339.

[45]Hazen, *Middle Eastern Subcultures*, p. 161.

[46]In Egypt half of the radios are in Cairo, in Iran sixty percent of the radios are in Tehran, and in Lebanon fifty percent of the radios are in Beirut, "Communications in the Middle East," *Middle Eastern Affairs* 7 (June-July 1956) : 248-56.

[47]Mowlana, "Mass Media Systems," p. 591.

[48]Huffard, "Agenda for Evangelization," p. 50.

[49]Mowlana, "Mass Media Systems," p. 584.

[50]Robert W. Crawford, "Cultural Change and Communications in Morocco," *Human Organization* 24 (Spring 1965) : 75.

[51]Hazen, *Middle Eastern Subcultures*, p. 163.

[52]Joyce, "Literature for Muslims," p. 2.

[53]Christian Goforth, "The Entree of Media Through Factors in Muslim Culture," in Shumaker, *Media in Islamic Culture*, p. 111.

[54]Gospel Recordings, Inc. is involved in this kind of work. Radio School of the Bible also provides cassettes in Arabic. Find the addresses in appendix 3.

[55]Butler, "Evangelism and the Media," p. 530.

[56]Ibid.

[57]Lerner, *Traditional Society*, pp. 180, 175, 338. Abu-Lughod discovered that radio in comparison to newspaper was the most effective medium of communication in Egyptian villages, "Mass Media," p. 104.

[58]Doob, *Communication*, p. 57.

[59]Arensberg, *Social Change*, p. 97.

[60]Rogers, *Innovations*, p. 252.

[61]Hall, *Silent Language*, p. 38.

[62]W. D. Brewer, "Patterns of Gesture Among the Levantine Arabs," *American Anthropologist* 53 (April-June 1951) : 233.

[63]Brewer, "Gesture," p. 234; and Robert A. Barakat, "Arabic Gestures," *Journal of Popular Culture* 6 (Spring 1973) : 752.

[64]Barakat, "Arabic Gestures," pp. 772-93.

[65]Hall, "A System for the Notation of Proxemic Behavior," *American Anthropologist* 68 (August 1966) : 971-85.

[66]O. Michael Watson and Theodore D. Graves, "Quantitative Research in Proxemic Behavior," *American Anthropologist* 68 (August 1966) :971-85.

[67]Watson, "Proxemic Behavior," p. 983.

[68]Hall, *The Hidden Dimension* (Garden City, New York: Doubleday, Anchor Books, 1966), pp. 154-64.

[69]Marsh, *Share Your Faith*, p. 91.

[70]Gulick, *Tripoli: A Modern Arab City* (Cambridge: Harvard University Press, 1967), p. 54.

[71]Howard H. Martin, "Communication Settings," in Andersen, *Speech Communication*, p. 73.

[72]Ibid., pp. 74-78.

[73]Nida, *Message and Mission*, p. 174.

[74]Huffard, "Agenda for Evangelization," pp. 41, 51.

[75]Barton, *Christian Approach*, p. 294.

[76]Arensberg, *Social Change*, p. 89.

[77]Huffard, "Agenda for Evangelization," p. 52.

[78]Ibid., p. 53.

[79]Huffard concludes that since one should never disagree with his guest on the subject of religion, that home Bible studies would be self-defeating, "Agenda for Evangelization," p. 18.

[80]Huffard, personal letter, January 24, 1977.

[81]Huffard, "Agenda for Evangelization," p. 75.

[82]Hazen, *Middle Eastern Subcultures*, p. 129.

[83]Hazen, *Middle Eastern Subcultures*, p. 130.

[84]Huffard, "Agenda for Evangelization," p. 18.

[85]Huffard, personal letter, January 24, 1977.

[86]Ibid.

[87]Brian W. Beeley, "The Turkish Village Coffeehouse as a Social Institution, "*Geographical Review* 60 (October 1970) : 475 : and American University, *Jordan*, p. 88.

[88]Beeley, "Coffeehouse," p. 482.

[89]Huffard observes that in Nazareth, Israel the coffee-house seems to lack credibility, personal letter, March 25, 1977.

[90]F. S. Khair-Ullah, "Muslims," p. 823.

[91]Gerrit D. Van Peursem, "Methods of Evangelism in Arabia *"Muslim World* 11 (July 1921) : 268.

[92]Ibid.

[93]Rogers, *Innovations*, p. 260.

[94]Ibid., p. 255.

[95]Ibid., p. 256.

[96]Rogers, *Innovations*, p. 256.

[97]Ibid., p. 259.

[98]Ibid., p. 262.

CHAPTER 6

[1]Slate, "What the Bible Teaches About World Evangelism," in *What the Bible Teaches: 1972 Bible Lectureship of Harding Graduate School of Religion* (Nashville: Gospel Advocate Company, 1972), p. 168.

[2]Doob, *Communication*, p. 48.

[3]Ibid., p. 52.

[4]Paul Tillich, *Theology of Culture*, ed. Robert G. Kimball (New York: Oxford University Press, 1959), p. 201.

[5]Alan R. Tippett, "Christopaganism or Indigenous Christianity," in *Christopaganism or Indigenous Christianity*, ed. Tetsunao Yamamori and Charles R. Taber (Pasadena: William Carey Library, 1975), p. 14.

[6]Ibid., p. 15.

[7]Ibid., p. 28.

[8]MacDonald, "The Essence of Christian Missions," *Muslim World* 22 (October 1932) : 327.

[9]Sa'adah, "Christianity and the Arabic Mind," *Muslim World* 29 (January 1939) : 31.

[10]Kraemer, *Christian Message*, p. 323.

[11]Ibid., p. 316.

[12]Badeau, *Lands Between*, p. 105.

[13]Charles H. Kraft, "Christian Conversion or Cultural Conversion," *Practical Anthropology* 10 (July-August 1963) : 179-87.

[14]Kraft, "Conversion," p. 181.

[15]Ibid., p. 183.

[16] Ibid., p. 184.

[17]Nida, *Message and Mission*, pp. 35-61.

[18]Ibid., p. 36.

[19]Nida, *Message and Mission*, p. 40. The form of the message is discussed in chapter seven.

[20]Ibid., p. 58.

[21]Luzbetak, "Unity in Diversity: Ethnotheological Sensitivity in Cross-Cultural Evangelism," *Missiology* 4 (April 1976) : 214.

[22]Doob, *Communication*, p. 11.

[23]Rogers, *Innovations*, p. 227.

[24]Rogers, *Innovations*, p. 228.

[25]Rogers, *Innovations*, p. 248. Achieving such a terminal relationship involves training indigenous leaders.

[26]Ibid.

[27]William W. Stennett, "The Christian Missionary Confronting the Moslem," (M. Th. thesis, Southeastern Baptist Theological Seminary, 1959), p. 25.

[28]It is the consensus of opinion among missiologists that the evangelist must know the local language in order to be effective: Nida, *Customs and Cultures*, p. 222; McGavran, *Church Growth*, p. 193; McCurry, "Muslim Evangelization," p. 280; Howard H. Norton, *The Eldership and the Missionary* (Oklahoma City: Oklahoma Christian College, 1971), p. 12; Dewayne Davenport, "Identification: The Bridge Between Missionary and National," in *Missions for the Seventies*, ed. Wayne Anderson, Jr. (Oklahoma City: Oklahoma Christian College, 1970), p. 238.

[29]McGavran, *Church Growth*, p. 193.

[30]Acts 26: 14.

[31]Acts 2: 6, 8, 11. See also Jacob A. Loewen, "Language that Communicates," *Evangelical Missions Quarterly* 8 (Spring 1972) : 147.

[32]McGavran, *Church Growth*, p. 195.

[33]Ibid., p. 196.

[34]Franklin E. Hoskins, "Language Study for Arabic-Speaking Missionaries," *Muslim World* 2 (October 1912) : 358. He goes on to say that the American Mission in Syria with ninety years experience of supporting 157 missionaries, is agreed that every new missionary should have three years of language study. Experience has shown that few men coming after they are twenty-seven years of age ever succeed in mastering the language.

[35]Bethmann, *Bridge to Islam*, p. 206.

[36]Ibid.

[37]Marsh, *Share Your Faith*, p. 59.

[38]Ibid., p. 60.

[39]Hall and Whyte, "Intercultural Communication," p. 218. For a thorough discussion of this see Shouby, "Arabic Language," pp. 284-302.

[40]Cor. 9: 19-23.

[41]McCurry, "Muslim Evangelism," p. 272.

[42]Ibid.

[43]McCurry, "Muslim Evangelism," p. 272.

[44]Nida, *Customs and Cultures*, p. 250.

[45]William D. Reyburn, "Identification in the Missionary Task," *Practical Anthropology* 7 (January-February 1960) : 6.

[46]John Van Ess, *Meet the Arab* (New York: John Day, 1943) P. 161.

[47]Hall, *Hidden Dimension*, p. 188; and Luzbetak, *Church and Cultures*, p. 77.

[48]Loewen, "Rules: Relating to an Alien Social Structure," *Missiology* 4 (April 1976) : 217.

[49]Ibid., p. 239.

[50]Dale W. Kietzman, "Conversion and Culture Change," *Practical Anthropology* 5 (September-December 1958) : 209.

[51]Kietzman and William A. Smalley, "The Missionary's Role in Culture Change," *Practical Anthropology*—Supplement (1960) : 90.

[52]Hall, "Intercultural Communication," p. 228.

[53]Badeau, "The Role of the Missionary in the Near East," *International Review of Missions* 43 (October 1954) : 400.

[54]Jennings, "Islamic Culture," p. 132.

[55]Nida, *Message and Mission*, pp. 168-70.

[56]Luzbetak, *Church and Cultures*, p. 98. One of the most helpful studies of culture shock is Bert M. Perry's *Missionary, Know Thyself* (Winona, Mississippi: J. C. Choate Publications, 1972), which was originally an M. A. thesis at Harding Graduate School of Religion.

[57]Rogers, *Innovations*, p. 237.

[58]McCurry, "Muslim Evangelization," p. 282.

[59]Nida, *Customs and Cultures*, p. 257.

[60]Kraft, "Conversion," p. 186.

[61]Delbert Rice, "Evangelism and the Decision-Making Processes," *Practical Anthropology* 16 (November-December 1969) : 264-73.

[62]Addison, *Christian Approach*, p. 304.

[63]Ibid., p. 305.

[64]Zwemer, "The Dynamics of Evangelism," *Muslim World* 31 (April 1941) : 112; *The Cross Above the Cresent* (Grand Rapids : Zondervan, 1941), p.250; Wilson, "Public Confession and the Church," *Muslim World* 31 (April 1941) : 137; and *Christian Message*, pp. 169-71.

[65]Jennings, "Cultural Features," p. 71.

[66]Farsoun, "Family Structure," pp. 295-96.

[67]"Evangelization Among Muslims," p. 825.

[68]McGavran, *Church Growth*, p. 190.

[69]Ibid.

[70]Ibid.

[71]McGavran, *Church Growth*, p. 191.

[72]Jennings, "Cultural Features," p. 76; Jennings, "Islamic Culture," p. 136. See also Robert B. Cunningham, "Dimensions of Family Loyalty in the Arab Middle East: The Case of Jordan," *Journal of Developing Areas* 8 (October 1973) : 63.

[73]Chua W. Hian, "Evangelization of Whole Families," in Douglas, *Let the Earth Hear*, p. 970; Jennings, "Islamic Culture," p. 136; and McGavran, *Church Growth*, p. 299.

[74]McGavran, *The Bridges of God* (New York: Friendship Press, 1955); McGavran, *Church Growth*, pp. 296-334; J. Waskom Pickett et al., *Church Growth and Group Conversion* (Pasadena: William Carey Library, 1973); A.R.

[74]Tippett, *Verdict Theology in Missionary Theory* (Pasadena: William Carey Library, 1973), pp. 133-47; and Tippett, *Church Growth and the Word of God* (Grand Rapids: Eerdmans, 1970), pp. 31-33.

[75]Patai, *Arab Mind*, p. 282.

[76] Patai, *Middle East*, p. 384.

[77]Patai, *Middle East*, p. 384.

[78]McGavran, *Church Growth*, p. 298.

[79]Ibid.

[80]Tippett, *Verdict Theology*, p. 124.

[81]Ibid., p. 87

[82]F. Peter Cotterell argues the necessity of such an experience in conversion, "The Conversion Crux," *Missiology* 2 (April 1974) : 183-89.

[83]Rogers, *Innovations*, p. 161.

[84]Rogers, *Innovations*, p. 163.

[85]Slate, "Church Planting," *Mission Strategy Bulletin* 3 (July-August 1976).

[86]Phillip W. Elkins, *Church-Sponsored Missions* (Austin, Texas: Firm Foundation, 1974), p. 79.

[87]Smalley, "Cultural Implications of an Indigenous Church," in Smalley, *Missionary Anthropology*, p. 147.

[88]Ibid., p. 149.

[89]Ibid., P. 150.

[90]Nida, *Message and Mission*, p. 185.

[91]Charles H. Kraft, "Dynamic Equivalence Churches," *Missiology* 1 (January 1973) : 39-57.

[92]Ibid., p. 48.

[93] Kraft, "Dynamic Equivalence Churches," p. 49.

[94] Ibid., p. 49.

[95] Watt, "Missionary Task of the Church," p. 160.

[96] Luther P. Gerlach and Virginia H. Hine, *People*, (New York: Bobbs-Merrill, 1970), p. xvii.

[97] Elkins, *Church-Sponsored Missions*, p. 74.

[98] Anyone attempting to develop indigenous forms of worship must become very familiar with Muslim forms of worship, and the following sources would be a good beginning place. Constance E. Padwick, *Muslim Devotions: A Study of Prayer-Manuals in Common Use* (London: S.P.C.K., 1961); G. E. Von Grunebaum, *Muhammadan Festivals* (New York: Henry Schuman, 1951); Geoffrey Parrinder, *Worship in the World's Religions* (New York: Association Press, 1961), pp. 185-205; and Arthur Jeffrey, *A Reader on Islam: Passages from Standard Arabic Writings Illustrative of the Beliefs and Practices of Muslims* (The Hague: Mouton, 1962), pp. 519-668.

[99] Gulick, *Middle East*, p. 196.

[100] "Evangelization Among Muslims," p. 826.

[101] Kerr, "Personal Encounters with Muslims and Their Faith," *Missiology* 4 (April 1976) : 329.

[102] Rolla Foley's book, *Song of the Arab* (New York: Macmillian, 1953), is recommended as a possible beginning place. Included in the book is a sixteen item bibliography on materials on Arabian music available in English.

[103] Bernard Howell, *Missions: Progress, Stalemate, or or Regression?* (Concord, California: Pacific Publishing Company, 1971), p. 95.

[104] Elkins, *Church-Sponsored Missions*, p. 20.

[105] Howell, *Missions*, p. 102.

[106] Elkins, *Church-Sponsored Missions*, p. 71.

[107] Howell, *Missions*, p. 109; and McGavran, *How Churches Grow* (New York: Friendship Press, 1966), p. 135.

108 Howell, *Missions*, p. 119.

109 Huffard, "Agenda for Evangelization," pp. 64-66.

110 A good selection of books in this field is available from the Church Growth Book Club, P.O. Box 128-C, Pasadena, California 91104.

111 Barakat, "Social Integration," p. 317.

112 Irene G. West, "Asmara Study Conference, April 1-9, 1959," *International Review of Missions* 48 (October 1959) : 433.

113 McGavran, "Loose the Churches: Let Them Go," *Missiology* 1 (April 1973) : 81-94.

114 Huffard, "Agenda for Evangelization," pp. 93-99; and Farsoun, "Family Structure," p. 96.

115 McGavran, *Church Growth*, p. 290.

116 Byang H. Kato, "The Gospel, Cultural Context and Religious Syncretism," in Douglas, *Let the Earth Hear*, p. 1217.

CHAPTER 7

1 Elkins, *Church-Sponsored Missions*, p. 78; and Addison, *Christian Approach*, p. 289.

2 Harold W. Fehderau, "Keys to Cultural Insights," *Practical Anthropology* 10 (September-October 1963) : 208.

3 Cragg, "Christian Literature for the Contemporary Muslim," *Muslim World* 43 (July 1953) : 201.

4 Nida, *Message and Mission*, p. 57.

5 Ibid., p. 59.

6 Addison, *Christian Approach*, p. 290.

[7]Addison, *Christian Approach*, p. 291; and Kraemer, *Christian Message*, p. 130.

[8]MacDonald, "The Vital Forces of Christianity and Islam, " *International Review of Missions* 2 (October 1913) : 673.

[9]This list was compiled from various sources: Barton, *Christian Approach*, pp. 272-78; Stewart Crawford, "The Vital Forces of Christianity and Islam," *International Review of Missions* 1 (October 1912) : 609; Godfrey Dale, " The Vital Forces of Christianity and Islam," *International Review of Missions* 2 (April 1913) : 310; Dwight M. Donaldson, "Suggestions for Friends of Muslims," *Muslim World* 42 (January 1952) : 1-7; and Siraji ud-Din, "The Vital Forces of Christianity and Islam," *International Review of Missions* 2 (January 1913) : 105-109.   These authors have had much contact with Muslims.

[10] Acts 14:8-18.

[11]Barnett, *Innovation*, pp. 330-33.

[12]Tippett, "Evangelization Among Animists," in Douglas, *Let the Earth Hear*, p. 850.

[13]Taylor, *Cultural Anthropology*, p. 45; and Luzbetak, *Church and Cultures*, p. 138.

[14]Rogers, *Innovations*, pp. 135-72.

[15]Ibid., p. 167.

[16]Ibid., p. 139.

[17]Ibid., p. 167.

[18]Ibid., p. 168.

[19]Ibid.

[20]Ibid., p. 168.

[21]Ibid., p. 157.

[22]Ibid., p. 159.

[23]Ibid., p. 160.

[24]Watt, "The Forces Now Moulding Islam," *Muslim World* 43
(July 1953) : 170.

[25]Nida, *Customs and Cultures*, p. 274.

[26]Barnett, *Innovation*, p. 97.

[27]Rogers, *Innovations*, p. 105.

[28]Barnett, *Innovation*, p. 97.

[29]See Barnett, *Innovation*, pp. 107-26, for a thorough
treatment of subliminal needs.

[30]Rogers, *Innovations*, p. 238; Niehoff, *Social Change*,
p. 25; Arensberg, *Social Change*, p. 114; and Margaret Mead,
Cultural Patterns and Technical Change (New York: New
American Library, 1955), p. 258.

[31]Rogers, *Innovations*, p. 239.

[32]Ibid., p. 104.

[33]Ibid.

[34]Sayigh, *Entrepreneurs*, p. 133. Note that Rogers and
Shoemaker do not use this study in their analysis.

[35]Ibid., p. 135.

[36]Niehoff, *Social Change*, p. 25.

[37]Niehoff, *Social Change*, p. 25; and Arensberg, *Social
Change*, p. 115.

[38]Rogers, *Innovations*, p. 148.

[39]Cragg, "Christian Literature," p. 200.

[40]Morrison, "Missions to Muslims," p. 612.

[41]Ibid. Felt needs are not involved in all of these
cases. Jesus told the rich young ruler that he had to give
up his riches (Lk. 18:18-25). But the fact remains that
Jesus adapted his message to what it would mean and what
it would demand of those who would follow Jesus. There is
a clash inherent in the Christian message.

[42]Tippett, "Christopaganism," p. 25. An illustration of how Christianity can become syncretistic if not related to the felt needs is given by Pat Hile, "A Relevant Message for the Quiche," A paper presented at Harding Graduate School of Relition, January 20, 1977, p. 17. (Soon to be published)

[43]McGavran, *Church Growth*, p. 150.

[44]Ibid.

[45]Ibid., p. 151.

[46]Ibid., p. 152.

[47]Acts 8:18-24.

[48]Luzbetak, *Church and Cultures*, p. 287.

[49]Cragg, "Christian Literature," p. 203. Cragg recommends the Levonian tracts in the Woodbrook series as examples of material that deals with the great problems of human existence.

[50]Ibid., p. 204. Cragg notes that little Christian literature deals with this problem except for two books by John Elder, *The Influence of Christianity on Society* and *The Path of Social Reform*.

[51]Gulick, *Middle East*, p. 122.

[52]Gulick, *Tripoli*, p. 196.

[53]Speight, "A Christian Apologetic to Islam," p. 204.

[54]Goldsmith, "Muslim Resistance," p. 320.

[55]Ibid.

[56]Ibid.

[57]Paul S. Minear, *Immages of the Church in the New Testament* (Philadelphia: Westminster Press, 1960).

[58]1 Tim. 1:17; John 5:23; Eph. 6:2; 1 Tim. 5:1-3; and Phil. 2:25, 29.

[59]Prov. 3:16; 11:16; 13:18; 15:33; 20:3; 21:21; 1 Sam. 2:30; and John 12:26.

[60]Mt. 25:35; Rom. 12:13; 1 Tim. 3:2; 5:10; Tit. 1:8;
Heb. 13:2; and 1 Pet. 4:9.

[61]Gen. 19:1-11; and Lk. 11:5-13.   Kenneth E. Bailey has
done an exegesis of this parable in light of his extensive
understanding of Arab culture, *Poet and Peasant: A
Literary-Cultural Approach to the Parables in Luke* (Grand
Rapids: Eerdmans, 1976), pp. 119-41.

[62]Gen. 18:1-8; 24:31-33; 43:31-34; 45:16-20; Josh. 2:
1-16; 2 Sam. 9:7-13; Lk. 10:38-42; Acts 16-14-15; Acts 28:
2, 7.

[63]Luzbetak, *Church and Cultures*, p. 180.

[64]Hile, " A Relevant Message for the Quiche," p. 22.

[65]The destructive force of the evil eye and the spirits
may very well be imaginary, but passages such as Eph. 6:
10-20 suggest that the Christian has power to resist such
forces through Christ.   To use the power encounter approach
in relation to such forces does not involve one in neo-
pentecostalism.

[66]Watt, "New Paths to Islam," *International Review of
Missions* 36 (January 1947) :78.

[67]Speight, "Christian Apologetic," p. 199.

[68]Barton, *Christian Approach*, p. 274; W. H. T. Gairdner,
"Christianity and Islam," in *The Jerusalem Meeting of the
International Missionary Council, March 24-April 8, 1928,*
8 vols. (New York: International Missionary Council,
1928).   vol. 1:   *The Christian Life and Message in Relation
to Non-Christian Systems of Thought and Life*, p. 199.

[69]Julius Basetti-Sani, "For A Dialogue Between Christians and Muslims," *Muslim World* 57 (April 1967) : 128.

[70]Brown, "Christian Encounter with Islam," p. 26.

[71]Gulick, *Middle East*, p. 196.

[72]Heb. 8:6; 9:15; 12:24.

[73]Barton, *Christian Approach*, p. 279.

[74]Barnett, *Innovation*, p.130.

[75]Gulick, *Lebanese Village*, p. 93.

[76]Gulick, *Middle East*, p. 189.

[77]Patai, *Middle East*, p. 388.

[78]A. R. Hargreaves, " A Method of Presenting Jesus Christ to Moslems," *Muslim World* 37 (October 1947) :255-65.

[79]Nida, *Message and Mission*, p. 76.

[80]Ibid.

[81]Jennings, "Islamic Culture," p. 139.

[82]McCurry, "Muslim Evangelism," p. 280.

[83]Nida, "Cross-Cultural Communication of the Christian Message," *Practical Anthropology* 2 (March-April 1955): 39.

[84]Jennings, "Cultural Features," p.68.

[85]John Mander, "Beirut, Damascus, Tel Aviv," *Encounter* 30 (February 1968) :9.

[86]Barton, *Christian Approach*, p. 245.

[87]Bailey, *Poet and Peasant*.

[88]Goldsmith, "Muslim Resistance," p. 321.

[89]Ibid., p. 322.

[90]Shouby, "Arabic Language," p.300.

[91]Shouby, "Arabic Language," p. 300.

[92]E. Terry Prothro, "Arab-American Differences in the Judgment of Written Messages," *Journal of Social Psychology* 42 (August 1955) :9.

[93]Ibid., p. 10.

Bibliography

Abou-Zeid, Ahmed. M. "Honour and Shame Among the Bedouins of Egypt." In *Honour and Shame: The Values of Mediterranean Society*, pp. 243-59. Edited by Jean G. Peristiany. Chicago: University of Chicago Press, 1966.

Abu-Lughod, Ibrahim. "The Mass Media and Egyptian Village Life." *Social Forces* 42 (October 1963) :97-104.

Abu-Lughod, Janet, and Amin, Lucy. "Egyptian Marriage Advertisements: Microcosm of a Changing Society." *Marriage and Family Living* 23 (May 1961) :127-36.

Adams, Charles J. "Islamic Religious Tradition." In *The Study of the Middle East: Research and Scholarship in the Humanities and the Social Sciences*, pp. 29-96. Edited by Leonard Binder. New York: John Wiley and Sons, 1976.

Adams, Michael, ed. *The Middle East: A Handbook*. New York: Praeger Publishers, 1971.

Addison, James T. *The Christian Approach to the Moslem: A Historical Study*. New York: Columbia University Press, 1942; reprint ed., New York: A.M.S. Press, 1966.

The American University. *Area Handbook for the Hashemite Kingdom of Jordan*. 2nd ed. Washington: U. S. Government Printing Office, 1974.

_____. *Area Handbook for Lebanon*. 2nd ed. Washington:
U. S. Government Printing Office, 1974.

_____. *Area Handbook for Syria*. Washington: U. S.
Government Printing Office, 1965.

Andersen, Kenneth E. "Variant Views of the Communicative
Act." In *Speech Communication*, pp. 2-23. Edited by
Howard H. Martin and Kenneth E. Andersen. Boston:
Allyn and Bacon, 1968.

Anderson, J. N. D. "The Christian Message to Islam."
Christianity Today 4 (December 22, 1958) :216-18.

Anderson, J. N. D. "Obstacles in the Muslim World." In
*One Race, One Gospel, One Task: World Congress on
Evangelism, Berlin 1966, Official Reference Volumes*.
2 vols., 1:281-84. Edited by Carl F. H. Henry and
W. Stanley Mooneyham. Minneapolis, Minnesota: World
Wide Publications, 1967.

Anthropological Quarterly 47 (January 1974): Visiting
Patterns and Social Dynamics in Eastern Mediterranean Communities.

Antoun, Richard T. "Anthropology." In *The Study of the
Middle East: Research and Scholarship in the
Humanities and Social Sciences*, pp. 137-228. Edited
by Leonard Binder. New York: John Wiley and Sons,
1976.

Arensberg, Conrad M., and Niehoff, Arthur H. *Introducing
Social Change: A Manual for Community Development*.
2nd ed. Chicago: Aldine Publishing Company, 1971.

Badeau, John S. "The Role of the Missionary in the Near
East." *International Review of Missions* 43 (October
1954): 397-403.

_____. *The Lands Between*. New York: Friendship Press,
1958.

Baer, Gabriel. *Population and Society in the Arab East*.
New York: Frederick A. Praeger, 1964.

Bailey, Kenneth. *The Cross and the Prodigal*. St. Louis:
Concordia Publishing House, 1973.

_____. *Poet and Peasant: A Literary-Cultural Approach to the Parables in Luke.* Grand Rapids: Eerdmans, 1976.

Barakat, Halim. "Social and Political Integration in Lebanon: A Case of Social Mosaic." *Middle East Journal* 27 (Summer 1973): 301-18.

Barakat, Robert A. "Arabic Gestures." *Journal of Popular Culture* 6 (Spring 1973): 749-93.

Barnett, Homer G. *Innovation: The Basis of Cultural Change.* New York: McGraw-Hill, 1953.

Barton, James L. *The Christian Approach to Islam.* Boston: Pilgrim Press, 1918.

Basetti-Sani, Julius. "For a Dialogue Between Christians and Muslims." *Muslim World* 57 (April 1967): 126-37.

Beaumont, Peter; Blake, Gerald H.; and Wagstaff, J.Malcolm. *The Middle East: A Geographical Study.* New York: John Wiley and Sons, 1976.

Beck, Dorthy F. "The Changing Moslem Family of the Middle East." *Marriage and Family Living* 19 (November 1957): 340-47.

Beeley, Brian W. "The Turkish Village Coffeehouse as a Social Institution." *Geographical Review* 60 (October 1970): 475-93.

Benedict, Ruth. *Patterns of Culture.* New York: New American Library, 1934.

Benet, F. "The Ideology of Islamic Urbanization." In *Urbanism and Urbanization*, pp. 111-26. Edited by Nels Anderson. Leiden: E. J. Brill, 1964.

Bentley, Livingston. "Christ and the Cross." *Muslim World* 41 (January 1951): 5-10.

Berger, Morroe. *The Arab World Today.* Garden City, New York: Doubleday, Anchor Books, 1962.

_____.*The New Metropolis in the Arab World.* New Delhi: Allied Publishers, 1963.

Bethmann, Erich W. *Bridge to Islam: A Study of the Religious Forces of Islam and Christianity in the Near East*. London: George Allen and Unwin, 1953.

Binder, Leonard, ed. *The Study of the Middle East: Research and Scholarship in the Humanities and Social Sciences*. New York: John Wiley and Sons, 1976.

Bishop, Eric F. F. "Impressions of the Bhamdum Conference: 1954." *Muslim World* 45 (January 1955): 37-44.

Blasdell, R. A. "The Muslim Attitude Toward Sin." *Muslim World* 31 (April 1941): 145-48.

Borthwick, Bruce M. "The Islamic Sermon As A Channel of Political Communication." *Middle East Journal* 21 (Summer 1967): 299-313.

Brewer, W. D. "Patterns of Gesture Among the Levantine Arabs." *American Anthropologist* 53 (April-June 1951): 232-37.

Brown, David. "The Christian Encounter with Islam." *Theology* 70 (January 1967): 23-29.

Brown, Ina C. *Understanding Other Cultures*. Englewood Cliffs, New Jersey: Prentice-Hall, 1963.

Brown, Leon Carl. *From Madina to Metropolis, Heritage and Change in the Near East City*. Princeton, New Jersey: The Darwin Press, 1973.

Browne, Lawrence E. *The Quickening Word: A Theological Answer to the Challenge of Islam*. Cambridge: W. Heffer and Sons, 1955.

_____. "Theological Problems in the Presentations of Christianity to Muslims." *Review and Expositor* 58 (January 1961): 91-104.

Butler, Philip. "Evangelism and the Media: A Theological Basis for Action." In *Let the Earth Hear His Voice*, pp. 526-32. Edited by J. D. Douglas. Minneapolis, Minnesota: World Wide Publications, 1975.

Calverley, Edwin E. "The Fundamental Structure of Islam." *Muslim World* 29 (July 1939): 364-84.

_____. "Christian Theology and the Qur'an." *Muslim World* 47 (October 1957): 283-89.

Campbell, James C. "Using Audiovisual Resources." In *Communication: Learning for Churchmen*, pp. 233-97. Edited by B. F. Jackson. Nashville: Abingdon Press, 1968.

Chamberlayne, John H. "The Family in Islam." *Numen* 15 (May 1968): 119-41.

Chamoun, Mounir. *Les Superstitions Au Liban: Aspects Sociologuques*. Beirut: Dar el-Machreq Editeurs, 1973.

Chejne, Anwar G. "Arabic: Its Significance and Place In Arab-Muslim Society." *Middle East Journal* 19 (Autumn 1965): 447-70.

Churchill, Charles W. *The City of Beirut: A Socio-Economic Survey*. Beirut: Dar el-Kitab, 1954.

Clark, John I., and Fisher, W.B. eds. *Population of the Middle East and North Africa*. New York: Africana Publishing Corporation, 1972.

"Communications in the Middle East." *Middle Eastern Affairs* 7 (June-July 1956): 248-56.

Cooke, Francis T. "Sins and Their Punishment in Islam." *Muslim World* 28 (July 1938): 272-78.

Coon, Carleton S. *Caravan: The Story of the Middle East*. rev. ed. New York: Holt, Rinehart, and Winston, 1958.

Cotterell, F. Peter. "The Conversion Crux." *Missiology* 2 (April 1974): 183-89.

Cragg, Kenneth. "The Arab World and the Christian Debt." *International Review of Missions* 42 (April 1953): 151-61.

_____. "Christian Literature for the Contemporary Muslim. *Muslim World* 43 (July 1953): 197-207.

_____. Review of *Al-Tabshir Wa-1-Ishti'mar Fi-1-Biladi-1 Arabiyya* (Missions and Imperialism, Being an Account

of Mission Work in the Arab World as a Medium of
Cultural Expansion and a Preparation for Political
Intervention), by Mustafa Khalidy and Omar A. Farrukh.
International Review of Missions 43 (January 1954):
90-93.

_____. *The Call of the Minaret*. New York: Oxford
University Press, 1956.

Crawford, Robert W. "Cultural Change and Communications in
Morocco." *Human Organization* 24 (Spring 1965): 73-77.

Crawford, Stewart. "The Vital Forces of Christianity and
Islam." *International Review of Missions* 1 (October
1912): 601-17.

Cunningham, Robert B. "Dimensions of Family Loyalty in the
Arab Middle East: The Case of Jordan." *Journal of
Developing Areas* 8 (October 1973): 55-64.

Dale, Godfrey. "The Vital Forces of Christianity and
Islam." *International Review of Missions* 2 (April
1913): 305-17.

Darity, William A. "Some Sociocultural Factors in the
Administration of Technical Assistance and Training
in Health." *Human Organization* 24 (Spring 1965):
78-82.

Davenport, Dewayne. "Identification: The Bridge Between
Missionary and National." In *Missions for the
Seventies*, pp. 233-48. Edited by Wayne Anderson, Jr.
Oklahoma City: Oklahoma Christian College, 1970.

Dawn, C. Ernest. "Arab Islam in the Modern Age." *Middle
East Journal* 19 (Autumn 1965): 435-46.

Dermenghem, Emile. *Le Culte Des Saints Dans L'Islam
Maghrebin*. Paris: Gallimard, 1954.

Donaldson, Bess. A. *The Wild Rue: A Study of Muhammadan
Magic and Folklore in Iran*. New York: Arno Press,
1973.

Donaldson, Dwight M. "Suggestions for Friends of Muslims."
Muslim World 42 (January 1952): 1-7.

Doob, Leonard W. *Communication in Africa*. New Haven: Yale
University Press, 1961.

Dorman, Henry G., Jr. *Toward Understanding Islam: Contemporary Apologetic of Islam and Missionary Policy.* New York: Bureau of Publications, Teachers College, Columbia University, 1948.

Douglas, Elmer H. "Christian Witness in the World of Islam." *South East Asia Journal of Theology* 8 (April 1967): 6-16.

Douglas, J. D., ed. *Let the Earth Hear His Voice.* Minneapolis, Minnesota: World Wide Publications, 1975.

Elder, E. E. "The Development of the Muslim Doctrine of Sins and Their Forgiveness." *Muslim World* 29 (April 1939): 178-88.

Elder, John. "Family Life in Shi-ah Islam." *Muslim World* 18 (July 1928): 250-55.

Elkins, Phillip W. *Church-Sponsored Missions.* Austin, Texas: Firm Foundation, 1974.

Engel, James F. "The Audience for Christian Communication." In *Let the Earth Hear His Voice*, pp. 533-39. Edited by J. D. Douglas. Mineapolis, Minnesota: World Wide Publications, 1975.

Erdman, Paul. "The Arabic Version of the Bible." *Muslim World* 27 (July 1937): 218-36.

Farsoun, Samih K. "Family Structure and Society in Modern Lebanon." In *Peoples and Cultures of the Middle East.* 2 vols., 2:257-307. Edited by Louise E. Sweet. Garden City, New York: Doubleday, 1970.

_____., and Farsoun, Karen. "Class and Patterns of Association Among Kinsmen in Contemporary Lebanon." *Anthropological Quarterly* 47 (January 1974): 93-111.

Fehderau, Harold W. "Keys to Cultural Insights." *Practical Anthropology* 10 (September-October 1963): 193-98.

Fernea, Elizabeth W. *Guests of the Sheik.* Garden City, New York: Doubleday, Anchor Books, 1965.

Fisher, Harold A. "Communicating the Christian Message: A
    Study Directed Toward the Needs of Muslims but Based
    on a Thorough Examination of the Process of Communi-
    cation." STM Thesis, San Francisco Theological Semi-
    nary, 1959.

Fisher, Sydney N., ed. *Social Forces in the Middle East.*
    Ithaca, New York: Cornell University Press, 1968.

Foley, Rolla. *Song of the Arab: The Religious Ceremonies,
    Shrines, and Folk Music of the Holy Land Christian
    Arab.* New York: Macmillan, 1953.

Foster, George M. *Traditional Cultures: And the Impact of
    Technological Change.* New York: Harper and Row, 1962.

Fry, C. George. "Christianity's Greatest Challenge."
    Christianity Today 14 (November 7, 1969): 113-16.

Fuller, Anne H. *Buarij: Portrait of a Lebanese Muslim
    Village.* Cambridge: Harvard University Press, 1961.

Gairdner, W. H. T. "The Doctrine of the Unity in Trinity."
    Muslim World 1 (October 1911): 381-407.

_____. "Christianity and Islam." In *The Jerusalem Meeting
    of the International Missionary Council, March 24 -
    April 8, 1928.* 8 vols. New York: International
    Missionary Council, 1928. Vol. 1: *The Christian
    Life and Message in Relation to Non-Christian Systems
    of Thought and Life.*

_____. "The Essentiality of the Cross." *Muslim World* 23
    (July 1933): 230-51.

Gellner, Ernest. *Saints of the Atlas.* Chicago: University
    of Chicago Press, 1969.

Gerlack, Luther P., and Hine, Virginia H. *People, Power,
    Change Movements of Social Transformation.*
    Indianapolis: Bobbs-Merrill, 1970.

Gibb, H. A. R. "The Structure of Religious Thought in Islam,
    I: The Animistic Substrate." *Muslim World* 38
    (January 1948): 17-28.

Gilsenan, Michael. *Saint and Sufi in Modern Egypt: An Essay in the Sociology of Religion.* Oxford: Clarendon Press, 1973.

Glover, R. H. *The Progress of World Wide Missions.* Revised and enlarged by J. Herbert Kane. New York: Harper and Row, 1960.

Goforth, Christian. "The Entree of Media Through Factors in Muslim Culture." In *Conference on Media in Islamic Culture*, pp.107-12. Edited by Richard C. Shumaker. Toronto: Fellowship of Faith for Muslims, 1974.

Goldsmith, Martin, "Community and Controversy: Key Causes of Muslim Resistance." *Missiology* 4 (July 1976): 317-24.

Goodsell, Fred F. "A New Venture of Faith: Communicating the Gospel to Muslims." *International Review of Missions* 43 (April 1954): 162-69.

Gulick, John. *Social Structure and Culture Change in a Lebanese Village.* New York: Wenner-Gren Foundation for Anthropological Research, 1955.

_____. "Old Values and New Institutions in a Lebanese Arab City." *Human Organization* 24 (Spring 1965): 49-52.

_____. *Tripoli: A Modern Arab City.* Cambridge: Harvard University Press, 1967.

_____. "The Arab Levant." In *The Central Middle East: A Handbook of Anthropology and Published Research on the Nile Valley, the Arab Levant, Southern Mesopotamia, the Arabian Peninsula, and Israel*, pp. 79-170. Edited by Louise E. Sweet. New Haven: Human Relations Area Files Press, 1971.

_____. *The Middle East: An Anthropological Perspective.* Pacific Palisades, California: Goodyear Publishing Company, 1976.

Hacker, Jane M. *Modern Amman: A Social Study.* Durham: University of Durham, 1960.

Hahn, Ernest. *Jesus in Islam: A Christian View.* Vaniyam-badi, India: Concordia Press, 1975.

226   REACHING THE ARABS

Hall, Edward T. *The Silent Language*. Garden City, New
    York: Doubleday, Anchor Books, 1959.

_____. "A System for the Notation of Proxemic Behavior."
    American Anthropologist 65 (October 1963): 1003-26.

_____. *The Hidden Dimension*. Garden City, New York:
    Doubleday, Anchor Books, 1966.

_____., and Whyte, William F. "Intercultural Communication:
    A Guide to Men of Action." *Practical Anthropology* 10
    (September-October 1963): 216-29.

Hamady, Sania. *Temperament and Character of Arabs*. New
    York: Twayne Publishers, 1960.

Hamalian, Arpi. "The Shirkets: Visiting Pattern of Armen-
    ians in Lebanon." *Anthropological Quarterly* 47
    (January 1974): 71-92.

Hargreaves, A. R. "A Method of Presenting Jesus Christ to
    Moslems." *Muslim World* 37 (October 1947): 255-65.

Harik, Iliya F. *The Political Mobilization of Peasants:
    A Study of An Egyptian Community*. Bloomington:
    Indiana University Press, 1974.

Harris, George K. *How to Lead Moslems to Christ*. Philadel-
    phia: China Inland Mission, 1949.

Hayek, Michel. *Le Christ De L'Islam*. Paris: Editions du
    Seuil, 1959.

Hazen, William, and Mughisuddin, Mohammed, eds. *Middle
    Eastern Subcultures: A Regional Approach*.
    Lexington, Massachusetts: Lexington Books, 1975.

Hesselgrave, David J. "Dimensions of Crosscultural Commu-
    nication." *Practical Anthropology* 19 (January-
    February 1972): 1-12.

Hian, Chua W. "Evangelization of Whole Families." In *Let
    the Earth Hear His Voice*, pp. 968-73. Edited by
    J. D. Douglas. Minneapolis, Minnesota: World Wide
    Publications, 1975.

Hile, Pat. "A Relevant Message for the Quiche." A Paper
   presented at Harding Graduate School of Religion,
   January 20, 1977 (soon to be published).

Hitti, Philip K. *Capital Cities of Arab Islam.* Minneapolis:
   University of Minnesota Press, 1973.

The Holy Bible; Revised Standard Version. London: Collins,
   1952.

Hoskins, Franklin E. "Language Study for Arabic-Speaking
   Missionaries." *Muslim World* 2 (October 1912): 358-66.

Hovannisian, Richard G. "The Ebb and Flow of the Armenian
   Minority in the Arab Middle East." *Middle East
   Journal* 28 (Winter 1974): 19-32.

Howell, Bernard. *Missions: Progress, Stalemate, or Regression?* Concord, California: Pacific Publishing
   Company, 1971.

Huffard, Everett W. "An Agenda for the Evangelization of
   Egypt, Jordan, and Lebanon with Specific Reference
   to the Effect of Modernization on Receptivity." M.A.
   Thesis, Harding Graduate School of Religion, 1973.

_____. Personal Letter, February 24, 1977.

_____. Personal Letter, March 25, 1977.

Al-Husayni, Isaq M. "Christ in the Qur'an and in Modern
   Arabic Literature." *Muslim World* 50 (October 1960):
   297-302.

Ingrams, Doreen. "The Position of Women in the Middle
   Eastern Arab Society." In *The Middle East: A
   Handbook*, pp. 526-31. Edited by Michael Adams. New
   York: Praeger Publishers, 1971.

Jabra, Jabra I. "Arab Language and Culture." In *The Middle
   East: A Handbook*, pp. 174-78. Edited by Michael
   Adams. London: Anthony Blond, 1971.

Jennings, George J. "Islamic Culture and Christian
   Missions." *Practical Anthropology* 18 (May-June 1971):
   128-44.

_____. "Cultural Features Important to Missionaries in
    Lebanese Villages." *Practical Anthropology* 19 (March-
    April 1972): 59-82.

Johnson, R. Park. "Renewal of the Christian Mission to
    Islam: Reflections on the Asmara Conference."
    International Review of Missions 48 (October 1959):
    438-44.

Johnstone, T. M. "The Languages of the Middle East." In
    Peoples and Cultures of the Middle East. 2 vols.,
    1: 114-23. Edited by Louise E. Sweet. Garden City,
    New York: Doubleday, 1970.

Jones, L. Bevan. *The People of the Mosque*. London: S.C.M.
    Press, 1932.

Joyce, Raymond H. "Literature for Muslims." A Paper
    prepared for the Evangelical Alliance's Conference
    on the World of Islam Today. Great Britain, January
    6-9, 1976.

Karmi, H. S. "The Family as a Developing Social Group in
    Islam." *Asian Affairs* 62 (February 1975): 61-68.

Katchadourian, Herant. "A Comparative Study of Mental
    Illness Among the Christians and Moslems of Lebanon."
    International Journal of Social Psychiatry 20 (Spring-
    Summer 1974): 56-67.

Kato, Byang H. "The Gospel, Cultural Context and Religious
    Syncretism." In *Let the Earth Hear His Voice*, pp.
    1216-23. Edited by J. D. Douglas. Minneapolis,
    Minnesota: World Wide Publications, 1975.

Keay, Frank E. "The Challenge of Islam." *Christianity
    Today* 3 (December 22, 1958): 10-12.

Kerr, David. "Personal Encounters with Muslims and Their
    Faith." *Missiology* 4 (July 1976): 325-30.

Khair-Ullah, Frank. "Evangelization Amoung Muslims." In
    Let the Earth Hear His Voice, pp. 816-24. Edited by
    J. D. Douglas. Minneapolis, Minnesota: World Wide
    Publications, 1975.

_____. "Linguistic Hang-Ups in Communicating with Muslims."
Missiology 4 (July 1976): 301-16.

Khayat, Marie K., and Keatinge, Margaret, C. *Lebanon:
Land of the Cedars*, rev. ed. Beirut: Khayats, 1960.

Khuri, Fuad I. " A Comparative Study of Migration Patterns
in Two Lebanese Villages. *Human Organization* 26
(Winter 1967): 206-13.

Khuri, Fuad I. "The Etiquette of Bargaining in the Middle
East." *American Anthropologist* 70 (August 1968):
698-706.

_____. "The Changing Class Structure in Lebanon." *Middle
East Journal* 23 (Winter 1969): 29-44.

_____. *From Village to Suburb: Order and Change in
Greater Beirut*. Chicago: University of Chicago
Press, 1974.

Kietzman, Dale W. "Conversion and Culture Change."
Practical Anthropology 5 (September-December 1958):
203-10.

_____., and Smalley, William A. "The Missionary's Role in
Culture Change." *Practical Anthropology*, Supplement (1960): 85-90.

Kilgour, R. W. "Arabic Versions of the Bible." *Muslim
World* 6 (October 1916): 383-88.

Korson, J. Henry. "Students Attitudes Toward Mate Selection
in a Muslim Society: Pakistan." *Journal of Marriage
and the Family* 31 (February 1969): 153-65.

Kraemer, Hendrik. *The Christian Message in a Non-Christian
World*. 3rd ed. Grand Rapids: Kregel Publications,
1956.

_____. "Islamic Culture and Missionary Adequacy." *Muslim
World* 50 (October 1960): 244-51.

Kraft, Charles H. "Christian Conversion or Cultural Conversion?" *Practical Anthropology* 10 (July-August
1963): 179-87.

_____. "Dynamic Equivalence Churches." *Missiology* 1
    (January 1973): 39-57.

Kriss, Rudolph, and Kriss-Heinrich, Hubert. *Volksglaube im
    Bereich des Islams*. 2 vols. Wiesbaden: Harrassowitz,
    1960-62.

Lapidus, Ira M. ed. *Middle Eastern Cities*. Berkeley:
    University of California Press, 1969.

Lazerfeld, Paul F.; Berelson, Bernard; and Gaudet, Hazel.
    *The People's Choice: How the Voter Makes Up His Mind
    in a Presidential Campaign*. 2nd ed. New York:
    Columbia University Press, 1948.

Lerner, Daniel, *The Passing of Traditional Society:
    Modernizing in the Middle East*. New York: Free Press,
    1958.

Levonian, Lootfy. "Islam and the Evangelical Churches in
    the Near East." *International Review of Missions* 24
    (July 1935): 392-96.

_____. "Muslim Evangelization: A Psychological Study."
    International Review of Missions 29 (April 1940):
    236-40.

_____. *Studies in the Relationship Between Islam and
    Christianity: Psychological and Historical*. London:
    George Allen and Unwin, 1940.

Levy, Reuben. *The Social Structure of Islam*. New York:
    Cambridge University Press, 1962.

Lichtenstadter, Ilse. "An Arab-Egyptian Family." *Middle
    East Journal* 6 (Autumn 1952): 379-99.

Loewen, Jacob A. "Language That Communicates." *Evangelical
    Missions Quarterly* 8 (Spring 1972): 147-52.

_____. "Roles: Relating to an Alien Social Structure."
    Missiology 4 (April 1976): 217-42.

Lutfiyya, Abdulla M. *Baytin: A Jordanian Village*. London:
    Mouton and Company, 1966.

Luzbetak, Louis J. "Toward an Applied Missionary Anthropo-
     logy." *Practical Anthropology* 10 (September–October
     1963): 199–209.

_____. *The Church and Cultures: An Applied Anthropology
     For The Religious Worker.* Techny, Illinois: Divine
     Word Publications, 1970; reprint ed., Pasadena: William
     Carey Library, 1975.

_____. "Unity in Diversity: Ethnotheological Sensitivity
     in Cross-Cultural Evangelism." *Missiology* 4 (April
     1976): 207–16.

McCurry, Don M. "Cross-Cultural Models for Muslim Evan-
     gelism." *Missiology* 4 (July 1976): 267–84.

MacDonald, Duncan B. "The Vital Forces of Christianity
     and Islam." *International Review of Missions* 2
     (October 1913): 657–73.

_____. "The Essense of Christian Missions." *Muslim World*
     22 (October 1932): 327–30.

MacDonald, Duncan B. *The Religious Attitude and Life in
     Islam.* Beirut: Khayats, 1965.

McGavran, Donald A. *The Bridges of God: A Study in the
     Strategy of Missions.* New York: Friendship Press,
     1955.

_____. *Understanding Church Growth.* Grand Rapids:
     Eerdmans, 1970.

_____. "Loose the Churches: Let Them Co." *Missiology* 1
     (April 1973): 81–94.

Madany, B. M. "Preparation of Radio Programs to Reach
     Muslims." *Report of 1964 Conference: Committee of
     Evangelical Missionaries to Islam,* pp. 26–33.
     Hackensack, New Jersey: n.p., 1964.

Mander, John. "Beirut, Damascus, Tel Aviv." *Encounter* 30
     (February 1968): 9–15.

Marsh, Charles R. *Share Your Faith With a Muslim.* Chicago:
     Moody Press, 1975.

Matheny, Tim. "Teaching the Gospel in an Arab Culture, Field
    Notes." Unpublished Paper, Summer 1976.

Mead, Margaret. *Cultural Patterns and Technical Change.*
    New York: New American Library, 1955.

Melikian, Levon H., and Diab, Lutfy N. "Group Affiliations
    of University Students in the Arab Middle East."
    Journal of Social Psychology 49 (May 1959): 145-59.

Middle East and North Africa, 1976-77. 23rd ed. London:
    Europa Publications, 1976.

Miller, Wesley. "Demonstration of Media Solution." In
    Conference on Media in Islamic Culture, pp. 124-25.
    Edited by Richard C. Shumaker. Toronto: Fellowship
    of Faith for Muslims, 1974.

Miller, William M. "The Presentation to Muslims of the
    Christian Doctrines of the Deity of Christ, the
    Trinity, the Atonement and the Inspiration of the
    Scriptures." In *International Missionary Council.*
    Madras Series. 6 vols. New York: International
    Missionary Council, 1939. Vol. 3: *Evangelism*, pp.
    215-36.

_____. *A Christian's Response to Islam.* Nutley, New
    Jersey: Presbyterian and Reformed Publishing Company,
    1976.

Minear, Paul S. *Images of the Church in the New Testament.*
    Philadelphia: Westminster Press, 1960.

Morrison, S. A. "The Indigenous Churches and Muslim Evan-
    gelization." *International Review of Missions* 25
    (July 1936): 306-20.

_____. "Missions to Muslims." *International Review of
    Missions* 27 (October 1938): 601-15.

Mowlana, Hamid. "Mass Media Systems and Communication
    Behavior." In *The Middle East: A Handbook*, pp.
    584-98. Edited by Michael Adams. New York: Praeger
    Publishers, 1971.

Muhyi, Ibrahim A. "Women in the Arab Middle East." In
    The Modern Middle East, pp. 124-40. Edited by
    Richard H. Nolte. New York: Atherton Press, 1963.

Neill, Stephen. *Christian Faith and Other Faiths: The Christian Dialogue with Other Religions.* 2nd ed. London: Oxford University Press, 1970.

Nida, Eugene A. *Customs and Cultures: Anthropology for Christian Missions.* New York: Harper and Row, 1954; reprint ed., Pasadena: William Carey Library, 1975.

_____. "Cross-Cultural Communication of the Christian Message." *Practical Anthropology* 2 (March-April 1955): 36-42.

_____. *Message and Mission: The Communication of the Christian Faith.* New York: Harper and Row, 1960; reprint ed., Pasadena: William Carey Library, 1972.

_____. *Religion Across Cultures: A Study in the Communication of the Christian Faith.* New York: Harper and Row, 1968.

_____. "Linguistic Models for Religious Behavior." *Practical Anthropology* 19 (January-February 1972): 13-26.

_____. "Are We Really Monotheists?" In *Readings in Missionary Anthropology*, pp. 223-28. Edited by William A. Smalley. South Pasadena: William Carey Library, 1974.

Niehoff, Arthur H. ed. *A Casebook of Social Change.* Chicago: Aldine Publishing Company, 1966.

Nielsen, Alfred. "Difficulties in Presenting the Gospel to Moslems." *Muslim World* 19 (January 1929): 41-46.

Norton, Howard W. *The Eldership and the Missionary.* Oklahoma City: O.C.C. Educational Associates, 1971.

Al-Nowaihi, Mohamed. "Religion of Islam: A Presentation to Christians." *International Review of Mission* 65 (April 1976): 216-25.

Ogawa, Matthew S., and Rossman, Vern. "Evangelism through
    the Mass Media and Audio Visual Materials."
    International Review of Missions 50 (October 1961):
    417-29.

Opler, Morris E. "Themes as Dynamic Forces in Culture."
    American Journal of Sociology 51 (November 1945):
    198-206.

Padwick, Constance E. "North African Reverie." *Interna-
    tional Review of Missions* 27 (July 1938): 346.

Parrinder, Geoffrey. *Jesus in the Qur'an.* London: Faber,
    1965.

Parshall, Phil. *The Fortress and the Fire: Jesus Christ
    and the Challenge of Islam.* Bombay: Gospel Literature
    Service, 1975.

Patai, Raphael. *The Arab Mind.* New York: Charles
    Scribner's S ons, 1973.

_____. *Society, Culture, and Change in the Middle East.*
    3rd ed. Philadelphia: University of Pennsylvania
    Press, 1969.

Peristiany, Jean G., ed. *Honour and Shame: The Values of
    Mediterranean Society.* Chicago: University of
    Chicago Press, 1966.

Perry, Bert M. *Missionary Know Thyself.* Winona,
    Mississippi: J. C. Choate Publications, 1973.

Peursem, Gerrit D. Van. "Methods of Evangelism in Arabia."
    Muslim World 11 (July 1921): 267-71.

Pickett, J. W.; Warnshuis, A. L.; Singh, G. H.; and
    McGavran, D. A. *Church Growth and Group Conversion.*
    5th ed. Pasadena: William Carey Library, 1973.

Pickthall, Mohammed M. trans. *The Meaning of the Glorious
    Koran.* New York; New American Library, 1953.

Pierce, Joe E. *Understanding the Middle East.* Rutland,
    Vermont: Charles E. Tuttle, 1971.

Pitt-Rivers, Julian. "Honour and Social Status." In *Honour and Shame: The Values of Mediterranean Society*, pp. 19-77. Edited by Jean G. Peristiany. Chicago: University of Chicago Press, 1966.

Prothro, E. Terry. "Arab-American Differences in the Judgment of Written Messages." *Journal of Social Psychology* 42 (August 1955): 3-11.

_____., and Melikian, Levon. "Social Distance and Social Change in the Near East." *Sociology and Social Research* 37 (September 1952): 3-11.

_____. "Generalized Ethnic Attitudes in the Arab Near East." *Sociology and Social Research* 37 (July 1953): 375-79.

Rand McNally Illustrated Atlas of the Middle East. Chicago: Rand McNally, 1975.

Report of the 1964 Conference: Committee of Evangelical Missionaries to Islam. Hackensack, New Jersey: n.p., 1964.

Report of the 1966 Conference: Committee of Evangelical Missionaries to Islam. Hackensack, New Jersey: n.p., 1966.

Reyburn, William O. "Identification in the Missionary Task." *Practical Anthropology* 7 (January-February 1960): 1-15.

Rice, Delbert. "Evangelism and the Decision-Making Processes." *Practical Anthropology* 16 (November-December 1969): 264-73.

Riggs, Henry H. "Shall We Try Unbeated Paths in Working For Moslems." *Muslim World* 31 (April 1941): 116-26.

Rogers, Everett M., and Svenning, Lynne. *Modernization Among Peasants: The Impact of Communication.* New York: Holt, Rinehart, and Winston, 1969.

Rogers, Everett M., and Shoemaker, F. Floyd. *Communication of Innovations: A Cross-Cultural Approach.* 2nd ed. New York: Free Press, 1971.

Saab, Hassan. "Communication Between Christianity and
     Islam." *Middle East Journal* 19 (Winter 1964): 41-62.

Sa'adah, Mounir R. "Christianity and the Arabic Mind."
     Muslim World 29 (January 1939): 31-36.

Saunders, Denys. "Visual Aids and the Communication of the
     Gospel." *International Review of Missions* 45 (July
     1956): 314-22.

Sayigh, Yusif A. *Entrepreneurs of Lebanon: The Role of
     the Business Leader in a Developing Economy.*
     Cambridge: Harvard University Press, 1962.

Schimmel, Annemarie. "Islam." In *Historia Religionum:
     Handbook for the History of Religions*, pp. 125-210.
     Edited by C. Jouco Bleeker and Geo Widengren.
     Leiden: E.J. Brill, 1971.

Schneider, Robert. "Reaching Muslims Through Bible Corres-
     pondence Courses." *Report of 1964 Conference: Com-
     mittee of Evangelical Missionaries to Islam*, pp.
     36-40. Hackensack, New Jersey: n.p., 1964.

Scott, Frances E. *Dare and Persevere: The Story of One
     Hundred Years of Evangelism in Syria and Lebanon,
     From 1860 to 1960.* London: Lebanon Evangelical
     Mission, 1960.

Shouby, Eli. "The Influence of the Arabic Language on
     Arab Psychology." *Middle East Journal* 5 (Summer
     1951): 284-302.

Shumaker, C. Richard, ed. *Conference on Media in Islamic
     Culture.* Toronto: Fellowship of Faith for Muslims,
     1974.

Slate, C. Philip. "What the Bible Teaches About World
     Evangelism." In *What the Bible Teaches: 1972 Bible
     Lectureship of Harding Graduate School of Religion*,
     pp. 161-78. Nashville: Gospel Advocate Company, 1972.

_____. "Modes of Perception: Cross-Cultural Considera-
     tions." Fall 1974 (Typewritten).

_____. "Church Planting." *Mission Strategy Bulletin* 3
     (July-August 1976).

_____. Class Notes, Applied Anthropology, Fall 1976. Harding Graduate School of Religion.

Smalley, William A. "Cultural Implications of an Indigenous Church." In *Readings in Missionary Anthropology*, pp. 255-57. Edited by William A. Smalley. Pasadena: William Carey Library, 1974.

_____. "Report and Ethnocentrism." In *Readings in Missionary Anthropology*, pp. 255-57. Edited by William A. Smalley. Pasadena: William Carey Library, 1974.

Smith, Donald K. "Changing People's Minds." *Practical Anthropology* 18 (July-August 1971): 167-76.

Smith, Percy. "A Plea for the Use of Versions of Scripture and of Other Literature in the Vulgar Arabic." *Muslim World* 4 (January 1914): 52-63.

Speight, Marston. "Some Bases for a Christian Apologetic to Islam." *International Review of Missions* 54 (April 1965): 193-205.

Spencer, Harold. "Humpty Dumpty." *International Review of Missions* 40 (April 1951): 185-89.

Steele, Francis R. "Islam: The Continuing Threat." *Christianity Today* 8 (July 31, 1964): 19.

Stennett, William W. "The Christian Missionary Confronting the Moslem." M. Th. Thesis, Southeastern Baptist Theological Seminary, 1959.

Stycos, J. Mayone. "Patterns of Communication in a Rural Greek Village." *Public Opinion Quarterly* 16 (Spring 1952): 58-70.

Sweet, Louise E., ed. *Peoples and Cultures of the Middle East.* 2 vols. Garden City, New York: Doubleday, 1970.

_____., ed. *The Central Middle East: A Handbook of Anthropology and Published Research on the Nile Valley, the Arab Levant, Southern Mesopotamia, the Arabian Peninsula, and Israel.* New Haven: Human Relations Area Files Press, 1971.

Sweetman, J. Windrow. *Islam and Christian Theology*. London:
    Lutterworth Press, 1945.

Taylor, Robert B. *Introduction to Cultural Anthropology*.
    Boston: Allyn and Bacon, 1973.

Tillich, Paul. *Theology of Culture*. Edited by Robert C.
    Kimball. New York: Oxford University Press, 1959.

Tippett, Alan R. *Church Growth and the Word of God*. Grand
    Rapids: Eerdmans, 1970.

_____. *Verdict Theology in Missionary Theory*. Pasadena:
William Carey Library, 1973.

_____. "Christopaganism or Indigenous Christianity." In
Christopaganism or Indigenous Christianity, pp. 13-34.
Edited by Tetsunao Yamamori and Charles R. Taber.
Pasadena: William Carey Library, 1975.

_____. "Evangelization Among Animists." In *Let the Earth
Hear His Voice*, pp. 844-55. Edited by J. D. Douglas.
Minneapolis, Minnesota: World Wide Publications, 1975.

Tomeh, Aida K. "The Impact of Reference Groups on the
    Educational and Occupational Aspirations of Women
    College Students." *Journal of Marriage and the Family*
    30 (February 1968): 102-10.

Ud-Din, R. Siraj. "The Vital Forces of Christianity and
    Islam." *International Review of Missions* 2 (January
    1913): 96-117.

Van Ess, Dorothy L. "Arab Customs." *Practical Anthropology*
    6 (September-October 1959): 219-22.

Van Ess, John. *Meet the Arab*. New York: John Day, 1943.

Vinogradov, Amal. "Visiting Patterns and Social Dynamics
    in Eastern Mediterranean Communities: Introduction."
    Anthropological Quarterly 47 (January 1974): 2-8.

Warren, Thomas J. P. "The Problem of the Convert From
    Islam." *Muslim World* 8 (April 1918): 149-57.

Watson, O. Michael, and Graves, Theodore D. "Quantitative
    Research in Proxemic Behavior." *American Anthropo-
    logist* 68 (August 1966): 971-85.

Watt, W. Montgomery. "New Paths to Islam." *International Review of Missions* 36 (January 1947): 74-80.

_____. "The Missionary Task of the Church in Palestine and Syria." *International Review of Missions* 36 (April 1947): 153-62.

_____. "The Forces Now Moulding Islam." *Muslim World* 43 (July 1953): 161-72.

_____. "The Use of the Word 'Allah' in English." *Muslim World* 43 (October 1953): 245-47.

Webster, Warren. "Why Do So Few Muslims Become Christians?" *Report of the 1966 Conference: Committee of Evangelical Missionaries to Islam.* Hackensack, New Jersey: n.p., 1966.

West, Irene G. "Asmara Study Conference, A pril 1-9, 1959." *International Review of Missions* 48 (October 1959): 433-37.

Westermack, Edward. *Pagan Survivals in Mohammedan Civilization.* Amsterdam, Netherlands: Philo Press, 1973.

Wilber, Donald N. *United Arab Republic, Egypt: Its Peoples, Its Society, Its Culture.* New Haven: Human Relations Area Files Press, 1969.

Williams, Judith R. *The Youth of Haouch El Harimi: A Lebanese Village.* Cambridge: Harvard University Press, 1968.

Wilson, J. Christy. "Public Confession and the Church." *Muslim World* 31 (April 1941): 127-39.

_____. "Evangelism for Mohammedans." *Muslim World* 36 (October 1946): 288-305.

_____. *The Christian Message to Islam.* New York: Fleming H. Revell, 1950.

_____. *Introducing Islam.* rev.ed. New York: Friendship Press, 1958.

Wonderly, William L., and Nida, Eugene A. "Cultural Differ-
    ences and the Communication of Christian Values."
    Practical Anthropology 10 (November–December 1963):
    241–58.

Wysham, William N. "The Use of Literature in Evangelism."
    Muslim World 27 (January 1937): 56–64.

Yousef, Fathi S. "Cross–Cultural Communication: Aspects
    of Contrastive Social Values Between North Americans
    and Middle Easterners." *Human Organization* 33 (Winter
    1974): 383–87.

Zaehner, R. C. *Christianity and Other Religions.* New York:
    Hawthorn Books, 1964.

Zwemer, Samuel M. *The Moslem Doctrine of God.* New York:
    Young People's Missionary Movement, 1905.

Zwemer, Samuel M. *The Moslem Christ: An Essay on the Teach-
    ings of Jesus Christ According to the Koran and
    Orthodox Traditions.* Edinburgh: Oliphant, Anderson,
    and Ferrier, 1912.

_____. "The Present Attitude of Educated Moslems Towards
    Jesus Christ and the Scriptures." *International
    Review of Missions* 3 (October 1914): 696–707.

_____.*The Influence of Animism on Islam.* New York:
    Macmillan, 1920.

_____. "The Dynamics of Evangelism." *Muslim World* 31
    (April 1941): 109–15.

_____. *The Cross Above the Crescent: The Validity,
    Necessity, and Urgency of Missions to Moslems.*
    Grand Rapids: Zondervan, 1941.

_____. "The Doctrine of the Trinity." *Muslim World* 35
    (January 1945): 1–5.

Index

Tim Matheny lived in Beirut, Lebanon as a child between the ages of nine and sixteen. During this time his parents, Carl and Betty Lou Matheny, were engaged in evangelistic work for the churches of Christ. In those seven years Tim developed a keen interest in the Arab people which has had a profound effect upon his life.

In 1974 he completed the B.A. degree majoring in speech and Bible at Harding University, and in 1977 he completed the M.Th. degree at Harding Graduate School of Religion. This book is a result of the research he did at that time.

Tim Matheny was selected to appear in *Who's Who Among Students in American Universities and Colleges* and *Outstanding Young Men of America* in 1977. Since that time, he has served as the minister of evangelism at the Madison Church of Christ in Tennessee.

525385